# LINCOLN
# ÜBER ALLES

# LINCOLN ÜBER ALLES

## Dictatorship Comes to America

John Avery Emison

PELICAN PUBLISHING COMPANY
GRETNA 2009

*The word "Pelican" and the depiction of a pelican are trademarks
of Pelican Publishing Company, Inc., and are registered in the
U.S. Patent and Trademark Office.*

**Library of Congress Cataloging-in-Publication Data**

Emison, John Avery.
  Lincoln über alles : dictatorship comes to America / John Avery Emison.
    p. cm.
  Includes bibliographical references and index.
  ISBN 978-1-58980-692-4 (hardcover : alk. paper) 1. Lincoln, Abraham,
1809-1865—Political and social views. 2. Lincoln, Abraham, 1809-
1865—Military leadership. 3. Lincoln, Abraham, 1809-1865—Relations
with German Americans. 4. German Americans—History—19th century
5. Forty-Eighters (American immigrants) 6. Germany—History—
Revolution, 1848-1849—Refugees. 7. United States—History—Civil War,
1861-1865—Causes. 8. United States—Politics and government—1861-
1865. 9. Federal government—United States—History—19th century. 10.
Secession—United States. I. Title.
  E457.2.E483 2009
  973.7092—dc22

                  2009023777

Printed in the United States of America

Published by Pelican Publishing Company, Inc.
1000 Burmaster Street, Gretna, Louisiana 70053

*In memoriam to a small-town lawyer and Southern gentleman,
my father, Theophilus James Emison (1915-2008)*


*Dedicated to men and women everywhere who love liberty*

# Contents

CHAPTER ONE
Introduction . . . . . . . . . . . . . . . . . . . . . . . . . . . . . . . . . . . . . . .11

CHAPTER TWO
Race: The Eight-Hundred-Pound Gorilla of American
History . . . . . . . . . . . . . . . . . . . . . . . . . . . . . . . . . . . . . . . . . .29

CHAPTER THREE
The German Forty-Eighters: Lincoln's Indispensable Allies . . .71

CHAPTER FOUR
Lincoln's Call for Troops: Six Governors Say "No" . . . . . . . . . . .99

CHAPTER FIVE
Secession, the Constitution, and Law . . . . . . . . . . . . . . . . . . .119

CHAPTER SIX
Sovereignty and the Historical Context of Secession . . . . . . . .169

CHAPTER SEVEN
War Crimes: Lincoln Prosecutes the War on the South . . . . . .199

CHAPTER EIGHT
Secession: Legal in 1860, Legal Today . . . . . . . . . . . . . . . . . . .255

CHAPTER NINE
One Nation Under Surveillance: Will the Republic
Terminate in an Empire? . . . . . . . . . . . . . . . . . . . . . . . . . . . .277

Notes . . . . . . . . . . . . . . . . . . . . . . . . . . . . . . . . . . . . . . . . . . . .301

Index . . . . . . . . . . . . . . . . . . . . . . . . . . . . . . . . . . . . . . . . . . . .317

# LINCOLN
# ÜBER ALLES

# CHAPTER ONE

# Introduction

*"The opposite of a correct statement is a false statement. But the opposite of a profound truth may well be another profound truth."*

—William Jennings Bryan

This book takes almost everything you learned in school about the Civil War and turns it right side up. Even the name of the conflict is wrong. What you know, or think you know, about the Civil War, Abraham Lincoln, secession, slavery, emancipation, racial justice in nineteenth-century America, and the effects of these events on our lives today is almost entirely mistaken.

Some may ask, "So what?" It's a reasonable question that has been answered at least in part by former New York governor Mario Cuomo in his 2004 book, *Why Lincoln Matters: Today More than Ever.*[1]

The front flap of Cuomo's book claims "the contemporary relevance of Lincoln's message" includes among others, the issue of "the role of government," which is part of the "American scripture," that Cuomo asserts was revealed to us by our storied and hallowed sixteenth president. Historian Gabor Boritt applies the word "Gospel" to Lincoln's utterances. Say, "Hallelujah," say "Amen."

Cuomo is correct that Lincoln does indeed matter; that the Leviathan-like role of the central government matters; that the statists and central planners of America's contemporary welfare/warfare/nanny-state worship, revere, absolve, and deify Lincoln for all the things he had no legal authority to do but did anyway, and all the things he is credited with doing but never actually accomplished. (And with the completion of this paragraph, there is nothing else with which to agree with Governor Cuomo).

The central truth about the Civil War is that it *was not* simply a conflict between North and South; it was a conflict between the

11

Southern states and the federal government. The federal government won, and the Feds have been winning ever since.

Today, the federal government decides how much water we flush down the toilet. It decides how much rat feces is an acceptable amount of rodent droppings in the nation's grain supply (which equates to how much feces the government allows in your box of Wheaties®). It decides how many glass shards are permitted in a bottle of baby food. It decides which county will be a "corn" county or a "cotton," "dairy," "tobacco," "rice," or "sugar" county. It has gradually federalized the learning curriculum in public and private schools, virtually erasing the differences between the two. It has federalized charitable response to disasters through the Federal Emergency Management Agency and its "partnering" with the American Red Cross. It decides the rules of golf and the temperature of hot coffee.

Since there is nothing in the Constitution that authorizes the federal government to do any of these things, one might conclude that the government has no more right to tell a farmer what crops he can or cannot grow on his land than it has to tell the farmer's daughter whom she may or may not marry. Yet the power to tell us what we cannot do, and to tell us what we must do, was usurped by Lincoln in 1861 and aggrandized by almost every president since.

Some seem to think that the power of the federal government extends only to those activities that are objectively good. This view is sadly naïve. The federal government took to itself the power to release massive clouds of radioactive iodine, deliberately and secretly exposing the public, because it placed a higher value on research data on the health effects of radiation than it did the actual health of its citizens. It is the largest polluter in the history of man. It has interred American citizens against their will—citizens who were not even accused of breaking the law—because it thought they might. It confiscated Americans' gold money and gave them paper in return. It has even burned women and children to death in the name of protecting them from what it considered a dangerous religious cult.

The Federal Bureau of Investigation (FBI) can now monitor the books you check out of the library, the e-mail you send, and the Internet chat rooms you visit without bothering with a warrant, all under the presumption that such monitoring protects us from acts of terrorism. A recent U.S. president has asserted that surreptitious surveillance of citizens is his duty.

America has become a combination of a "police" as well as a "nanny" state. The federal government wants to protect us against crime, and the Justice Department reports that the United States has the highest percentage of adult male citizens behind bars of any country in the world. Prison construction is a growth industry.

The federal government offers entertainment and warns us about things that might hurt us, just as a good nanny would do. Many federal agencies offer coloring books to indoctrinate children in the value of the "village" that one prominent U.S. politician says is needed to raise them. The federal government warns us that eating too much will make us fat; that drinking too much will make us drunk; that eating rancid meat will make us sick; that smoking will kill us. The Consumer Product Safety Commission issued a voluntary recall of Martha Stewart Everyday®-brand candles, which it claimed, "May ignite, posing a fire and burn hazard." (Isn't this what candles are supposed to do?) It is reminiscent of the Ronald Reagan retort to the National Park Service's published warning that insects crawling into the ears of hikers could lead to a painful condition: "You know we'd have never thought of that one by ourselves."

In the near future, the National Transportation Safety Board wants to track your car in real time 24/7 using an aerospace-type "black box" enhanced with global positioning system technology. The Department of Agriculture wants to implant a chip in every farm animal and household pet. Are we next? The implementation of a national identity card by the Department of Homeland Security is well underway (papers please). The Food and Drug Administration wants to use miniature radio transmitters to track your prescription pain medicine and Viagra from the pharmacy to your home. National security bureaucrats have access to your every credit and debit card purchase in the "mother of all databases." Video surveillance of public and private places can track you as you move from place to place. Eye-, face-, voice-, and handprint-recognition systems know where you have been. Traffic cameras nab you when you transgress (even though the police have no probable cause to surveil your activities). Bar codes record what you buy, where you shop, and when you shop. Passwords record where or to what you have gained access. Computer "cookies" record your every move on the Internet. Between "don't-fly" lists, digital cell phones, computerized ID badges for schoolchildren, spyware on your computer, and IRS records, "Big Brother" is already watching you, and he always wants to know more.

Technology has made our lives transparent; Lincoln paved the way for this Leviathan-like role of government with his "American scripture" in everyday life—the Father Abraham of the Messianic American republic *cum* empire. Just ask Mario Cuomo.

The essence of the Lincoln counterrevolution was the overthrow of the principle of "consent of the governed," at first only as it applied to the consent of the states, then increasingly to the individual citizen who is defenseless before the government behemoth. Just as the fictional computer Hal (in Arthur C. Clark's epic book and film *2001: A Space Odyssey*) morphed from the role of servant to master, so too the Feds have demoted the individual from the status of citizen to subject, whose consent is no longer needed, sought, or relevant.

Thus begins the end of the experiment of limited government commenced by the Founding Fathers. Their distrust of government has evolved into government's distrust of us.

The following sections in this chapter address the basic argument of this book, which is secession of the Southern states was legal and the counterrevolution Lincoln perpetrated in the name of "preserving the Union" was illegal.

### Secession was Legal

Secession was the acid test of the American Revolution and the Confederates were the true defenders of the natural rights of man that were asserted by the Colonies and the people in the Declaration of Independence and codified (for the most part) in the Bill of Rights to the Constitution.

*The nation failed the test.*

The most obvious legal argument supporting secession relates to sovereignty. Numerous Supreme Court rulings spanning the eighteenth through twenty-first centuries hold that the people of the states are sovereign. They alone, *not the federal government*, ultimately hold the reins of political power. In 1787-90, they alone created the

Constitution through the ratification process of conventions in each state, just as today they hold the sole and exclusive political authority to amend the Constitution. Three-quarters of the states, acting through their individual legislatures, must agree to any amendment to the Constitution.

Southern secession was legal by application of three Supreme Court doctrines expounded in numerous rulings that were the law of the land at the time and remain so today.

The unmistakability doctrine is one of the three current Supreme Court doctrines that support a state's right to withdraw from the union of states. Unmistakability holds that in contracts between the government and private parties, the government cannot transfer any attribute of sovereignty except in unmistakable terms. This doctrine applies to the federal government and state and local government and their agencies. A contract is nothing more than a voluntary agreement among parties. In fact, if any agreement is not voluntarily adopted by the parties to it (in other words if one party coerces the other to agree to the contract), it is not a valid contract and cannot be enforced. Under the unmistakability doctrine, since states cannot transfer attributes of sovereignty in private agreements, how can they do so in public agreements (such as the ratification of the U.S. Constitution) except in unmistakable terms? We will see later that no form of the word "sovereign" is in the Constitution because the Founding Fathers believed it would make it impossible to obtain ratification.

Another current doctrine of the court is known as "legislative entrenchment." This doctrine is traced from English common law hundreds of years ago, yet it originated in the Roman Republic a century before Christ.

This doctrine holds that one legislature cannot bind a future legislature by a simple act. In other words, any action that a past legislature was competent to enact, a future legislature is competent to modify or repeal.

Here's how legislative entrenchment applies to the question of secession. If the legislatures of the four Southern states (that would secede in 1860-61) were competent to enact a mechanism to choose a convention to ratify the Constitution in 1787-90, they were equally competent to convene a convention with the same authority in 1860-61, which is to say the authority to rescind ratification and sever political ties with the United States. This is precisely what South Carolina, Georgia, Virginia, and North Carolina did; they simply rescinded their prior ratification of the Constitution. Virginia even titled its secession ordinance "An Ordinance to repeal the ratification of the Constitution of the United States of America by the State of Virginia . . ." These states' actions were in perfect harmony also with the right of revolution, i.e., the right to alter or abolish the form of government over them, a right that remains in the wording of many state constitutions even in the twenty-first century, the same right upon which the Colonies declared their independence.

All the other Southern states (as well as Northern) have the same rights and prerogatives of the original Thirteen Colonies under the Supreme Court doctrine of the equality of the states, also known as the equal footing doctrine. This doctrine, which is still in force today, holds that by constitutional necessity every state is admitted to the Union on an equal footing with the original states just as if they had been one of the original thirteen. Upon Tennessee's statehood in 1796, Congress included a clause in the act of admission that provided Tennessee entered the Union "on an equal footing with the original states in all respects whatever." Prior to Tennessee's admission, Vermont and Kentucky had been admitted with conceptually similar language. Since Tennessee's admission, every subsequent state has had the same language in their statehood-enabling act.

In addition to these current doctrines of the court, secession is a "reserved power" under the Tenth Amendment. The Tenth Amendment was the final part of the Bill of Rights. It is one of the shortest amendments:

> The powers not delegated to the United States by the Constitution, nor prohibited by it to the states, are reserved to the states respectively, or to the people.

The Constitution is silent on whether it is a perpetual and irreversible commitment of union by and among the states. It is silent on whether the states and the people have given up their right to alter or abolish forms of government over them. It is silent on the severing of political ties by or among the states. Clearly, such powers are "not delegated to the United States by the Constitution, nor prohibited by it to the states." Therefore these powers, *including secession,* "are reserved to the states respectively, or to the people." Following the Civil War, Congress required the occupied Southern states renounce the right of secession before they were readmitted to the Union. How does one renounce a right without legitimately possessing it to start with?

So we see that the people are sovereign in all states, or they are sovereign not at all. They retain their rights and prerogatives unless they have unmistakably transferred them to the federal government. The legislatures of the states and the people retain the right to "alter or abolish" forms of government that no longer serve their interests and to repeal any existing political arrangement that was agreed-to previously. Otherwise, the issue of the permanence and indivisibility of the central government has been illegally entrenched, and the people no longer have sovereign authority to address these issues.

### The Civil War was an Illegal Counterrevolution to Free the Federal Government from Constitutional Restrictions of Power

The war was an illegal counterrevolution for the purpose of severing what Jefferson referred to as the "chains" of the Constitution, to leave the federal government free to do whatever it could get away with politically and militarily. In its place came the central government that we have today with virtual unlimited power to plunder society and transfer wealth to politically favored groups and industries, i.e., corporate welfare.

Lincoln operated under his theory that as commander in chief he had extraordinary power do whatever he determined was warranted to "preserve the Union," with or without the consent of Congress, even if the authority he exercised was beyond the enumerated powers of Congress (Article I) or the president (Article II).Of course, his actions were almost entirely outside the law. He carried out a Machiavellian counterrevolution to establish the federal government's *carte blanche* role in re-creating the nation into the image of his choosing.

The war also overturned the most sacred and fundamental principle in the Declaration of Independence, that "governments are instituted among men, deriving their just powers *from the consent of the governed.*"

It was imperative for Lincoln to overturn the principle of consent in order to defeat secession. As long as states believed their consent was optional and could be withdrawn via secession, it was impossible to remake the federal government into today's Leviathan. It would always be a self-limiting process if any state, or group of states, were pushed too far by the federal government. Secession stood in the way of the dream of the almighty, dominant central state.

As long as secession existed as at least a debatable option, the federal government could never become more than the loose confederation that it had been under Lincoln's fifteen predecessors. Pres. Franklin Pierce referred to this confederation as "the congress of sovereignties," an explicit acknowledgment that sovereignty resided in the citizens of the states rather than the federal government. It was the people who created what was widely referred to as the American "experiment" in government, and at no time have the people willingly or consciously forsaken the right to alter or abolish it.

It was the boys wearing the butternut and gray, not the boys in blue, who fought to save that principle. As H. L. Mencken noted, Lincoln's argument in the Gettysburg Address was that the Union soldiers who died there "sacrificed their lives to the cause of self-determination—that government of the people, by the people, for the people, would not perish of the earth." Mencken emphatically disagrees: "It is difficult to imagine anything more untrue. The Union soldiers in the battle actually fought against self-determination; it was the Confederates who fought for the right of their people to govern themselves."

Today, the federal government supervises and polices the ethical standards in state government, as if government at the federal level is free of corruption. It routinely entraps and prosecutes members of state legislatures even while those law-making bodies are in session. Often these entrapment schemes violate state law. What law gives the FBI agents the right to violate state law? Which is the greater corruption of the Constitution: the state official caught by the FBI with his hand in the till, or the FBI agent who tramples state law in pursuit of a headline arrest?

When the chains of the Constitution were shed, they were replaced with the raw exercise of power that is a law unto itself, no longer limited by the Constitution. The Founding Fathers feared such an eventuality, and that is why they deliberately distributed political power in order to avoid the tyranny that would result from its centralization.

### The War Neither "Freed the Slaves" Nor Did It "Preserve the Union"

The initiation of the war had nothing to do with either ending slavery or preserving the Union. Technically speaking, it did neither. The Thirteenth Amendment freed the slaves, and it did not come until months after Lee surrendered. All slaves held in bondage at the beginning of the war in what Lincoln referred to as the "loyal" slave-holding states of Missouri, Kentucky, and Maryland (as well as Delaware) remained in bondage when the guns fell silent.

In 1863, when Lincoln signed the congressional act that admitted the State of West Virginia to the Union—a *federally approved albeit legally dubious secession* from Virginia—it was admitted as a slave state.

When slavery was legally ended one by one in the Northern states, not a single slave owner who lost his chattel property did so without receiving compensation. Slavery was abolished gradually in every Northern state that chose to end it. There was no immediate, instantaneous emancipation anywhere in the North. Nor did Lincoln emancipate any slaves, anywhere, at any time. Indeed, he reversed emancipation announced by one of his commanders in Missouri. Moreover, when time came for his Emancipation Proclamation, it was carefully written in legal double-talk to appear to emancipate slaves when in fact it craftily avoided emancipation in occupied areas of Tennessee and Louisiana (where he had the actual power to bring it about). When John Wilkes Booth assassinated the so-called Great Emancipator, he had freed not a single slave by law.

In addition, if the war was fought to "preserve the Union," why is it that the conquered Southern states were required by the federal government to be readmitted in order to obtain representation in Congress? Each such readmitted state was voted on by Congress just as Congress had done when the first "new" state, Vermont, fourteenth in order of admission, and every state thereafter was admitted. Even four of the original thirteen states of Lincoln's preserved Union were forced to be readmitted just as if they had never been part of the nation.

Since the federal government won this war to preserve the Union, why did it impose military governments on the Southern states whose place in that Union it had preserved? Why did the U.S. Army dictate the terms of several new state constitutions in the preserved Union? The citizens of Mississippi and Texas labored the longest—six years—under military government without the benefit of representation in Congress. What was it about the preserved Union of those states that the federal government was certain justified the slaughter of 620,000 Americans? In victory, the federal government's actions looked a lot more like conquest than preservation.


**Northerners Had No Interest in Racial Justice**
Perhaps the most powerful misconception about the Civil War is that the Northern states were on the right side of the race issue and relished the idea of freeing Southern-held slaves. The fact is that Northerners had no interest in dying for racial justice in 1861. For the most part, they despised and hounded free blacks and enacted Jim Crow laws as a means of preventing them from crossing the borders of Northern states. In short, they wanted to keep all blacks out of the Northern states and maintain the western territories as white only. Negro exclusion laws worked quite well in the North as hundreds of communities from Ohio to Iowa remain segregated, virtually white only today.

On the eve of the Civil War, Ohio was one of several states that required free blacks to post a $1,000 good-behavior bond in order to cross its border. Virtually no one, white or black, had $1,000 cash at that time. In Illinois, it was a crime for a white person to aid a free black in crossing into the state. In Indiana, free blacks had virtually no rights. Even the term "free" state (the opposite of "slave" state) is a misnomer in that forms of slave bondage survived in New Jersey and Illinois, and perhaps other Northern states, up to and during the Civil War.

Prior to the Civil War, free blacks could not vote in any Northern state outside four New England states, Massachusetts, Vermont, New Hampshire, and Maine, where virtually no blacks lived. Previously, Connecticut and Rhode Island had allowed Negro suffrage but took it away in 1818 and 1836, respectively. White voters in Wisconsin defeated black suffrage four separate times, including on the eve of the war and again at the war's end in 1865. At least twenty-five statewide referenda for black suffrage in Northern states in the prewar era through 1868 ended in failure. Not a single one passed. Except for Massachusetts, no black man had served on a jury prior to 1860 in the North. Blacks could not testify against a white man in most Northern courts even if they were the victims of violence at the hands of a white perpetrator.

In 1859, two years before the war, Congress voted to admit Oregon, which became the only state to have a race-based exclusion clause in its constitution at the time of statehood. During the war in 1862, Illinois voters passed a Negro exclusion amendment to their state Constitution.

Northern business interests and port workers continued to benefit from participation in the illegal Atlantic slave trade for decades after it was abolished in 1808, right up to the virtual eve of Civil War hostilities. Northern intellectuals were also hostile toward Jews. Books, articles, speeches, and sermons by New England universalist-dominated clergy and intelligentsia were filled with anti-Semitic terms and references. By contrast, Charleston had the most influential Jewish community during the Colonial and pre-Lincoln periods, and the first three Jewish members of the U.S. Senate were all Southerners (David Yulee of Florida and Judah P. Benjamin and Benjamin F. Jonas both of Louisiana). It was almost a century before a Jew represented any Northern state in the Senate chamber.

**"The Final Solution of the Indian Problem"**
And then there was the Indian problem.

Before the war ended (and extending for another two decades after the war), the federal government committed itself to a policy of racial genocide of the Plains Indians, who were in the way of the railroads. After the war, William Sherman even coined the term "final solution of the Indian problem," which had precisely the same connotation for Jews in Europe when the Nazis borrowed the term seventy-five years later.

It is illustrative as to the racial attitude of Lincoln that he *approved in his own handwriting* the largest mass execution in the history of North America, consisting of thirty-eight Indians and "half-breeds" (Lincoln's words) who were all hanged together in Minnesota the day after Christmas 1862. They were arrested, tried, predictably convicted, and executed by the U.S. Army without benefit of the civilian courts.

Ask yourself, how can a government wage a war of racial justice in one part of the country while simultaneously carrying out racial genocide in another?

### War Criminals Under Their Own Military Code of Justice

Abraham Lincoln, Ulysses Grant, William Sherman, Henry Halleck, and others were war criminals under the Lieber Code, which was commissioned by Lincoln and issued by his generals. If the federal government had lost the war, they would likely have been hanged.

Historians credit Sherman as the father of "total warfare," war on the civilian population. His military superiors, Grant and Halleck, also knew and approved of his actions by both omission and commission. Lincoln searched desperately for a combination of generals to win at any cost and found them with Grant commanding the Army of the Potomac and Sherman the Army of the Tennessee.

The crimes were systematic, pervasive, and deliberate. Starvation of civilians; house burnings; kidnapping; forced labor; the use of slave labor; the use of Confederate soldiers as human shields in combat; the murder of soldiers who were attempting to surrender; threats and actual acts of retaliation and retribution on both military and civilians; banishment of Jews; revenge killings; torture; and wanton destruction of private property were all illegal under the U.S. Army's Lieber Code and placed the Union high command as well as Lincoln in jeopardy of their liberty and lives.

These developments are important because a direct line in the history of warfare on civilians as well as the development of the international law of war crimes can be traced from Vicksburg, Atlanta, and Savannah to the fire bombings of German civilian population centers, Hiroshima, the My Lai village, and the Abu Ghraib prison.

America's federal Leviathan is in the historically unenviable position of demanding a level of conduct and justice from others that is infinitely higher than anything it has enforced on itself.

## Enter the European Revolutionaries

European revolutionaries, including Karl Marx, influenced the radical wing of the Republican Party, which was politically assisted by thousands of revolutionaries from Central Europe who immigrated to America following the failed revolutions of 1848. Lincoln's nomination as the Republican presidential candidate in 1860 would have been much less likely without the support of recent German dogmatic émigrés, thousands of whom had literally taken up arms and participated in the 1848 European revolutions. Lincoln's election as president would have been impossible without their support.

The German immigrants who participated in those revolutions and came to America are known in history as the Forty-Eighters. They came to American shores with their own unique *weltanschauung:* A political agenda to remake their new homeland into the strong central state that would enforce their views of equality throughout the nation and the rest of the world. They were antiprivate-property statists who opposed the relatively weak confederacy of the existing federalism of the Founding Fathers just as they opposed the weak, fractured confederacy of states and principalities in the Fatherland.

Though they failed to break the power of the aristocracy in Germany in the 1840s, they contributed enormously to Lincoln's counterrevolution of the 1860s to break the chains of the Constitution and establish a powerful and dominant federal government. Otto von Bismarck emulated the Lincoln model in his Fatherland in the 1870s just as Adolf Hitler and Joseph Goebbels perhaps patterned the Nazi policy of *lebensraum* in Eastern Europe on the Lincoln/Sherman/Grant model for dealing with the Plains Indians.

## Secession Is Political Divorce

Secession is the philosophical equivalent to divorce. It is a political divorce where a party to the political marriage believes it is no longer in its interest to maintain the relationship. As a marriage between a man and a woman is not legal without the consent of both parties, so it is with political unions. Yet the parties to political divorce have no more legal, moral, or philosophical justification to preserve the relationship by force of arms and loss of life than do the parties of an actual divorce. If the opposite were true, the use of physical force by the more powerful of the parties to divorce would be commonplace and the result would be predictable.

Divorce often is painful, traumatic, contentious, regrettable, expensive, and sometimes avoidable. However, no contemporary Western society recognizes any right to use force to prevent divorce, much less to restore a broken union. Likewise, the law of the land can grant every imaginable right and prerogative to a marriage partner save one—the right of peaceable separation and divorce—and all the other rights are meaningless. Just as with secession, if one partner of the marriage withdraws consent to the union and desires peaceable separation and divorce rather than coerced union, but the other partner has the right to use force to "preserve the union," the first partner has no rights at all.

If violence is an unacceptable method of maintaining a union between individuals, if the parties who consensually create a union have the right to withdraw without fear of violence from the other party, so it must be among political unions of civilized people who are ruled by law rather than coercive force. Political divorce neither demands nor justifies the murder of either party.

Emory University philosophy professor Dr. Donald W. Livingston uses the dissolution of the Soviet Union as a modern-day example. Livingston has noted the irony that peaceful secession was allowed in a totalitarian communist state (the former U.S.S.R.), yet war was the answer to secession in the liberal Western democracy of America. He asks rhetorically, whether we consider Mikhail Gorbachev a failure because he did not precipitate a war to "preserve the [Soviet] Union?"

### What Were the Politically Centrifugal Forces Pulling North and South Apart?

The Civil War was a struggle between political partners who, as many married partners discover about their own relationships, grew apart and over the years became increasingly dissimilar.

The dissimilarities between North and South loomed significant and apparent. By 1860, the economies of the two regions could not have been more different. The South remained almost exclusively agrarian while the North had experienced nearly a century of industrialization. The labor systems that evolved in these two economies, a combination of free and slave labor in the South and exclusively wage labor in the North, were also different.

These economic systems produced different political interests. The South exported food and fiber and imported manufactured goods from Europe. Free trade was the South's preference. The North wanted high tariffs to protect its uncompetitive industry and preferential access to the Southern market. In addition, tariff was the government's main source of tax revenue. This meant the Southerners paid most of the taxes, subsidizing the industrial North.

Perhaps the most fundamental difference between these two partners was the biracial nature of Southern culture (by then more than two hundred years old) versus the almost all white culture of the North.

During the antebellum period, mostly Celtic peoples settled in the backwoods and frontier South while the North was predominantly Anglo-Saxon. These groups didn't much like each other in the Old World, and little changed when they migrated to the New.

There were deep religious differences between North and South. The North was home to numerous radical or new religions, various social reform movements, and utopian communities. For many Southerners, it seemed that the Northern proclivity to chase after new religions and try to reform the world was evidence of cultural imperialism. The most glaring example of religious extremism was the so-called Burned-over District of central and western New York. Historian Whitney Cross gave the name to this area because it was so repeatedly swept with evangelistic fervor during the antebellum period that eventually there was no fuel, or unevangelized people, left to burn, or convert. This stands in stark contrast to religious beliefs and practices in the South, where people were more conservative, resistant to change, orthodox in religious thought and practice, and unsympathetic to popular convulsions in the North.

From the early Colonial years, there were the austere Puritans of New England, at war with nature, with Native Americans, with the Salem witches, and always with their own human nature. Religious perturbance in the North continued during the antebellum period, which saw the founding of the Mormon Church in New York by Vermonter Joseph Smith, Jr.; the Seventh Day Adventist movement (New York); the spiritualist movement (séances) by the Fox sisters (New York); the socialist Owenites of the Harmony Society (Pennsylvania and Indiana); the Community of True Inspiration (Amana Colonies of Iowa); the Zoar Separatists (Ohio); the Marxists of the Aurora Colony (Oregon); and the Oneida, New York, commune of John Humphrey Noyes, who taught that Christ returned in 70 A.D. and it was up to man to bring about his millennial kingdom on Earth. One of Noyes' followers assassinated President Garfield after the war. The period also saw the emergence of the Unitarian-Universalist movement, which most Southern Protestants and Catholics believed to be heresy because it rejected the Trinity. The Harvard Divinity School was founded by Unitarians who dominated the official state church in Massachusetts. The Massachusetts state church was not disestablished until 1831.

It should be no surprise that either of these partners eventually concluded that it made no sense for them to live together, unequally yoked in the same political union. Their economics were different; their politics were different; they worked differently; they were different in race, religion, climate, diet, accent, and culture. Most importantly, they had different and irreconcilable views of themselves, each other, and the world. Many in the North wanted to "save" the nation or even the world from one boogeyman or another. Most in the South just wanted to be left alone.

**What Do We Call This War?**
A "civil war" is a conflict between rival factions, parties, or regions to control the central government of a nation. The Lincoln scholars prefer the term "civil war" because it mischaracterizes the nature of the conflict. Spain had a civil war in 1936-39 with the Nationalists defeating the Republicans for control of the entire country. The events of 1861-65 in America were not a civil war because there was no effort or interest on the part of the South to control the national government. There was no struggle over which side would rule in Washington, as there was in Madrid. The Southern states merely wanted separation. Therefore, it cannot correctly be called a civil war.

Nor can it be called a rebellion. A rebellion connotes an overthrowing of the form of government that had previous jurisdiction and its replacement with something entirely different. The Russians had a revolution in 1917. The Romanov dynasty ruled Russia under the divine right of kings for more than three hundred years until it was overthrown and replaced briefly with a republican form of government that was subsequently overthrown by a communist dictatorship. So the conflict in America was not a rebellion.

Many Southerners, including Southern historians, prefer the term "War Between the States" (WBTS) because it avoids the use of the word "rebellion," and it avoids the term preferred in the North, "Civil War." While WBTS is significantly less inaccurate than calling it a civil war, it is still inaccurate. Though the conflict involved units from some states invading and destroying other states, it was actually a conflict between the Southern states and the federal government. (It was the Southern states' great error to leave the structure of the federal government in undisputed and exclusive control of Northern politicians during the secession winter of 1860-61.)

Some Southerners prefer to call it the War of Northern Aggression. This is also inaccurate to the extent that the aggression came from the federal government and not the Northern states per se. Calling it a war of Northern aggression places the blame on a subset of states rather than the federal government.

What then do we call it?

The conflict in 1861 was identical to the conflict in 1776. In 1861, the South wanted out from under the heavy hand of the federal government just as in 1776 when the Colonies had wanted out from under the heavy hand of King George III. The Colonies wanted to rule themselves separate from George III and made no demand on England that it change its government or overthrow its king. The parallel to Southern secession is identical in that Southern states demanded self-determination without placing any demands on the federal government to overthrow President Lincoln. It would seem, therefore, that both conflicts could be called wars for independence. Many people use the term the War for Independence to describe the 1776 conflict. One could accurately refer to the conflict in 1861 as the War for Southern Independence. However, a more accurate way of describing both of these wars is that they were wars of secession. The first war of secession was for independence from England. As the late Ross Hoffman (chairman of the history department at Fordham University) put it, the Revolutionary War was an *"American secession from the British Empire."* The second war of secession was for Southern independence. Thus, the most accurate term for the 1861 conflict is the "Second War of Secession." The use of this term provides a more complete historic context of both conflicts. The Lincoln scholars will, no doubt, ridicule this term because it implies legitimacy to the concept of secession that they thoroughly reject.


**Conclusion**

Virtually everything Lincoln did to defeat secession by force of arms was illegal: The declaration of war without a vote of Congress; the invasion of states and overthrow of duly elected state governments; the blockade of Southern ports; the arbitrary impressments of Southerners into U.S. Army ranks; and, borrowing Pres. Franklin Roosevelt's words two generations hence, the "unprovoked and dastardly attack" on civilian noncombatants and deliberate destruction of private property.

Likewise, Lincoln's dictatorial suppression of political opposition in the North was also illegal. The arrest of civilians, mayors and other Northern officials by the U.S. Army; the numerous suspensions of habeas corpus by executive order; the shutting down of opposition newspapers and arresting editors; the trial of Northern civilians in military courts; the financing of the war with worthless paper money; and even the threatened arrest of Chief Justice Roger Taney was illegal, morally wrong, and profoundly counterrevolutionary.

In the twenty-first century, America is haunted by Lincoln's blood lust for a coercive, dominant, unitary, unaccountable, debt-laden central government. This government's primary function has become the plunder of society and the redistribution of wealth to the politically privileged elite and their collection of political sycophants who help keep them in power. In this regard, the two major political parties have become the party of Lincoln, each a metastatic twin of the other. The political, social, economic, and legal landscape increasingly resembles the Mexican oligarchy, where one class holds all the assets, and the one-party system that they control holds all the power.

This is why this book matters. Abraham Lincoln opened the door to the Leviathan central state that mandates, manipulates, and regulates virtually every aspect of life in America and seeks unilateral hegemony around the globe.

# CHAPTER TWO

# Race: The Eight-Hundred-Pound Gorilla of American History

*"We want no more poetry about striking off chains and bidding the oppressed go. Plain people want to know whether the chains will not be put upon white limbs; and whither the oppressed are to go. . . . If they are to go to Ohio and the North, we want to know it. Nay, we want, if we can, to stop it."*
—Ohio Congressman Samuel S. Cox,
On the floor of Congress, 1862

The idea that the federal government, white Northerners, or Northern "free" states fought the Civil War to end slavery, or were on the right side of the racial-justice issue, is preposterous. This position, which is advocated by Princeton University historian James McPherson, Arthur Schlesinger, Jr., and other statists, is nothing short of gullible self-deception, bordering on simple-mindedness.

One must be mindful that as regions, neither the North nor the South has clean hands in regards to racial justice. The harsh truth is that there were slaveholding plantations in New York, New Jersey, and Massachusetts. Archaeological evidence clearly shows that "full-fledged plantations" in these states held African American slaves under conditions similar to those in the South. "Historians are stunned by some of the evidence," says one historical archaeologist.[1] And in several Northern states, child slavery stubbornly survived long after adult slavery ceased to exist.

Though conditions on those Northern plantations were similar to Southern plantations, the manner in which slavery was ended in the North was not. Before the Thirteenth Amendment was ratified in 1865, granting instantaneous freedom to all slaves, each Northern state that voluntarily ended slavery did so under a system of manumission. Manumission provided that a child born of a slave mother after a date set by each state's legislature was born free but bound to service to his mother's master for a specific number of years (which varied from state to state). The slave parents of the freeborn child remained in slavery. "Under such arrangements, slaveholders suffered no losses on existing male slaves or on female slaves who were already past their childbearing years."[2] Thus, manumission was a gradual form of emancipation that incorporated compensation to slave owners who were rewarded with productive years of forced labor as compensation for the expense of raising the freeborn child who would eventually discharge all labor obligations to his mother's master.

New York's 1799 manumission law (An Act for the Gradual Abolition of Slavery) was typical. Female children born of slave women after July 4, 1799, would be free at age twenty-five, men at age twenty-eight. Slowly, slavery would end as slave women aged beyond child-bearing years and their children reached the age of release in the 1830s, '40s, and '50s. Thus, manumission allowed slavery to die out in a literal sense, as it did not free a single person already a slave. The *Journal of Negro History* says manumission was a "very fair" way of ending slavery:

> All things considered, this was a very fair way of putting an end to slavery in New York. No slaves were to be suddenly cast loose in the world without means of support . . . and no masters were to be deprived of their slaves against their consent.[3]

This gradual approach of ending New York slavery, the largest Northern slave-holding state, was enacted to protect the economic interests of slave owners, according to David N. Gellman, a lecturer in early American history at Northwestern University and expert on the abolition movement in New York. "It certainly beats the Civil War, if that's the alternative," says Gellman, ". . . though it seems appalling that real human beings should be subject to this give and take."[4]

If there were any truth to the proposition that the North was on the correct side of the racial-justice issue in 1861, and that the war was fought to free the slaves, then history would record the humane treatment of free blacks in the North. Or, history would record progressively better treatment of free blacks in the North. Or, history would record a progressively sympathetic attitude towards free blacks among Northerners. The harsh reality of history is precisely the opposite on all points.

The fact is that free blacks were exploited, marginalized, maligned, made fun of, and hated in every Northern state where they were present before the war. To call free blacks "second-class" citizens in the North at that time would be to describe a legal and social status that was far superior to the reality of their lives. Free blacks were not citizens of any Northern state. The argument that Northern whites were willing to fight and die for racial justice in the South while they simultaneously perpetrated systematic exploitation of free blacks in the North is an argument with no supporting facts. There was no more prewar racial justice in the North than there was in the South. In fact, there is a strong argument to be made that there was more actual opportunity for free blacks in the South than there was in the North.

**Atlantic Slave Trade**
The Atlantic slave trade was likely the most vicious atrocity ever perpetrated by one man upon another. It lasted for two centuries because it was enormously profitable for all who touched it, on both sides of the Atlantic. First and foremost, slavery was a lucrative system of labor.

Slavery was profitable for the African nations who sold members of their own race into slavery; it was profitable for the Portuguese, Dutch, British, and later American (primarily New England) shipping interests who transported human cargo; it was profitable for the New England shipbuilders who built or outfitted many of the slavers; it was profitable for the suppliers in the ports that supported the trade; it was profitable for the financial interests who owned the slave expeditions; it was profitable for the middle-men merchants who conducted the auctions and filled the orders for human servants; and it was profitable for the slave master in America, Brazil, Cuba, and elsewhere in the New World.

All such interests North and South and on both sides of the Atlantic participated and profited. They all shared a common motive, money. The historic record indicates there was plenty of it.

The sale of slaves to European traders on the African coast from the sixteenth through eighteenth centuries was dominated by the three kingdoms of Benin, Dahomey, and Oyo, according to Herbert S. Klein in his 1999 book *The Atlantic Slave Trade*. These kingdoms granted royal monopolies and heavily taxed the slave trade and "derived significant wealth" therefrom.[5] Other historians suggest that numerous small political entities were involved in the slave trade.

Part of this wealth came from the heavy taxation levied by the African nations on the slave trade as well as from the sale of the slaves themselves. Taxes were levied on the right to conduct the trade; there were required payments "for royal officials handing movement of slaves to the ships," for the costs for interpreters, and even a final export tax.[6]

The *Journal of Black Studies* states that the sale of Africans on the coast tended to displace legitimate trade in other goods and foodstuffs because "the profit to be made from the sale of slaves was far greater than that which could be made from traditional forms of trade."[7] Africans were sold into bondage "because there was economic incentive to enslave them."[8]

Europeans slave buyers "were totally dependent on African sellers for the delivery of slaves."[9] Slaves "usually saw their first European only when the slaves arrived at the coast of Africa [from the interior]. Their fates to that point had been entirely in the hands of other Africans."[10]

Warfare was only one source of slaves but "was not the primary mechanism for obtaining slaves." How, then, was the supply of souls furnished? Klein answers: "Given the long-term and very steady nature of slave exports from [Africa], it is evident that the trade was obtaining slaves from systematic raiding on the frontier as well as from local religious, judicial, and political sources all along the trade routes in the interior."[11] Not surprisingly, victims caught in raids and other mechanisms were usually "people outside of the immediate political unit or kinship grouping" of their African kidnappers.[12]

Popular American culture of the late twentieth century and beyond focuses its blame for slavery on the stereotypical Southern planter, so it may shock some to learn that the *Journal of Negro History* reports "slavery in Africa is as old as the people . . . an old and well established organized traffic in slaves existed long before the first Europeans came to the Guinea coast."[13]

Klein notes, "Both an internal and international slave trade existed in Africa before the arrival of Europeans," and the Europeans simply availed themselves of "markets and trading arrangements already in place. An extensive slave market already existed before the arrival of the Europeans and though domestic slavery in Africa would be substantially different from commercial slavery in America, the whole process of seizing war captives, enslaving criminals and debtors, taxing dependent groups for slaves, and even raiding defenseless peasants constituted well-known market activities." [14]

Africans not only owned other Africans and sold them to Europeans, they also sold African slaves to Middle Eastern, Mediterranean, and Asian markets, including Islamic states in North Africa and the Near East. [15]

The slave trade in America was immensely profitable for shippers, ship builders, shipping suppliers, and for those who owned the human cargoes of the expeditions to Africa.

As Donald Livingston has noted, it was New England that "opened the slave trade with Africa and grew rich selling slaves throughout the [W]estern [H]emisphere." Livingston says the slave trade, conducted mainly by New England, provided the "seed money for the industrial revolution" which would open new economic possibilities in the North. [16]

Historian David Harper on his Web site www.slavenorth.com states that the slave trade was "one of the foundations of New England's economic structure." In the final one hundred years of legal international slave trade, Harper writes, "Rhode Island merchants sponsored at least 934 slaving voyages to the coast of Africa and carried an estimated 106,544 slaves to the New World." [17]

Indeed, in 2003, Dr. Ruth J. Simmons, the first black president of an Ivy League school and first woman president of Brown University, commissioned a Steering Committee on Slavery and Justice to investigate and discuss, among other things, Brown University's connection to slavery. Simmons explains that when Brown was founded in 1764, it was "a period in our nation's history when nearly all commerce and wealth was in some manner entangled with the slave trade." She reveals that Providence-area slave labor was "involved" with the construction of the university's first building. [18]

Much of the historic record of the wealth of the Brown family and its connection to the slave trade is well known. At least six of the Browns, "James and his brother Obadiah, and James' four sons,

Nicholas, John, Joseph, and Moses ran one of the biggest slave-trading businesses in New England, and for more than half a century the family reaped huge profits from the slave trade." The slave trade was the "foundation" for the Brown fortune and, their donations to Rhode Island College "were so generous that the name was changed to Brown University."

The Browns were not the only Rhode Islanders to get a piece of the action. More than two hundred Rhode Islanders owned a share in a slave voyage at one time or another. Until the abolition of the international slave trade by the United States in 1808, slavery provided Rhode Island with a major profit sector.

Moreover, what was good for Rhode Island was good for Massachusetts and the rest of New England. At the time of the American Revolution, the slave trade had "[woven] itself into the entire regional economy of New England. The Massachusetts slave trade gave work to coopers, tanners, sail makers, and rope makers. Countless agents, insurers, lawyers, clerks, and scriveners handled the paperwork for slave merchants." In the New England fishing ports and backwoods, the slave trade supported fisherman, loggers, and livestock farmers.[19]

Much the same could be said of New York. The slave trade was "one of the cornerstones of New York's commercial prosperity in the eighteenth century." It was "enormously profitable to the business community."[20]

By the time of the American Revolution, "the entire community had a stake in the [slave] trade. Newspapers depended upon it for much of their advertising revenue. . . . Lawyers and scriveners also played an important role in arranging slave transactions."[21] Shippers from New York and other homeports conducted the slave trade for "the profits made by supplying the demand for slaves."[22]

However, Northern participation and profits in the slave trade did not simply end when the United States and Great Britain abolished the international slave trade in 1808. The navies of both countries patrolled the Atlantic to interdict slave ships, but because the U.S. was one of the few nations that did not allow the British Navy to board its ships, the slave traders continued to bring slaves to Brazil and Cuba under the U.S. flag. Many of these ships were built for that purpose by Northern shipyards, in ventures financed by Northerners.

One of the most notorious examples of the continuing illegal slave trade from Northern ports was the schooner-yacht *Wanderer*, "pride of the New York Yacht Club." Virtually on the eve of the Civil War, April 1858, a half-century after the federal government abolished the Atlantic slave trade, the *Wanderer* sailed to Port Jefferson, New York, to be fitted out for that purpose. Port officials and workers looked the other way, which to Harper suggests, "This kind of thing was not unusual." But the port surveyor reported the ship to federal authorities who towed it to New York, where her captain talked his way out of trouble and finished fitting her out. The *Wanderer* cleared customs and set sail to Africa "where she took aboard some 600 Blacks. On Nov. 28, 1858, she reached Jekyll Island, Georgia, where she illegally unloaded the 465 survivors of what is generally called the last shipment of slaves to arrive in the United States."[23]

The 2005 book *Complicity* states that in the peak years of New York's participation in the illegal slave trade (1859-60), by one "cautious estimate," at least two ships per month departed for Africa. In 1861, just as it was about to be interrupted by war, New York's illegal slave trade was so "brazen" that anyone who read a newspaper would have known about it.[23A]

Slavery was also profitable for the middlemen and retailers. In New York, "The retail markup was so high—at least 100 percent—that almost anyone with sufficient capital to import a small parcel of slaves could set up a lucrative business."[24]

Lawyers and scriveners also played an important and lucrative role as New York slavery middlemen. "Their particular specialty was the operation of slave registries which contained detailed information on slaves for sale."[25] The business was also profitable for the slave owner, whether he was a planter, who may have owned dozens or hundreds of slaves, or a much smaller farmer who owned a few slaves, or a businessman who owned a few slaves who worked in mills or factories as skilled artisans.

The 1974 book on Negro slavery by Johns Hopkins' economists Robert William Fogel and Stanley L. Engerman, *Time on the Cross*, explodes several myths about slavery in America, and as one might expect, it created a firestorm of controversy among historians.

One such myth is that slavery on the eve of the Civil War was "economically moribund," a dying institution. Fogel and Engerman found just the opposite. "As the Civil War approached, slavery as an economic institution was never stronger."[26] And there was a reason for this because the investment in slave labor in the South was as profitable to the slave owner as any investment opportunity in the North among industrialists. "The purchase of a slave was generally a highly profitable investment which yielded rates of return that compared favorably with the most outstanding investment opportunities in manufacturing."[27]

Nor was slavery just a Southern problem. Slavery was a national problem. It stained the history of the entire country because its profitability was just too much for any section or group to resist. Even the Society of Friends (the Quakers), who were the first group in America to reject slavery as morally wrong, did so only after its members had owned and traded in slaves for more than one hundred years.

When the Northern states began the slow process of the manumission of slaves held in their jurisdiction, a number of disquieting facts are worth noting because they are so frequently untold and unknown to most people:

- Slave owners in the North were compensated for the loss of every slave to emancipation, without exception;
- No slave was granted immediate emancipation in any Northern state when those states individually abolished slavery, and in some states, the process took as long as twenty-eight years (the process of manumission or gradual emancipation);
- Many Northern slaves whose children would have been born free under manumission laws in the North, were legally sold to Southern slave owners, where those children would be born as slaves;
- Northern ports, shipbuilders, shippers, suppliers, banks, and other investors continued to reap profits from the illegal Atlantic slave trade that they dominated, up to the eve of the Civil War;
- At least two so-called "free" states, New Jersey and Illinois, had legal loopholes that allowed them to claim they were "free" when in fact slavery was never eradicated before the Civil War.

The error of slavery does not stop at the Atlantic shore, for without the centuries-old market of human bondage on the coast of Africa, there could have been no Negro slavery in America.

In an article titled "Rattling the Chains," Thomas Sowell points out, "Slavery was an ugly, dirty business but people of virtually every race, color, and creed engaged in it on every inhabited continent. And the people they enslaved were also of virtually every race, color and creed."[28]

The origin of the word "slave," which is an Anglicized corruption for the word "Slav," reveals that the Islamic conquest of the Balkans drove perhaps millions of Europeans into slavery in the Muslim world, so much so that the name of this Eastern European ethnic group became synonymous with the condition of human bondage.

Sowell notes that "no race, country, or civilization ha[s] clean hands" when it comes to slavery. Caesar had British slaves, Muslims had European and African slaves, Europeans enslaved other Europeans and Africans, and Americans had African slaves. "It was the same story in Asia, Africa, and among the Polynesians and the indigenous peoples of the Western Hemisphere."[29] In another article, Sowell states, "People of every race and color were enslaved—and enslaved others. White people were still being bought and sold as slaves in the Ottoman Empire, decades after American blacks were freed."[30]

Indeed, slavery was not formally abolished on the Arabian peninsula, specifically Saudi Arabia, until 1962 (1962, not 1862). It is "one of the most ancient [and] long-lived forms of economic and social organization."[31]

Of the 9.5 million souls kidnapped in Africa and forcibly transported across the Atlantic as slaves to the New World, only six percent were imported to the United States, about the same number of slaves that were transported to tiny Dutch, Danish, and Swedish Caribbean colonies. The nation of Brazil alone received at least six times the number of slaves than did the South.[32]

Nevertheless, by the time of the Civil War, the South had become the largest slave-holding region in the Western Hemisphere, even surpassing Brazil. This was due to "the unusually high rate of natural increase of its slave population," in other words the relatively low mortality rate of the Southern slave versus the typical slave in Brazil.[33]

Slavery continues to be a world problem into the twenty-first century. The U.S. State Department has issued numerous reports regarding its effort to end human trafficking, which primarily involves sex slavery.


### Racial Attitudes in the North

University of California, Berkeley historian Leon Litwack reveals in scores of instances in his seminal book *North of Slavery*, the true attitudes of Northern whites about free blacks leading up to the Civil War. It is not a pretty picture.

Though Litwack carefully documents a few, scattered instances of progress of free blacks in the North prior to the war, the overwhelming attitude was against the Negro race. Blacks were held in with "chains of a stronger kind [that] manacled their limbs, from which no legislative act could free them; a mental and moral subordination and inferiority, to which tyrant custom has here subjected all the sons and daughters of Africa."[34]

Other historians draw the same conclusion. In an article in the *Mississippi Valley Historical Review,* Jacque Voegeli notes that the states of the old northwest (Ohio, Indiana, Illinois, Michigan, Wisconsin, Minnesota, and Iowa) were bastions of white supremacy.[35] Even during the war, as late as 1862, there were "insistent voices" in the northwest, Pennsylvania, and New Jersey clamoring for action "to shield the North from a Negro invasion" should the South collapse militarily or the slaves free themselves by insurrection.[36]

Nor was racial justice to be found in the heart of Abraham Lincoln or his cabinet. Secretary of Treasury (and future chief justice) Salmon P. Chase wrote, "Many honest men really think they [Negroes] are not to be permitted to reside permanently in Northern states." Chase realized that forced expulsion of free blacks from the North was a popular idea. Though he did not personally object to the presence of free blacks in his home state of Ohio, Chase nevertheless believed that most free blacks in the North would move south if given the chance. "Let, therefore, the South be opened to negro emigration by emancipation along the Gulf, and it is easy to see that the blacks of the North will slide southward, and leave behind them no question to quarrel about as far as they are concerned."[37] Chase's attitude toward free blacks was "good riddance."

According to Litwack the negative racial attitude toward free blacks in the North was all pervasive:

> Legal and extralegal discrimination restricted Northern Negroes in virtually every phase of existence. Where laws were lacking or ineffectual, public opinion provided its own remedies. Indeed, few held out any hope for the successful or peaceful integration of the Negro into white-dominated society.[38]

French nobleman Alexis de Tocqueville traveled extensively through the northern and southern regions of the United States in the early 1830s and subsequently wrote *Democracy in America*. Having associated the plight of blacks with the institution of slavery, de Tocqueville expresses astonishment at the treatment of free blacks in the North and finds that "custom and popular prejudices exerted a decisive influence." He observes that racial prejudice "appears to be stronger in the states that have abolished slavery than in those where it still exists; and nowhere is it so intolerant as in those states [parts of New England and the Midwest] where servitude has never been known." Noting that free blacks are discriminated against by white churches and white cemeteries in the North, de Tocqueville concludes, "Thus the Negro is free, but he can neither share the rights, nor the pleasures, nor the labors, nor the afflictions, nor the tomb of him whose equal he been declared to be; and he cannot meet him upon fair terms in life or in death."[39]

Even "scientific" knowledge in the nineteenth-century North was prejudiced against the black man, excluding him from equality with whites on the basis that blacks form a separate species. In the 1840s, New York attorney William Frederick Van Amringe published *An Investigation of the Theories of the Natural History of Man*, in which he argued that humans are divided into four species (not merely races): Caucasian, Oriental, Aboriginal, and Negroid.[40]

Some views were as equally prejudiced against American Indians as they were against blacks. In 1842, Dr. Samuel George Morton, a physician, presented a paper to the Boston Society of Natural History that advanced the argument that Indians are a race "peculiar, and distinct from all others," and he argued, naturally inferior. Two of Morton's followers, also physicians, Dr. Josiah C. Nott of Mobile,

Alabama, and Dr. Henry S. Patterson of Philadelphia, were vehement white supremacists. Nott wrote in 1844, the "Indian and the Negro are now and have been in all ages and places inferior to the Caucasian." In 1853, Patterson advocated racial genocide against the Plains Indians who he referred to as "the cinnamon-colored vermin west of the Mississippi."[41]

**Statutory Barriers and Political Realities in Prewar Northern States**
And it was not just attitudes that held back the free black man in the North, he also faced numerous legal barriers, such as Jim Crow laws, put in place deliberately to exploit and stop free blacks from entering communities where they were not already present. Even

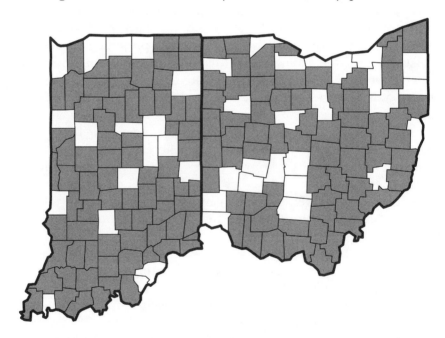

*Racial settlement patterns of Indiana and Ohio Counties from 2000 Census data. Shading shows counties that remain virtually all white (>93.33% white) into the twenty-first century, a legacy of Negro exclusion laws that were on the books when both states were settled in the early nineteenth century and admitted to the Union.* (U.S. Census Bureau, Census 2000 Redistricting Data, Summary File, Matrices PL1 and PL2.)

Lincoln voted for Jim Crow when he was a member of the Illinois legislature. According to Lerone Bennett, Jr., Lincoln voted for a resolution that stated, "The elective franchise should be kept pure from contamination by the admission of colored votes."[42] These barriers worked quite well, especially in Illinois where the total percentage of blacks fell with every census from 1820 to 1860. By the time of the Civil War, 249 of every 250 people in Illinois were white. Jim Crow was almost as effective in Indiana and Ohio, where the percentage of blacks hovered around one to five percent during that period.

When Lincoln called for the invasion of the South, there were more free blacks in Virginia than Illinois, Indiana, and Ohio combined. Very little has changed in 145 years. According to the 2000 U.S. Census, there are still almost five hundred counties in the states of Ohio, Michigan, Indiana, Illinois, Wisconsin, Iowa, and Minnesota that remain as they always have been: Lily White. Table 1 shows the number and percentage of virtually all-white counties in those states. Each of these states had Negro exclusion laws on the books upon statehood. Free blacks were literally excluded by law.

**Table 1. States Admitted from the Northwest Territory, 1803-1848**

| State | Total No. of Counties | White-Only* Counties |
|---|---|---|
| Illinois | 102 | 64 counties (63%) |
| Indiana | 92 | 75 counties (82%) |
| Iowa | 99 | 88 counties (89%) |
| Michigan | 83 | 53 counties (64%) |
| Minnesota | 87 | 73 counties (84%) |
| Ohio | 88 | 64 counties (73%) |
| Wisconsin | 72 | 55 counties (76%) |
| **TOTAL** | 623 | 472 counties (76%) |

*White-Only counties are defined as those in which at least 14 of every 15 individuals (or >93.33%) are white. Source: U.S. Census Bureau, Census 2000 Redistricting Data, Summary File, Matrices PL1 and PL2.

Free blacks could not vote in the prewar North in any state outside New England, except for Pennsylvania and that right was taken away in 1838. Moreover, before there was a law prohibiting free blacks from voting in Pennsylvania, public opinion was a powerful weapon discouraging the exercise. In the 1830s, an English visitor to Pennsylvania asked why free blacks did not vote. He was told, "Just let them try!"[43]

Following Maine's statehood in 1819, every state admitted to the Union until after the end of the Civil War confined the privilege of voting to white males.[44] Yet, slavery existed even in Maine. Upon statehood, according to Sue Macy's article "A Look Back at Slavery in Maine," "Wealthy people and aristocratic families who owned slaves kept them." It was as simple as that. Slaves were chattel property, and if you owned slaves when Maine was separated from Massachusetts and became a state, you simply "kept them." This article challenges the accuracy of the U.S. Census that shows several hundred free blacks in Maine in the early decades of the nineteenth century, but only records two slaves in the 1830 Census. Citing baptism records, Macy makes a compelling case that many of the blacks counted as freemen in the Maine census were actually slaves.[45]

The fact that slavery existed in Maine at the time of statehood means that slavery existed in Massachusetts and was tolerated there despite it being a "free" state. Perhaps there were other "wealthy people and aristocratic families" in Massachusetts who kept their slaves.

Since each state is admitted to the Union by an act of Congress with presidential approval, the systematic withholding of the vote from blacks by Southern and Northern states carried with it a certain acquiescence by every Congress and every president in office when any statehood was approved (except for Maine) during this period. This includes the Great Emancipator, Lincoln himself, who signed the act of statehood for West Virginia admitting it in 1863 technically as a slave state. The Lincoln scholars are quick to point out that the West Virginia Constitution abolished adult slavery and therefore qualifies for the "racially just" category of "free state." However, it is difficult to ignore that Lincoln put *his signature* on the enabling act that approved *child slavery* in West Virginia. Voting was also withheld from free backs there.

Table 2 displays the extent of Jim Crow laws passed in order to limit the liberty of free blacks in Northern states in the prewar ear. It is by no means intended to be an exhaustive list.

## Table 2. Jim Crow Laws in the North

| Year | Location | Jim Crow Law |
|---|---|---|
| 1777 | Vermont | Convention adopts constitution that protects child slavery and Atlantic slave trade.[1] |
| 1786 | Vermont | Vermont Constitution of 1786 contains identical protection for child slavery and the Atlantic slave trade that their 1777 Constitution contained.[2] |
| 1792 | Delaware | Constitution limits franchise to "free white males." |
| 1802 | District of Columbia | Congress establishes municipal government in D.C. that limits the franchise to "free white male" inhabitants.[3] |
| 1803 | Ohio | Upon statehood free blacks prohibited from voting; Ohio Constitution protects "virtual slavery" of Negro children.[4, 8] |
| 1804 | Ohio | Anti-Negro "Black Laws" restrict liberties of free blacks.[8] |
| 1807 | New Jersey | Legislature restricts the franchise to "free white male citizens."[3] |
| 1811 | New York | Legislature requires free blacks to produce "certificate of freedom" to vote.[3] |
| 1814 | Connecticut | Legislature restricts franchise to free white males.[6] |
| 1815 | New York | Legislature reenacts 1811 law requiring "certificate of freedom" and voids certificates obtained under an 1813 law.[3] |
| 1815 | New Hampshire | Legislature restricts enrollment in the militia to free white males.[10] |
| 1816 | Indiana | Upon statehood, legislature prohibits free blacks from voting.[4] |
| 1818 | Connecticut | Constitution disenfranchises free blacks not already registered to vote.[3] |
| 1818 | Illinois | Constitution at statehood protects human property of slaveholders already in the state.[7] |
| 1819 | Illinois | Legislature enacts Negro exclusion law.[9] |
| 1820 | New Jersey | Legislature reaffirms law that prohibits free black franchise.[3] |

| 1820 | District of Columbia | By charter Congress authorizes municipal government of D.C. "to restrain and prohibit the nightly and other disorderly meetings of slaves, free Negroes, and mulattoes."[10] |
|------|------|------|
| 1821 | New York | Voters amend state constitution, restrict free black franchise.[4] |
| 1822 | Rhode Island | Legislature restricts franchise to "white" males and bans interracial marriage.[6, 10] |
| 1823 | Illinois | By two-thirds vote the legislature places on the ballot constitutional amendment to make Illinois a slave state. Narrowly defeated by voters.[11] |
| 1827 | Michigan Territory | Territorial legislature enacts Negro exclusion law.[9] |
| 1829 | Illinois | Legislature renews Negro exclusion law.[9] |
| 1831 | Indiana | Legislature enacts Negro exclusion law.[9] |
| 1833 | Connecticut | State Supreme Court allows a lower court ruling to stand that Negroes and Indians are not citizens.[21] |
| 1833 | Connecticut | Legislature criminalizes the establishment of any school for persons of the African race.[10] |
| 1836 | Rhode Island | Legislature amends suffrage law but still applied to "white male persons" only.[6] |
| 1836 | Massachusetts | Legislature renews ban on interracial marriage.[10] |
| 1836 | Illinois | Illinois House of Representatives passes a resolution by two-thirds vote that "the elective franchise should be kept pure from contamination by the admission of colored votes." State Rep. Abraham Lincoln supported the resolution.[22] |
| 1837 | Pennsylvania | State Supreme Court rules that Negroes and mulattos are not entitled to vote.[4] |
| 1837 | Michigan | From statehood, the Michigan Constitution restricts franchise to "white males."[12] |
| 1838 | Pennsylvania | Voters amend state constitution and disenfranchise free blacks.[4] |
| 1839 | Ohio | Ohio House of Representatives passes a resolution that Negroes have no right to petition the legislature "for any purpose whatever."[5] |
| 1839 | Iowa Territory | Legislature enacts Negro exclusion law.[4] |
| 1845 | Connecticut | Constitutional amendment restricts franchise to "white" males.[6] |
| 1846 | Wisconsin Territory | Voters reject free black suffrage.[9] |

| 1846 | Iowa | Voters reject free black suffrage in original state constitution.[12] |
|------|------|------|
| 1846 | New York | Voters reject free black suffrage constitutional amendment.[4] |
| 1847 | Illinois | Voters reject free black suffrage constitutional amendment.[12] |
| 1847 | Connecticut | Legislature blocks proposal that would permit free blacks to vote.[3] |
| 1848 | Oregon Territory | From the organization as a territory, the legislature withholds exercise of the franchise from free blacks.[4] |
| 1849 | Wisconsin | Voters reject free black suffrage for a second time.[9] |
| 1850 | California | From statehood, the California Constitution prohibits free blacks from exercising the franchise.[19] |
| 1850 | Utah Territory | From the organization as a territory, the legislature withholds exercise of the franchise from free blacks.[4] |
| 1851 | Indiana | Voters ratify new state constitution that disenfranchises free blacks.[15] |
| 1851 | Ohio | Voters ratify new state constitution that disenfranchises free blacks.[16] |
| 1854 | Kansas Territory | From the organization as a territory, the legislature withholds exercise of the franchise from free blacks.[4] |
| 1854 | Nebraska Territory | From the organization as a territory, the legislature withholds exercise of the franchise from free blacks.[4] |
| 1855 | Connecticut | Voters adopt constitutional amendment requiring proof of literacy to vote.[12] |
| 1857 | Wisconsin | Voters reject free black suffrage for a third time.[9] |
| 1857 | Massachusetts | Voters adopt constitutional amendment requiring proof of literacy to vote.[12] |
| 1857 | Minnesota | From statehood, the Minnesota Constitution prohibits free blacks from exercising the franchise.[12] |
| 1857 | Iowa | Voters ratify a new constitution that retains the disenfranchisement of free blacks.[17] |
| 1857 | Oregon | Voters approve constitution 8 to 1, and in 1859, Oregon became the only state admitted to the Union with a racial exclusion provision in the state constitution; also prohibited exercising the franchise for free blacks, mulattos, and Chinese; prohibited property ownership for blacks and mulattos.[9, 18] |

| | | |
|---|---|---|
| 1859 | Ohio | Legislature requires election officials to reject the vote of a person "who has a distinct and visible admixture of African blood."[4] |
| 1860 | New York | Voters reject free black suffrage constitutional amendment for a second time.[4] |
| 1861 | Nevada Territory | From the organization as a territory, the legislature withholds exercise of the franchise from free blacks.[4] |
| 1861 | Colorado Territory | From the organization as a territory, the legislature withholds exercise of the franchise from free blacks.[4] |
| 1861 | Kansas | Admitted as a "free" state but withheld exercise of the franchise from free blacks.[4] |
| 1862 | Illinois | Voters reject free black suffrage; adopt a racial exclusion amendment to the Illinois Constitution.[13] |
| 1863 | West Virginia | Admitted to the Union during the war as a slave state; also prohibited free black franchise.[20] |
| 1864 | Nevada | Prohibited free black franchise from statehood.[4] |
| 1865 | Connecticut | Voters reject black suffrage proposal.[4] |
| 1865 | Minnesota | Voters reject black suffrage proposal.[23] |
| 1865 | Wisconsin | Voters reject free black suffrage for a fourth time.[9] |
| 1865 | Colorado Territory | Voters reject black suffrage proposal.[23] |
| 1865 | District of Columbia | Voters in the nation's capital reject black suffrage proposal.[23] |
| 1866 | Nebraska Territory | Voters reject black suffrage proposal.[23] |
| 1867 | Ohio | Voters reject black suffrage proposal.[4] |
| 1867 | Connecticut | Voters reject black suffrage in special election.[14] |
| 1867 | Minnesota | Voters reject black suffrage proposal a second time.[23] |
| 1867 | New Jersey | Lower house of legislature refuses a proposed amendment to strike the word "white" from the New Jersey Constitution.[14] |
| 1867 | Kansas | Voters reject black suffrage.[4] |
| 1868 | Pennsylvania | Lower house of legislature votes 64 to 14 against a proposed constitutional amendment for black suffrage.[14] |
| 1868 | Ohio | Legislature rejects black suffrage.[12] |
| 1868 | Michigan | Legislature rejects a proposed amendment to strike the word "white" from the Michigan Constitution.[12] |
| 1868 | New York | Voters reject free black suffrage constitutional amendment for a third time.[4] |

**Sources:**

1. Vermont Constitution of 1777.

2. Vermont Constitution of 1786.

3. Charles H. Wesley, "Negro Suffrage in the Period of Constitution-Making, 1787-1865," *The Journal of Negro History* 32, no. 2 (April 1947): 143-68.

4. Stephen B. Weeks, "The History of Negro Suffrage in the South," *Political Science Quarterly* 9, no. 4 (December 1894): 671-703.

5. Leon F. Litwack, *North of Slavery* (Chicago: University of Chicago Press, 1961)

6. James Truslow Adams, "Disfranchisement of Negroes in New England," *The American Historical Review* 30, no. 3 (April 1925): 543-47.

7. Illinois Constitution of 1818.

8. James H. Rodabaugh, "The Negro in Ohio," *The Journal of Negro History* 31, no. 1 (January 1946): 9-29.

9. Douglas Harper, www.slavenorth.com.

10. *Dred Scott* v. *John F. A. Sandford,* 60 U.S. 393 (1856)

11. Illinois State Historical Library, www.state.il.us.com.

12. Leo Alilunas, "A Review of Negro Suffrage Policies Prior to 1915," *The Journal of Negro History* 25, no. 2 (April 1940): 153-60.

13. Jacque Voegeli, "The Northwest and the Race Issue, 1861-1862," *The Mississippi Valley Historical Review* 50, no. 2 (September 1963): 235-51.

14, Leslie H. Fishel, Jr., "Northern Prejudice and Negro Suffrage 1865-1870," *The Journal of Negro History* 39, no. 1 (January 1954): 8-26.

15. Indiana Constitution of 1851.

16. Ohio Constitution of 1851.

17. Iowa Constitution of 1857.

18. Oregon Constitution of 1857.

19. California Constitution of 1849.

20. West Virginia Division of Culture and History, www.wvculture.org.

21. *Crandall* v. *Connecticut,* 10 Conn., Rep. 340.

22. Lerone Bennett, Jr., *Forced Into Glory* (Chicago: Johnson Publishing Co., 2000).

23. William Gillette, *The Right to Vote: Politics and the Passage of the Fifteenth Amendment* (Baltimore: John Hopkins Press, 1965).

Though incongruous to the argument that the war was fought for racial justice, these actions are perfectly consistent with a long string of congressional legislation, including limiting naturalization (citizenship) to white aliens (1790); organizing a "white only" militia (1792); excluding Negroes from carrying the mail (1810); and providing for "white only" municipal officials in Washington, D.C. (1820). Litwack concludes that before the war, Congress (*not* just the legislatures of Southern states) "resolved to treat Negroes neither as citizens nor aliens."[46]

Neither citizens nor aliens is perhaps the most apt characterization of the federal government's position on free blacks prior to the war. In 1843, U.S. Atty. Gen. Hugh Legare decided that free blacks occupy an intermediate position between citizens and aliens.[47] The U.S. State Department's policy regarding the issuance of passports for blacks is also prejudicial. In 1839, Secretary of State John Forsyth (the Van Buren administration) rejected the application for a passport by a free black from Philadelphia on the grounds that Pennsylvania's Constitution of 1838 did not recognize Negroes as citizens. In 1847, Secretary of State (and future president) James Buchanan said that free blacks are not issued a passport "in the ordinary form, recognizing them as citizens, but a certificate suited to the nature of the case." Buchanan's successor as secretary of state, John M. Clayton, stated in 1849 that passports "are not granted by this department to persons of color."[48]

In spite of such statements, the State Department actually issued a few passports to free blacks in the 1830s, '40s, and as late as 1854. However, the State Department's position hardened in 1856 when eleven free blacks applied for passports for the purpose of lecturing and raising money for the abolitionist movement. Secretary William L. Marcy (a New Yorker serving in the Pierce administration) refused to issue the passports and declared that the question of Black citizenship "has repeatedly arisen in the administration of both the national and State governments." Marcy cited an opinion by U.S. Atty. Gen. William Wirt in 1821 that free Negroes are not citizens. In 1858, Secretary Lewis Cass (a Northerner) asserted that passports "being a certificate of citizenship, has never since the foundation of the Government, been grated to persons of color."[49]

Their object of study, Lincoln himself, contradicts Lincoln

scholars. Making comments on the 1857 *Dred Scott* decision that were recorded in the *Daily Illinois State Journal*, Springfield, (June 29, 1857), Lincoln said,

> It is grossly incorrect to say or assume, that the public estimate of the negro is more favorable now [1857] than it was at the origin of the government.

Far from seeing real improvement in the condition of free blacks in the North, Lincoln referred to scattered advancements as nothing more than "trifling particulars" and that the trend, in fact, was in the wrong direction. In that same speech, Lincoln said, "All the powers of earth seem rapidly combining against him" (the black man).

Pennsylvania congressman David Wilmot, the prominent abolitionist who introduced the Wilmot proviso to ban slavery from the western territories, explained that his concern was not for blacks, but for whites. He said he possessed "no squeamish sensitiveness upon the subject of slavery, no morbid sympathy for the slave."[50]

Even among Northern abolitionists, the plight of the black slave in the South seemed no worse than the plight of the white hourly industrial worker in Northern cities. Abolitionist George Henry Evans concluded that the wage system under which whites labored in the industrialized North bred "crowded cities, debased servitude, rent exaction, disease, crime and prostitution" and was worse than slave life in the South. He noted that the Negro slave had a master in sickness and in health, but the Northern white worker was a freeman only as long and he could labor and when he could no longer toil became a pauper. The industrial worker—a "freeman"—was "worked by everybody and cared for by nobody."[51]

Labor advocate and publisher Horace Greeley wrote in the New York *Weekly Tribune* that he was more sympathetic to the plight of white workers in the North than slaves in the South. "If I am less troubled concerning slavery prevalent in Charleston or New Orleans, it is because I see so much slavery in New York." He said Southern slavery "is no more hideous in kind and degree than that which prevails in the North."[52]

The belief that Negroes were inferior and unfit to associate with or live on equal terms with whites was common among Northern

workingmen. John Campbell, a Philadelphia typesetter, published
these ideas in his book, *Negro-Mania*, 1851:

> Will the white race ever agree that the blacks shall stand beside us
> in election day, upon the rostrum, in the ranks of the army, in our
> places of amusement, in places of public worship, ride in the same
> coaches, railway cars or steamships? Never! Never![53]

The nation's leading abolitionist, William Lloyd Garrison,
publisher of *The Liberator,* revealed much of his true feelings about
the Negro race when he used an orangutan analogy to describe
blacks. Garrison also wrote that blacks, due to facial features that
are distinguishable from whites, "are branded by the hand of nature
with a perpetual mark of disgrace."[54]

Indiana congressman W. H. English was no less harsh than
Garrison. Speaking on the floor of the House of Representatives,
May 2, 1860, English's insult:

> The truth is, the free negro, as a general thing, is unfit to govern
> himself; and, under the most favorable circumstances, in free States,
> it is said he has but three rounds in the ladder of his ambition—to
> be a boss barber, have a banjo, and a white wife.

Congressman English went on to invoke the name of the Almighty
who, he observed, has made the Negro a Negro, "and it is not in the
power of all the Abolitionists and Republicans on earth to make him
anything else."[55]

Even after the war, House Speaker (and future vice president)
Schuyler Colfax of Indiana told a Detroit audience in 1866, "I
never believed in Negro equality." He said God made the white race
superior for his own purposes, and he did not believe in the racial
equality of Indians, Chinese, or other nonwhite races. "But I think
I can say without any impiety, I wish He had made all these races
white, for had he done so, there would not be a Democrat today."[56]

With the prevalence of such attitudes, it is no surprise that Ohio,
Indiana, and Illinois adopted laws requiring Negroes to post "good
behavior" bonds of up to $1,000 before moving into the state. Negroes
also had to produce legal documents verifying they were freemen.

Voters in the Northern states weren't any more sympathetic than

Northern politicians and legislatures. In statewide votes, Wisconsin refused to grant the vote to free blacks while still a territory in 1846 and three more times after statehood, 1849, 1857, and 1865. Eventually, the Wisconsin Supreme Court did what voters refused to do. Even in Illinois, "the land of Lincoln," there was great hostility toward the Negro race. Anti-immigration laws designed to keep Illinois "white only" passed the legislature in 1819, 1829, and 1853. In a statewide referendum in June 1862, Illinois voters approved a constitutional amendment that prohibited Negroes from settling in the state and denied suffrage and public office to Negroes and mulattoes. It passed by a vote of 171,896 to 71,806.[57] Indiana followed suit with anti-immigration laws of its own in 1831 and 1852. Michigan didn't wait for statehood as its territorial legislature passed a Negro exclusion law in 1827. Iowa Territory did the same in 1839 and followed up after statehood with another exclusion law in 1852.

Even into the war year of 1862, Voegeli notes that events "warned of intensifying hostility toward the black race." These events included "anti-Negro" race riots in New Albany, Indiana, Chicago, Toledo, and Cincinnati. In the 1862 fall election campaign, the Democratic Party of Wisconsin took the formal position that social equality of the races defied the laws of nature: "Nature never placed the races together; when brought together the servitude of the inferior is the best condition for both races."[58]

Also in the summer of 1862, talk about emancipating the slaves by act of Congress or by presidential proclamation (the Emancipation Proclamation was issued September 22, 1862) stirred up a great deal of opposition in the North. Ohio congressman Samuel S. Cox said on the floor of the House:

> We want no more poetry about striking off chains and bidding the oppressed go. Plain people want to know whether the chains will not be put upon white limbs; and whither the oppressed are to go. If the industry of the North is to be fettered with their support; if they are to go to Ohio and the North, we want to know it. Nay, we want, if we can, to stop it.[59]

Following Lincoln's issuance of the Emancipation Proclamation, the Republicans lost their majority in Congress to the Democrats in November 1862. Opposition to emancipation by Northern voters "was primarily the product of Negrophobia aggravated by the threat of a massive influx of Negroes." H.S. Bundy, an unsuccessful Unionist candidate for Congress in Ohio wrote Salmon P. Chase that Lincoln's proclamation was delivered just in time to defeat him and many other Unionist congressional candidates in Indiana and Ohio. Bundy wrote, "I had thought until this year the cry of 'nigger' & 'abolitionism,' were played out but they never had as much power & effect in this part of the state as at the recent elections."[60]

There was no integrated public education anywhere in the North, and even segregated public education (separate but equal) for free blacks was almost nonexistent. The courts in Ohio upheld segregation and found a great deal of public ill will against mixing the races. Regarding mingling of black and white children in schools, the courts held there is "an almost invincible repugnance to such communion and fellowship."[61]

Sen. James Harlan of Iowa acknowledged the "objection to the association of colored children with white children" in Iowa schools. Harlan addressed this "problem" on the floor of the U.S. Senate in 1860:

> This prejudice exists in my own state. It would be impossible to carry a proposition in Iowa to educate the few colored children that now live in that State in the same schools with the white children. It would be impossible, I think, in any one of the States of the Northwest.[62]

Vehement objection to biracial education was also present in Yankee New England. Litwack chronicles the tribulations of several academies, boarding schools, and colleges when they attempted to integrate. Negroes in the student body aroused irresistible opposition at Wesleyan University in Middletown, Connecticut; Noyes Academy in New Canaan, New Hampshire; and at a girls' boarding school in Canterbury, Connecticut, where townspeople poisoned the school's well by filling it with manure. Each of these schools were forced to back away from integration by popular opposition.[63] In New Haven, Connecticut, in 1831, townspeople voted 700-4 against opening a school for blacks near Yale University.[63A]

Openly favoring exclusion of free blacks, or worse, during the prewar years was accepted by Northern politicians. New York congressman Henry C. Murphy favored severe laws "against any who shall bring the wretched beings [blacks] into our Free States, there to taint the blood of the whites, or to destroy their race by vicious courses."[64] In debate on the floor of the U.S. Senate in 1855, John Pettit of Indiana stated that all blacks would be better off as slaves:

> I say today, that, in my solemn judgment, the slaves in Louisiana, where slavery is supposed to exist in its worst aspect, are in a better and happier condition than the same number of free negroes in Indiana. I do not entertain a doubt that, if, as a friend of the race, I desired them to increase in number, to multiply their progeny, I would advise them that slavery was their proper condition.[65]

Even some reformers argued for exclusion of the Negro race from the North on humanitarian grounds. Indiana politician and reformer Robert Dale Owen, questioned rhetorically if Negroes were permitted in Indiana would they not "remain then as now a race legally and socially excommunicated, as the Helots of Sparta—as the Pariah of India—disfranchised outcasts; a separate and degraded caste, to whom no honorable career is open; hopeless menials; the hewers of wood and drawers of water of those among whom they are tolerated, not received?"[66]

Nor did free blacks receive any better treatment in the courts in the North than they did at the hands of public opinion or Northern legislatures. In most Northern states, blacks had no access to the courts. In an 1838 Pennsylvania court case in which Democratic candidates in Bucks County protested the election results on the premise that black voters provided the vote margin against them, Judge John Fox of the Bucks County Court ruled that blacks do not have a right to vote and their race was not even contemplated by the framers of the state constitution. Judge Fox asked,

> What white man would not feel himself insulted by a serious imputation that he was a negro, and who, having believed himself to be of the white race, if he should be found to be strongly tainted with black blood, would not feel and experience that he had fallen greatly in the social scale?

Judge Fox also asserted that blacks had never voted in Philadelphia, where most of them lived, or in other parts of Pennsylvania.[67]

Five states (Illinois, Ohio, Indiana, Iowa, and California) prohibited Negro court testimony where a white man was a party to the case. The California Supreme Court ruled that in a criminal case against a white man, a Negro, even if he were the victim of violent crime, could not testify. Litwack concludes,

> A white man could assault, rob, or even murder a Negro in the midst of a number of Negro witnesses and escape prosecution unless another white man had been present and had agreed to testify.[68]

### Constitutional Barriers in Prewar Northern States

Another means of judging whether Northern states and whites had their hearts set on racial justice is to examine the constitutions of those states in the pre-Civil War years. What was the legal status of blacks in the North? How were they treated? This section will examine a number of constitutions of Northern states in chronological order so as to discern trends.

Vermont is often cited as the first state to end slavery. Indeed, Vermont's Constitution of 1777 is the first such document to address the ending of adult slavery. Chapter I of that document, "A Declaration of the Rights of the Inhabitants of the State of Vermont," Part I, states the following:

> Therefore, no male person, born in this country, or brought from over sea, ought to be holden by law, to serve any person, as a servant, slave or apprentice, after he arrives to the age of twenty-one Years, nor female, in like manner, after she arrives to the age of eighteen years, unless they are bound by their own consent, after they arrive to such age, or bound by law, for the payment of debts, damages, fines, costs, or the like.

This clause prohibits only adult slavery and provides for manumission, a gradual form of emancipation. In other words, *child slavery* was protected by Vermont's first constitution. In fact, human trafficking from the Atlantic slave trade was also protected, as it recognized that there are some persons "brought from over sea" for the purpose of coerced servitude. Vermont adopted another constitution only nine years later, in 1786. Chapter I, Part I in the 1786 Constitution contains language identical to the 1777 Constitution. The only difference is that three semicolons replaced commas in the same part of the latter document.

Interestingly, neither of these facts is mentioned on the State of Vermont's Department of Tourism and Marketing Web site (see www.vermontvacation.com). Under the topic of Vermont history and "Firsts in the Nation" section, this Web site tells the unwary that Vermont had the first constitution to "outlaw slavery" in 1777. It conveniently overlooks that this same constitution protects both child slavery and the Atlantic slave trade.

If one believes the "party line," let's call it the Lincoln scholars' lie, that the Civil War was a war of racial justice fought to end slavery immediately in the South, then how does one explain that Vermonters in their first two constitutions actually protected child slavery and the Atlantic slave trade? Would such a people act to impose with violence on others what they were unwilling to impose democratically on themselves? It's true that Vermont was among the first to provide troops to Lincoln, but how can it be said its purpose was to end slavery immediately in the South when it had not done so in its own constitution? Actually, its own constitutional provisions guaranteed compensation to every slave owner in Vermont who lost his chattel property.

Vermont's history has been whitewashed to cleanse it from the dark blot of slavery as if child slavery doesn't really count. The Vermont legend, told first by Northern historians and Lincoln scholars and now by statists who credit the Lincolnian Leviathan with bringing racial justice to those evil, nineteenth-century Southerners, does not align with the facts. It is true Vermont was the first state to "end slavery" if one's definition of "ending slavery" includes ending slavery in any, but not all forms. Yet Vermont most certainly did not end child slavery by either of its first two constitutions. These documents did nothing more than provide for compensation to slave owners in Vermont who would get the teenage and early adulthood years of coerced service from young slaves before having to set them free.

Let's set the record straight. In 1777, Vermont took a laudable and bold first step toward the voluntary ending of slavery without resorting to armed conflict. It did so through the process of manumission in order for slave owners to obtain what eighteenth-century Vermonters considered to be just compensation for the loss of their human chattel. The adoption of the U.S. Constitution in 1789 ultimately ended the Atlantic slave trade after January 1, 1808.

There is nothing wrong with this actual record in the paragraph above, nor is there anything shameful about Vermont taking the first step in abolishing slavery within its borders. However, Vermont's officials and its tourism industry obviously believe the myth sounds and sells better than the reality.

Connecticut's 1818 Constitution is notable for the things it reversed. It disestablished the state-sponsored church and disenfranchised free blacks. Article 6, Part 2 restricted the franchise to white male citizens who also met property qualifications.

The Illinois Constitution of 1818 was adopted for the purpose of statehood, approved by Congress, and signed into law by Pres. James Monroe. It was a discriminatory document in that blacks and Indians were not counted as people when determining the population for the apportionment of the legislature.

Article II, Part 5 set the apportionment in both houses of the legislature "according to the number of white inhabitants." And in counting the population of the state for this purpose, Article II, Part 31 restricted the count to "white inhabitants."

The 1818 Illinois Constitution also withheld suffrage from free blacks. Article II, Part 27 states that only "white male inhabitants above the age of 21 years" had any right to vote. Nor did this document allow free blacks to enter the militia. Article V, Part 1 states, "The militia of the State of Illinois shall consist of all free able-bodied persons, negroes, mulattoes and Indians excepted, resident in the state, between the ages of 18 and 45 years." Article VI protected the slavery that had already taken root in Illinois.

The territorial government of Michigan adopted a constitution in 1835. Congress and Pres. Andrew Jackson approved this constitution, and Michigan was admitted to the Union in 1837. Under the terms of this constitution, free blacks could not vote. Article II, Part 1 restricts the Michigan franchise to "every white male citizen above the age of twenty-one years." Michigan amended its constitution in 1850 and eliminated the word "white." Considering that the U.S. Census shows that Michigan remained 99.4 percent white in the decades leading up to the Civil War, whether free blacks could vote bore no significance politically or socially.

Like Illinois, Michigan's first constitution had identical language about slavery. Article XI, Part 1 states, "Neither slavery nor involuntary servitude shall ever be introduced into this state." Unlike Illinois, there is no record that more than a few slaves were ever brought to Michigan before or after statehood.

In Pennsylvania, free blacks were permitted to vote from the Revolutionary War into the early decades of the nineteenth century. That changed in 1838 with amendments that were debated at a state constitutional convention and subsequently adopted by popular vote.

Litwack notes that the sizeable black population of Philadelphia argued that their fathers "bled to unite . . . taxation and representation" during the Revolutionary War and to take the vote away from free blacks would destroy this principle. Nevertheless, voters in Pennsylvania passed the amendment with a "decisive vote of approval." Free blacks would not vote again in Pennsylvania until 1869.[69]

California was admitted to the union in 1850 based on its Constitution of 1849, approved by Congress and signed into law by Pres. Millard Fillmore. That constitution restricted suffrage to "white male" citizens (article II, Section 1).

Both Indiana and Ohio adopted new state constitutions in 1851. Indiana adopted the harshest and extensive racial restrictions on free blacks of any state constitution at that time. The 1851 Constitution continued to withhold the right to vote from free blacks. Article 2, Section 5:"No Negro or Mulatto shall have the right of suffrage."

Nor could free blacks serve in the Indiana militia. Article 12, Section 1 restricted militia service to "able bodied white male persons."

Nor could free blacks enter into contracts; and white people who employed free blacks were subject to fines. Article 13, Section 2:

> All contracts made with any Negro or Mulatto coming into the State, contrary to the provisions of the foregoing section, shall be void; and any person who shall employ such Negro or Mulatto, or otherwise encourage him to remain in the State, shall be fined in any sum not less than ten dollars, nor more than five hundred dollars.

But it didn't end there. The money collected from those fines was to be used only for colonizing free blacks to some other part of the world. Article 13, Section 3:

> All fines which may be collected for a violation of the provisions of this article, or any law which may hereafter be passed for the purpose of carrying the same into execution, shall be set apart and appropriated for the colonization of such Negroes and Mulattoes, and their descendants, as may be in the State at the adoption of this Constitution, and may be willing to emigrate.

And the most severe restriction of all was the blatant prohibition that forbade blacks from entering Indiana. Article 13, Section 1 states, "No Negro or Mulatto shall come into or settle in the State, after the adoption of this Constitution."

There was no welcome mat for free blacks in prewar Indiana. The free black man could not settle in Indiana; he could not work in Indiana; he could not enter into a contract in Indiana; he could not vote in Indiana; and he could not serve in the militia in Indiana. The only thing he *could* do was leave. Moreover, the 1851 Constitution made provision to finance his departure.

Ohio's 1851 Constitution was much less sweeping, mostly because the restrictions that Indiana adopted by constitutional means were enacted in Ohio by statute. But just like its neighbors to the east (Pennsylvania), the north (Michigan), the west (Indiana), and the south (Kentucky), Ohio's 1851 Constitution continued the exclusion of free blacks from exercising the elective franchise. Article V, Section 1 states that voting is restricted to "white male citizens of the United States, of the age of twenty one years." And service in the Ohio militia was limited to "white male citizens" (Article IX, Section 1).

Iowa had been a state for only a decade when it selected a convention to scrap its original constitution and draft a new one. Race and voting were issues the convention submitted to the voters in a referendum. The voters defeated extension of the franchise to free blacks, and this restriction was made part of the Constitution of 1857 that was subsequently approved by the voters. Article II, "Electors," restricts the franchise to "white male" citizens.[70]

Minnesota adopted its first state constitution in 1857. That document was approved by Congress and signed into law by Pres.

James Buchanan, making Minnesota a state in 1858. Article 7, Section 1 limited the franchise to the following four "classes" of persons:

1. White citizens of the United States.

2. White persons of foreign birth, who shall have declared their intentions to become citizens, conformably to the laws of the Unites States upon the subject of naturalization.

3. Persons of mixed white and Indian blood, who have adopted the customs and habits of civilization.

4. Persons of Indian blood residing in this State who have adopted the language, customs and habits of civilization, after an examination before any District Court of the State, in such manner as may be provided by law, and shall have been pronounced by said Court capable of enjoying the rights of citizenship within the State.

Obviously, race was on the minds of the delegates to the Minnesota Constitutional Convention. They allowed white men to vote. They allowed white foreign men to vote if they stated their intention to become citizens. They allowed men of mixed white and Indian blood to vote if they lived like white men. They allowed Indian men to vote if they lived like white men, but they didn't allow free blacks to vote, period.

Oregon also adopted its state constitution in 1857. This was submitted to and approved by Congress and signed into law by President Buchanan in 1859. It contained numerous blatant discriminatory provisions.

Article II, Section 2 restricts the franchise to "white male" citizens. If the meaning of this language is not plain enough, there is another section of the same article that leaves no doubt. Article II, Section 6: "No Negro, Chinaman, or Mulatto shall have the right of suffrage."

Article XV, Section 8 further limits the rights of Chinese:

No Chinaman, not a resident of the State at the adoption of this Constitution, shall ever hold any real estate, or mining claims or work any mining claims therein.

However, it is Article I, Section 35 that contains the most sweeping, restrictive language in the history of state constitutions:

No free Negro, or Mulatto, not residing in this State at the time of the adoption of this Constitution, shall come, reside, or be within this State, or hold any real estate, or make any contracts, or maintain any suit therein; and the Legislative Assembly shall provide by penal laws, for the removal, by public officers, of all such Negroes, and Mulattoes, and for their effectual exclusion from the State, and for the punishment of persons who shall bring them into the state, or employ, or harbor them.

In Oregon, by constitutional restriction, free blacks could not visit, settle, work, own property, enter into contracts, or have access to the courts. These restrictions are for the "effectual exclusion from the state" of free blacks. This is what the Constitution of Oregon said when it was approved by Congress for statehood. It was the only state ever admitted to the Union that had a raced-based exclusion law in its constitution at the time of admission.

West Virginia was admitted in 1863, technically as a slave state. Congress voted on its constitution just as it has done with every new state, and President Lincoln signed the West Virginia statehood law.

The writing of a constitution for the state of West Virginia and its petition for admission to the Union presented a complex set of challenges and compromises. Ironically, one of the early arguments Lincoln used against secession of any state was the argument that if a state can secede then it must yield to any portion of the state that might wish to secede from it, thus further subdividing its territory. Yet this is precisely the situation that West Virginia presented the Lincoln Administration along with the problem of slavery.

The U.S. Constitution requires a state to grant its consent before a new state can be formed from its own territory. This "never occurred in the case of West Virginia," according to the Web site for the West Virginia Division of Culture and History. Nevertheless, West Virginia was admitted to the Union on June 20, 1863.[71]

**Rights of Free Blacks in the South**
It may be a shocking fact to many, but free blacks enjoyed rights in many Southern states that far surpassed the rights of free blacks in Northern states. The example of the elective franchise is the most glaring, though it is not the only one.

There are documented occurrences of free blacks voting in Tennessee, North Carolina, and Louisiana into the 1830s and beyond, decades after the franchise had been withdrawn from them in Ohio (1803), New Jersey (1807), New York (1811), and Connecticut (1814). Indeed, Congressman John Bell of Tennessee attributed his 1834 margin of victory to the votes of free blacks. Bell was elected speaker of the House of Representatives that term.[72] Another Tennessean, Cave Johnson, a former U.S. postmaster, also attributed his first election to Congress to the 145 free blacks he employed at his iron furnaces. In Louisiana, free blacks voted freely in one particular parish from 1838 through the entire antebellum period.[73]

In Virginia, free blacks were allowed to own property including slaves. Even free black women were property owners. In 1832, a slave brought a suit for freedom against her owner, Mary Quickly, who was herself a black woman. The court records show there was no claim against Ms. Quickly challenging the right of a black woman to own a slave.[74] Perhaps the most striking fact is that a slave, let alone a free black, was permitted to sue in any court at all in Virginia. By 1830, most Northern states had already closed court access to free blacks, if there ever was any.

In prewar South Carolina, free blacks were "contractors, merchants, coal and wood dealers, and artisans," positions achieved in Charleston that would have been impossible at that time in New York. One free black owned a hotel. A "considerable number" were sufficiently successful to reach business standing with banks. Prior to 1835, there were schools for free blacks and slaves in Charleston. But after a local slave uprising, the legislature officially banned the education of slaves. This ban was ignored in Charleston which had a long history of Negro education societies.[75] The Connecticut legislature beat South Carolina to the punch by two years when in 1833, it criminalized both the establishment of any school for the purpose of educating free blacks and providing instruction therein (*Crandall* v. *Connecticut,* 10 Conn., Rep. 340).

In Louisiana, there were many free blacks of "considerable property and intelligence," especially in New Orleans, indicating that both property ownership and education were tolerated. They were reputed to own one-fifth of the taxable property in New Orleans.[76]

In Tennessee, property ownership is evidenced by a 1839 law that forbade free blacks from keeping a "grocery or tippling house." There would be no point in passing a law that forbids them to own or conduct certain types of businesses if they had no right to own or conduct any business.[77]

### Illinois and New Jersey Were *De Facto* Slave States

The extremities to which two "free" states, Illinois and New Jersey, went to hold slaves without appearing to do so, deserves special attention.

Slavery existed in Illinois during territorial days, having been introduced earlier by the French. Neither the territorial nor the state governments, according to the Illinois State Historical Library's (ISHL) Web site, eradicated slavery. This fact is supported by the first census that covered the area that became the state of Illinois, the U.S. Census of 1800. That census counted 107 slaves in Illinois. By 1820, two years after Illinois's admission as a state, the number of slaves counted in the census rose to 917. (A limited amount of slavery was also tolerated in Indiana before and following admission as a state in 1816, see the U.S. Census 1810 and 1820).

What's more, slave property was actually protected by the state's first constitution. Article VI, Part 1 of the Illinois Constitution of 1818 states, "Neither slavery nor involuntary servitude shall hereafter be introduced into this state otherwise than for the punishment of crimes." But, as the ISHL points out and the U.S. Census confirms, *slavery had already been introduced* into Illinois. So what does this mean?

ISHL says this provision "was written by a pro-slavery majority in order to preserve the rights of existing slave holders living within the boundaries of Illinois."[78] Furthermore, the state's first constitution specifically provided for indentured servants to work the salt mines in Saline County through the year 1825 (Article VI, Part 2).

On top of all this, Illinois came very close to becoming a *de jure* slave state. The legislature enacted by a two-thirds vote a call for a constitutional convention to adopt slavery in Illinois. In 1823, just five years after statehood and during a bitter statewide campaign, the vote to call a convention failed 4,972 to 6,640. Thus, Illinois rather narrowly escaped the stigma of *de jure* slavery.[79]

Slavery continued to be tolerated in Saline County, Illinois, at least into the 1840s by salt mine operator John Crenshaw. Crenshaw kept and perhaps traded slaves from his home, which has now come to be known as the Old Slave House in Equality, Illinois, near Shawneetown. Crenshaw is also said to have kidnapped free blacks and sold them into slavery in the South in a reverse Underground Railroad-type operation.[80] So we see that in the "land of Lincoln" the term "free state" is a misnomer.

The story in New Jersey is even more bizarre. In 1804, the New Jersey legislature enacted manumission, a process of gradual emancipation, which allows slave owners to retain the involuntary service of the slave and the slave's children for a specified period of time. The New Jersey law provided that females born of slave parents after July 4, 1804, would be free at age twenty-one and males at age twenty-five. Slave owners in New Jersey could still sell their slaves or their "free" children into other states that still allowed slaveholding, or into long indentures that were still allowed in Pennsylvania. This loophole was not closed until an 1818 law banned the exportation of "slaves or servants of color."

One of the really strange provisions of the New Jersey manumission system was that slave owners could technically "free" the children of their slaves and turn them over to state overseers of the poor. The slave owner could then agree to have them "placed" in his own household and collect a $3 per month maintenance fee from the state. "The evidence suggests this practice was widespread, and the line item for 'abandoned blacks' rose to be 40 percent of the New Jersey budget by 1809. It was a tax on the entire state paid into the pockets of a few to maintain what were still, essentially, slaves," Harper notes.[81]

Historian Edgar J. McManus noted in *Black Bondage in the North* (1973) that New Jersey's approach to manumission "carefully protected" the rights of slave owners to ensure they lost no labor by freeing young Negroes. Moreover, the courts ruled that the right was a 'species of property,' transferrable 'from one citizen to another like other personal property.' . . . New Jersey retained slaveholding without technically remaining a slave state."[82] Although slavery was finally abolished in 1846, slaves in New Jersey are counted in the U.S. Census of 1860.

**Injustice against the Black Man**
What does all this mean?

One particular debate on the floor of the U.S. Senate in 1859 sums up the status of the free black man in the North and white Northerners' attitudes toward the black man. The debate occurred between Sen. Lyman Trumbull of Illinois, a close associate of Lincoln, and Sen. (future president) Andrew Johnson of Tennessee. Johnson made these derisive comments about the status of free blacks in the North:

> He is a freeman, and yet can exercise no franchise that pertains to a freeman! He is a worse slave, in fact, than the African who is in the South and in bondage; a great deal worse, for by these restrains and restrictions is made a slave; he enjoys the shadow and the name of being a freeman, but is stripped of all the franchises that constitute a freeman. He is a slave, in fact, without a master; and I think his is a great deal worse condition than that of a slave who has a master.[83]

Trumbull replied to Johnson by saying, "[He] would not give to the negro population the same political rights that [he] would to the white population in every case." He said he did not know that he would give such rights "in any case." Trumbull also said he would not give the same political rights "either to women or negroes that I would to the white male population."[84]

Litwack closes his powerful book with the comment that change was not imminent in the North in 1860. He said an accurate symbol of the plight of the Negro in the antebellum North was the public cemetery in Cincinnati, Ohio, where whites were buried east to west (the traditional Christian belief of facing the Resurrection), and Negroes were buried north to south. "After all, white supremacy had to be preserved, even among the dead."[85]

We see that the black man in the North, especially the free black man, was despised and ridiculed by public sentiment; caricatured and disdained by politicians; marginalized by legislatures; scorned and taunted by members of Congress, Supreme Court justices, and cabinet members; disparaged and parodied by publishers, reformers, and even abolitionists; hemmed in by the courts; and discriminated against by the churches in this world and the next. As Johnson said, the free black man in the prewar North enjoyed merely the "shadow" of freedom but was "stripped" of everything that actually pertained to freedom.

So much for the idea of political, social, popular, or even military will in the North to enforce racial justice. The only thing the Lincoln scholars have accomplished in foisting this lie onto the pages of our children's history books is to delay the day of reckoning that race was and remains a problem throughout the *entire nation*. More precisely, slavery was and is a *worldwide* problem. Blaming racial injustice, which slavery indeed was, exclusively on the South lets the North off the hook and falsely sanctifies the federal government. It is a phony racial reconciliation that satisfies only the shallow conscience of the statist, true believers—reconciliation on the cheap. No wonder many blacks feel the United States has not fully faced the race issue even with the election of a black president in 2008. Reconciliation cannot occur until the Lincoln scholars grow up, overcome their own denial, and see to it that their lies are removed from schoolbooks and the classroom.

**"Final Solution of the Indian Problem"**
Even if one were to swallow completely the fable that was fabricated by the Schlesingers, McPherson, and other Lincoln scholars, yet another problem must be overcome.

Daydream for a moment outside the bounds of reality. Ignore that Northern citizens, politicians, workers, publishers, immigrants, educators, farmers, doctors, judges, clergy, and military officers were overwhelmingly white supremacists who, like Lincoln, wished there were no blacks in America and were concerned only for that which was good for the white race to the exclusion of what was good for the black race.

In your daydream, pretend that none of the grizzly facts of racial hatred in the North is true. Even so, one would still be compelled to repudiate the myth of clean hands of the North based on the treatment of the Plains Indians. For, it is impossible to swallow the lie that the Union Army, the United States Army, was conducting a holy war of racial justice in the South when it was simultaneously conducting a war of racial genocide against the Indians. In today's terminology, we are describing hate crimes and domestic terrorism. Most people, at least the ones who are not historical sociopaths, will find it difficult to accept the proposition that an army said to be fighting for racial justice could also have the blood of Indian men, women, and children on its hands. It is an incongruous and inherently irreconcilable proposition, no matter how gullible one might be, or how much one might wish it were not so.

Genocide was carried out against the Indians by mass execution, massacres, and starvation. The Plains Indians were not the victims of European culture or Christianity. They were the victims of an imperial federal government that wanted what they had, land and lots of it.

In early December 1862, Lincoln ordered the largest mass execution ever to occur in North America when he sent thirty-eight Sioux Indians to the gallows in Mankato, Minnesota. Lincoln wrote out the execution order in his own handwriting and referred to them as "Indians and Half-breeds." The Sioux had been arrested, tried, and convicted under military law. They were hanged the day after Christmas 1862.

In January 1863, two hundred California volunteers under the command of Col. Patrick Edward Connor attacked a Northwestern Shoshoni winter village near the present Utah-Idaho border. The assault is known as the Bear River Massacre. Before Connor led his men from Salt Lake City north to Bear River, he had announced that he intended to take no prisoners. Approximately 250 Shoshoni were slain, including ninety women and children. After the slaughter ended, soldiers went through the Indian village raping women and using axes to bash in the heads of women and children who were already dying of wounds.[86]

In the fall of 1864, just as Sherman was making Georgia "howl" during his march to the sea, another atrocity unfolded in the west. On November 29, a federal detachment of the Colorado territorial militia attacked and massacred 150 Cheyenne and Arapaho Indians at an undefended village near Sand Creek. The attack was ordered by Col. John Milton Chivington, an ordained Methodist minister and avowed abolitionist. Some accounts of the massacre hold that the Indians were mutilated and body parts displayed. An investigation found no wrongdoing by Chivington.

Perhaps the most chilling part of the eradication of the Plains Indians was the coining of the term "final solution of the Indian problem" by Gen. William T. Sherman. Although Sherman did not use this term until 1875, it was his description of the killing of the hostile Indians and segregating the remnants onto remote reservations, a twenty-year-long process that began in the early 1860s to make way for the railroads.

In a December 27, 1875, letter to a Frederick T. Dent of St. Louis, Sherman writes of the "final solution of the Indian problem." Historian Michael Fellman observes that Sherman, Sheridan, and Grant (who was president by then) all believed that the "final solution" was "vigorous war against the Indians." The three considered the Indians to be "a less than human, and savage race." The three thought the Indians were "obstacles to the upward sweep of history, progress, wealth, and white destiny."[87] Thus the adaptation of the phrase, some sixty years later, by the Nazis found a perfect twin in operation, history, and philosophy.

Adolf Hitler and Joseph Goebbels admired Lincoln for forcefully creating a strong central government just as they admired Otto von Bismarck for the same reason. It is a macabre connection totally unknown to most Americans.

**Summary**

Consider these questions about the Civil War. If it was a war of racial justice (i.e., to free the slaves) one must resolve each of the following questions, which simply cannot be done.

- Why were Northerners afraid of a "Negro invasion?"
- Why did Northern scientists and physicians insist that the black man was a separate and inferior species?
- Why did slavery hang on in Illinois, New Jersey, and perhaps even Maine?
- Why did Ohio, Indiana, and Illinois require "good behavior" bonds from free blacks?
- Why did so many Northern states enact Negro exclusion laws?
- Why did Connecticut, New York, New Jersey, Pennsylvania, and Rhode Island withdraw voting rights from free blacks *before* Southern states followed suit?

- Why did voters in Connecticut, Illinois, Iowa, Kansas, Massachusetts, Minnesota, New York, Ohio, Pennsylvania, and Wisconsin repeatedly reject black suffrage?
- Why did the Connecticut Supreme Court rule that blacks and Indians were not citizens twenty years before the same question was addressed in the Dred Scott decision?
- Why did the California Supreme Court rule that a black man could not testify against a white man even if the white man had perpetrated a violent crime against the black man?
- Why was Horace Greeley openly more sympathetic to white hourly laborers in the North than he was slaves in the South?
- Why did the nation's leading abolitionist William Lloyd Garrison compare blacks to orangutans and refer to their facial features as "a perpetual mark of disgrace?"
- Why were books like *Negro-Mania* published and widely read in the North?
- Why is it that the speaker of the house, during the war, said he "never believed in Negro equality?"
- Why did Salmon P. Chase believe that free blacks in the North should move to the Gulf Coast?
- Why was there so much public opposition to the acceptance of black students in private schools and academies in New England?
- Why was Oregon admitted to the Union on the virtual eve of the Civil War (1859) with a blatant racial exclusion provision in its constitution?
- Why did voters in Illinois amend their Constitution during the war (1862) to add a racial exclusion provision?
- Why did Lincoln reverse the emancipation of slaves in Missouri that had been announced by the U.S. Army?
- Why was the Emancipation Proclamation carefully written to exclude the actual freeing of slaves in parts of Tennessee and Louisiana that were occupied by the U.S. Army?
- Why didn't Congress end slavery in the "loyal" border states of Delaware, Maryland, Kentucky, and Missouri during the war?

- Why was West Virginia admitted to the Union as a slave state during the war (1863)?
- Why did Lincoln favor the forced expulsion of free blacks from America?
- Why did Lincoln approve the largest mass execution in the history of North America?
- Why did the U.S. Army commence its ethnic cleansing of the Plains Indians during the war?
- Why were there anti-black riots in several Northern cities just before and during the war?
- Why did every territorial government established by Congress prior to 1868 prohibit free blacks from voting?
- Why did all ten Northern states admitted to the Union between 1820 and 1868 prohibit free blacks from voting?
- Why did every referendum on black suffrage fail in the ten Northern states that conducted such votes in the prewar years through 1868? (There were more than twenty such referenda).
- Why didn't the federal government confiscate Northern property and wealth accumulated as a direct result of the Atlantic slave trade to purchase the freedom of slaves and avoid war?
- Why weren't at least some slaves freed, somehow, somewhere, at some time during the war, other than by their own initiative of simply running away?

The Lincoln scholars would have you believe that there are no answers to these questions. The reality is that each of these questions has a straightforward, simple answer: The war was not fought to free the slaves. It was not a war of racial justice. No society has every fought a war of racial justice for people who were outcasts within its midst. Nor can it be claimed that any human government ever fought a war of racial justice while it simultaneously perpetrated systematic racial genocide against a separate ethnic minority group. The ugly reality is that the only blacks who were freed during the war freed themselves by running away. Yet the self-anointed, morally superior Lincoln scholars steal credit for the slaves' act of running away and give it to the federal government.

Just like the undisciplined child who is caught with his hand in the cookie jar, the Lincoln scholars have an elaborate explanation that they hope will convince you that you didn't see them swipe a handful of cookies. They prefer denial to facts, deification of their object of worship to reason. They are twice too clever, and not smart enough by half.

Where are the clean hands?

Having dispelled the myth of a war fought to free blacks from the oppression of slavery, we will look elsewhere to discover why Lincoln precipitated the bloodiest war in the history of man up to that time (in terms of battle deaths).

# CHAPTER THREE

# The German Forty-Eighters: Lincoln's Indispensable Allies

*"A man's mind stretched to a new idea never goes back to its original dimensions."*
—Oliver Wendell Holmes, Jr.

We Americans tend to be a spoiled, self-absorbed lot. We study American history as if it is the only history that matters. We tend to see the rest of the world only as it impinges on American history. Thus, the French and the Germans are relevant on D-Day (June 6), the British on July 4, the Arabs on September 11, the Japanese on December 7.

In no part of American history does the ignorance of how we were affected by another country compare to the intellectual black hole of the Civil War. The University of London's Brian Holden Reid puts it best:

> As a British student of the American Civil War, I have always been struck by the rather parochial attitude of American scholars to this tremendous upheaval, and their reluctance to consider its significance in relation to other nineteenth-century wars. On rare occasions when comparisons have been made, they are halting; at worst, distorted by chauvinism, at best touched by special pleading.[1]

In short, Professor Reid believes Americans think the Civil War is all about Americans and nothing more. After all, every schoolchild in America is taught that Lincoln freed the slaves that, of course, he did not do at all. In subtle undertones, we are indoctrinated to believe that the war was a costly but necessary confrontation between forces of good and evil needed to wipe out slavery and slavery could only have been eliminated by an armed conflict—a grotesquely false notion as we have already seen. The fact is in the nineteenth century, America was the only place on Earth where war was associated with the end of slavery. Slavery was either abolished or manumission commenced without war in Haiti (1804), Argentina, (1813), Colombia (1814), Chile (1823), Central America (1824), Mexico (1829), Bolivia (1831), all British colonies (1838), Uruguay (1842), all French colonies (1848), all Danish colonies (1848), Ecuador (1851), Peru (1854), Venezuela (1854), all Dutch colonies (1863), Puerto Rico (1873), Cuba (1886), and Brazil (1888).[2] There is ample evidence to support Reid's observation that American scholars have overlooked the context of events in other countries and how some of them affected events in America in the 1860s.

The whole truth is that there is a direct, even startling, linkage between the European revolutions of 1848, especially in Germany, and the political events and bloodshed experienced in America from 1860-65. Thousands of Germans who actually manned the street barricades in Berlin and other central European cities came to America following the failed 1848 revolutions. This group of revolutionaries is known as the "Forty-Eighters."

The Forty-Eighters worked in an effective and critical role to secure Lincoln's nomination at the Republican Party Convention and played nothing less than a pivotal role in his election as president in 1860. They were the source of most of the radical philosophies that sought to crush the South by destroying its labor system and capital reserves embodied in the institution of slavery. They sought to crush the rather loose confederacy of the states that existed prior to Lincoln (i.e., Jeffersonian federalism) and erect in its place a strong central government that would dole-out political privilege and subsidy. In the name of "democracy," they wanted a Leviathan central state with a free hand to enforce the will of the political majority over any political minority without the complex checks and balances of federalism, a sort of semilegal mob rule. They were internationalists, imperialists, and many were antiprivate-property Marxists.

"In a sense the American Civil War is a belated chapter of the German revolution of 1848," according to sociologist Heinrich H. Maurer, who published a 1917 paper on German nationalism in America. Maurer views the Civil War as "a liquidation of a European, not merely of an American, past." The Forty-Eighters "poured new wine into old bottles, and the dregs of European experience flavored the American vintage."[3]

This was nothing less than a sweeping rejection and a setting aside of the principle of the "consent of the governed" as articulated by the Founding Fathers in the Declaration of Independence. It was an elimination of the Founding Fathers' reliance on natural law, our "unalienable rights"—a smashing of the limits placed on government by the Constitution—Jefferson's "chains" of the Constitution, there to limit government's reach. There is one particular term that describes this process quite eloquently: "counterrevolution."

Lincoln and the Forty-Eighters pulled off a counterrevolution to smash the idea that government is limited only to those powers to which the citizens have given their consent. Their belief, which comes to greater fruition with each new U.S. president, is that majority rule has no limits; the will of the majority can be enforced on the minority. A not-so-subtle corollary is that all citizens, whether they represent the political majority or minority, exist to serve the government, not the other way around. They believed, as most politicians believe today, that government is the master and man is the subject, and in support of this belief, the Lincoln scholars pour all their intellectual capacity.

So who were these Forty-Eighters? What did they believe in? How did they pull it off?

**The Events of 1848**
In 1848, a revolt that had begun in France spread to Germany. Germans took to the streets demanding freedom and unity. This was instigated by the growing German bourgeois merchants (middle class) in the villages and towns who sought to protect and enhance their economic gains against the reactionary royalists, the aristocracy of landed barons.

They desired a strong central government that would replace the loose German Confederation of states and principalities. Both the bourgeois and the revolutionaries (an odd mixture of intellectual radicals, such as Marxists, and radicals from various workers' parties) wanted national unification in order to eliminate the complex system of tariffs and trade barriers among the German principalities; to establish some form of representative government that would seize power from the aristocracy; and to address the harsh reality of life for industrial workers during the formative years of the

Industrial Revolution. They opposed regional interests and political subdivisions.

The revolutionaries from the educated, professional class who operated the barricades side by side with workers and successfully battled the Prussian Army, at least for a while. The temporarily common goal of the revolutionaries and the bourgeois was "to substitute the domination of industrial capitalism for the rule of the landed aristocracy." However, when the actual revolt in the streets came, "the middle class preferred to make its peace with the reaction [the royalist aristocracy] rather than permit the movement to follow a truly radical course of action."[4] The result was that Germany was neither unified nor a republican form of government established, and the revolutionaries, as historian W. T. Block has noted, fled for America one-step ahead of the hangman's noose.

## What the Forty-Eighters Believed

The *Handbook of Texas Online* (www.tshaonline.org) estimates that four thousand German revolutionaries immigrated to the United States just after 1848, some one hundred settling in Texas. Other historical sources estimate a much larger number of Forty-Eighters, perhaps as many as ten thousand. Though the vast majority of Forty-Eighters settled in the North, there were many older German settlements in the South, the most numerous in Texas.

Unlike other immigrants (including many other ordinary Germans) who fled famine or religious and class persecution, the Forty-Eighters came with their own political ax to grind and ideas about nationalism, which they quickly attempted to assert in their new country. According to historian Carl Wittke:

> Many Forty-eighters honestly believed that they had a "cultural mission" to perform in their adopted fatherland. They refused to be used a mere "raw material" to build a Yankee nation which they found so disappointing in many respects. . . . They hated American sabbatarianism, blue laws, and "the temperance swindle," and the more radical ridiculed what they called the religious superstitions of the American people.[5]

What's more, many had a "long nursed hatred against the social order" in America, against a central government that tolerated slavery in any state. The mere restriction of slavery to states where it presently existed was "almost contemptible" in their eyes. "Their motive in civil war and reconstruction sprang from the international mind of social democracy," not from anything in the uniquely American experience.[6]

Wittke uses the word "discontent" to describe many of the Forty-Eighters, a great many of whom were, he says, agnostics and atheists. Wittke says some of the more extreme Forty-Eighters:

> Actually dreamed of an intellectual conquest of the United States, which would then become the fulcrum for world revolution. In this "storm and stress" period, many an intellectual German refugee wanted to play the role of world reformer, beginning with the Unites States.[7]

German ideas about government were somewhat different than American ideas, and anarchist Victor Yarros noted it was "equally certain" that German thought would affect American thought just as the opposite was true. One can see the connection between Northern centralizers and typical German ideas that individual endeavors "must be unreservedly subordinated" to government. Yarros wrote that government is "infinitely more valu[able] than all its subjects taken together. It may order them to fight foreigners, or one another, and it may keep up the fighting indefinitely, without condescending to give reasons."[8]

Within a very short period of time the natural leadership ability and intellectual background of the Forty-Eighters thrust them into leadership roles in German American communities though out the country. By the time of the Louisville, Kentucky, mass meeting of leading Germans in 1854, their influence was evident. The meeting called for a separate political organization by German Americans who did not trust the Democrats because the party supported the right of states to regulate or permit slavery. They did not trust the Whigs due to the nativist, anti-immigrant element. Though they would soon align with the Republicans, they did not trust them in the mid-1850s because they were viewed an insufficiently radical on the issue of immediate emancipation.[9] The resolutions of the Louisville meeting read in part:

Speculation has taken the place of duty, corruption the place of virtue and reaction is in power. . . . The people are replaced by parties, parties by cliques, congress is in the hands of privileged classes, and the resources of the nation are in the hands of predatory interests. The common interest are ignored, and popular measures are defeated.[10]

Although the rhetoric may sound similar to contemporary political debate, let us examine the specific themes contained in this statement.

"Speculation has taken the place of duty," meaning private enterprise, individualism, and the American pioneer spirit has trumped regimented and coerced service ("duty") to the state. "Congress is in the hands of privileged classes," which reads the states rather than the people elect members of the U.S. Senate, and the Senate serves its constitutionally designed function of slowing down legislative action. "The resources of the nation are in the hands of predatory interests," in other words the huge landmass of the west has not yet been given away to free, white settlers. (In reality, most of the vast land domain of the west was given away to big corporations, i.e., railroads).

"Common interests are ignored, and popular measures are defeated." This is just as the Founding Fathers intended. No one at the Philadelphia Convention of 1787 wanted unfettered democracy. They all believed just as John C. Calhoun believed about the revolutions of 1848 that the abuse of power is inherent in the nature of man, "and consequently [there is] as much to be feared from a numerical majority as from a single individual. It could be prevented only by some form of federal structure which left in the hands of the parts sufficient power to resist the abuses of their common rulers."[11]

A number of specific political planks were adopted at the 1854 Louisville meeting, including:

- Inheritance laws must be reformed to counteract the accumulation of "idle" capital, a distinctly Marxist notion;
- A Pacific railroad should be a national enterprise, i.e., nationalization of the railroads;
- Neutrality must be abandoned whenever "American interests" dictate–i.e., imperialism, the creation of an American Empire;

- Direct election by popular vote of all federal offices. This would have eliminated any semblance of federalism because the big cities (Boston, New York, and Philadelphia) would always carry the day politically;
- Candidates for Congress could stand for election in any state of the Union, another stake in the heart of federalism, the states, and anything that smacked of regional differences or characteristics.

These demands were dangerously inconsistent with the "unalienable rights" established during the American Revolution and articulated in the Declaration of Independence. They smacked of a tyranny of the majority *a la* the French Revolution and had a distinctly Marxist, internationalist, old European ring to them.

The same year as the Louisville meeting, the Texas Germans advocated numerous reforms at their annual state convention of German singing groups, known as Saengerfest. The convention was held in San Antonio in 1854 and was "instigated and dominated by the Freethinkers," meaning agnostics or atheists.[12] The reforms included:

- Progressive taxation—the higher the income the greater the tax, an antiproperty Marxist idea that found a home in the U.S. income tax some sixty years later;
- Complete secularization of society by abolition of religious instruction in schools, barring preachers from teaching school; opening Congress with prayer;, and Sunday closure laws (Blue laws);
- Abolition of capital punishment and the grand jury system;
- Laws should be enacted so simply and intelligibly that there would be no need for lawyers.

Scharf states, "The slave-holding and religious communities of San Antonio became highly incensed that these newcomers to America should propose such radical ideas."[13]

One cannot imagine any group, club, organization, movement, or governmental jurisdiction that would happily welcome "radical ideas" from "newcomers," much less embrace and accept the newcomers who appear to want to take over. Imagine the cold reaction to "radical ideas" offered by "newcomers" on the boards of the Brookings Institution,

Oral Roberts Ministries, the American Civil Liberties Union, the National Association for the Advancement of Colored People, Harvard, or Bob Jones University. The only common denominator among these diverse and often adversarial organizations is that each would predictably reject "radical ideas" offered by "newcomers" in their midst, who having had the temerity to propose such ideas would be marginalized if not asked to leave. It is no surprise that the Forty-Eighters encountered the same phenomenon.

### Leaders of the Forty-Eighters

The Forty-Eighters were unlike any other group of immigrants who came to America, or perhaps any other country at any time. Many had been Prussian Army officers before joining the revolution. Some were graduates of military academies in Germany and Austria. A large number were lawyers, doctors, journalists, teachers, writers, artists, and university professors. Many Forty-Eighters wrote in English- and German-language newspapers and other publications both in their newly adopted homeland and in Europe. They were keenly aware of political developments in America and Europe and worked very hard to influence those events on both continents.

Many immersed themselves in party politics of the 1850s after only three to four years in the United States, attending national political conventions. One became an actual presidential elector in New York after only a few years of residence. Yet few had the same degree of loyalty and attachment to their new homeland that was characteristic of other naturalized Americans.

Some Forty-Eighters had been government officials and even holders of elected office in Europe, and sought the same, often successfully, in America. Two became U.S. ambassadors. Many served in legislatures in the Northern states. At least ten became general officers in the U.S. Army. After the Civil War, once they felt they had accomplished their mission here, some returned home to Germany to live and to serve in political office. A few of the prominent Forty-Eighters are mentioned below. These are but a small number of thousands.

**Carl Schurz** was perhaps the most notable Forty-Eighter for his prominent leadership among Germans in America as well as his meteoric rise in power in his adopted homeland.

*In nine years, Carl Schurz rose from unknown immigrant to ambassador to Spain.* (Courtesy Library of Congress)

In the brief span of nine years, he went from unknown immigrant (1852) to the U.S. ambassador to Spain (1861). In 1856, just four years after arriving in America, Schurz was a delegate to the 1856 Republican National Convention that nominated John C. Fremont. By 1860, he was a member of the Republican National Committee.[14] He campaigned for Lincoln in 1860 among the German communities of Illinois, Indiana, Missouri, Ohio, Pennsylvania, New York, and Wisconsin with positive effect.[15] After the war, he served in the nation's highest legislative body as U.S. senator from Missouri. Later he served as secretary of the interior under Pres. Rutherford B. Hayes and was cofounder of the *Saturday Evening Post*.

While Schurz was a student in Bonn, he joined what would become the German revolutionary movement of 1848. He participated in the rebellions in the Rhineland, the Palatinate, and Baden. After defeat, Schurz escaped to Switzerland and made his way to New York in 1852 via Paris and London. He settled in Wisconsin in 1855 and was admitted to the bar.[16]

After a brief stint as ambassador, Schurz returned to the U.S. to press for the abolition of slavery. He was commissioned a brigadier general in the Wisconsin volunteers in 1862 and saw action at Second Manassas and Chancellorsville, both disastrous defeats of the U.S. Army.[17]

It is interesting how much Schurz resisted assimilation as an American even though he served at the highest levels of government and sat in on Lincoln's cabinet meetings. At the opening of the Chicago World's Fair in 1893, he used the third person plural ("their") when referring to his fellow Americans (among whom he had lived, worked, and participated in government for the previous forty-one years).

> I have always been in favor of a healthy Americanization, but that does not mean a complete disavowal of our German heritage. It means that our character should take on the best of that which is American, and combine it with the best of that which is German. By doing this, we can best serve the American people and their civilization.[18]

**Frederich Karl Franz Hecker** was elected to the Baden assembly in 1842. By 1846, he had established himself as a leader in the assembly on the extreme left. Hecker and his followers attempted a coup d'état in May 1848. The coup failed and Hecker fled to the United States in September 1848, where he was welcomed upon arrival in New York by the mayor and a crowd of over twenty thousand. He settled briefly in Cincinnati and later on a farm near Belleville, Illinois. He played an active role in the founding of the Republican Party in the mid-1850s including attending the 1856 Republican convention that nominated John C. Fremont. Hecker, Schurz, Frederich Kapp and other Forty-Eighters campaigned for Fremont among the Germans. In 1861, he assembled a regiment of mostly German immigrants (the Illinois Eighty-second) called the "Hecker

Regiment." He was wounded when the Confederates routed the U.S. Army at Chancellorsville.[19]

**Frederich Kapp** had a rise to prominence in Northern politics almost as rapid as Schurz. Kapp arrived in New York in 1850. In 1856, he and Schurz campaigned for Fremont in New York. Only ten years after arriving, he was a New York presidential elector for Lincoln in 1860. Kapp practiced law in New York from 1850 to 1870 when he returned to Germany where he was elected to the German Diet in 1871.

He was even more adamant about not becoming an American than Schurz. "Our home is in Europe," Kapp wrote. "It is a lie to say we can build a second home . . . one cannot have two fatherlands any more than two fathers." Kapp also had a very dim view of the role of faith in America. He said America "will occupy a decidedly higher place as soon as it gets rid of Christianity."[20]

**Louis Blenker** was a lieutenant in the Bavarian Legion before it was disbanded in 1837. He returned to his hometown of Worms and studied medicine. In 1849, he became a leading member of the revolutionary government of Worms, fighting in several successful engagements with the Prussians. However, the revolutionaries were crushed and Blenker fled to the United States through Switzerland.

Blenker settled in New York and was commissioned as a colonel in the Eighth New York in April 1861. His regiment helped cover the U.S. Army's retreat at the First Manassas disaster, 1861. He was promoted to brigadier general in August 1861. The following winter, Blenker was given command of a division of German brigades from the East and Midwest. Suffering "great hardships" in West Virginia from what Boatner says was a lack of basic military necessities, Blenker's command was "reduced to looting and thievery" to survive. He died in 1863 at his home in Rockland County, New York, from an injury sustained in a Virginia campaign.[21]

**Dr. Karl Adolph Douai** came to the United States in 1852. He was "an atheist, an abolitionist, and an admirer of Karl Marx's communist philosophies," according to historian W. T. Block. Douai attempted to settle in the German communities in Texas but was "run out of New Braunfels because of his radical statements and teachings, and immediately founded the German-language *San Antonio Zeitung*, which published abolition editorials and espoused an all-German free state in West Texas in which runaway slaves could take refuge."[22] By 1860, he was in Boston and involved in Massachusetts politics.[23] He published German-language socialist newspapers until his death in 1888.

**Franz Sigel** was a graduate of the German military academy. He resigned his commission in the Prussian Army in 1847 and took up arms in the revolution of 1848, but soon fled to the United States. He taught school in New York City and moved to St. Louis, where he was director of the schools when the war broke out. In May 1861, Sigel was commissioned as a colonel in the U.S. Army and was promoted to brigadier general in thirteen days. The following year, he was promoted to major general. Siegel's first action was at Wilson's Creek in southwest Missouri (August 1861); however, his failure to distinguish Confederate uniforms from Union led to the rout of his unit.[24]

Sigel is chiefly remembered in the North for his defeat by teenage Virginia Military Institute students at New Market, Virginia, in 1864, although he long remained an idol of German America. Led by one of their professors, Lt. Col. Scott Ship, 247 cadets attacked Sigel's troops. After Shipp was wounded, the cadets were commanded by Capt. Henry A. Wise, the former governor of Virginia. The cadets kept up the attack for several hours before Sigel withdrew. He was relieved of command four days later.[25]

Although military historian Mark Boatner describes him as an inept general, he says Siegel's ability to rally German Americans to the federal cause was important. *"I fights mit Siegel"* was their slogan. He resigned from the U.S. Army in May 1865 and went into journalism. He eventually found his way back to New York City where he was active in publishing and politics.[26]

**Edward S. Salomon, Frederick S. Salomon, and Charles E. Salomon** were brothers who were born in Prussia and fled Germany in 1848 after fighting on the losing side of the revolution.

Edward S. Salomon was a lawyer who was a regent of the state university system when he was elected lieutenant governor of Wisconsin in 1861. He took the office of governor the following year upon the death of his predecessor. Edward moved to New York City in 1869 and eventually back to Prussia, where he died in 1909 and is buried.

*Gen. Franz Sigel was an officer in the Prussian Army who resigned in 1847 to join revolutionary forces the next year, but he soon fled to the United States. Sigel was relieved of his command days after he was defeated by Virginia Military Institute cadets at New Market, Virginia.* (Courtesy Library of Congress)

Frederick S. Salomon was a surveyor and engineer. He was commissioned as a captain in the U.S. Army May 1861, promoted to brigadier general in 1862 and major general before war's end. Frederick saw action through out the western theater. He moved to the Utah Territory after the war.

Charles E. Salomon was commissioned as a captain in the U.S. Army in May 1861 and promoted to brigadier general September 1862. He mustered out in November 1864.[27]

**Joseph Weydemeyer** was a Prussian-born Marxist and artillery officer in the Prussian Army from 1839-45. He was a member of Marx and Friedrich Engles' Communist Correspondence Committee of Brussels in 1846 and worked to establish similar groups in Germany. After the revolution failed, he fled to Switzerland and on to the United States in 1851.[28] He received a commission in the U.S. Army and commanded the Fortieth Missouri Regiment during the war.[29]

**Emil Pretorius** escaped the failed revolution and became editor of a respected German-language daily newspaper in St. Louis, the *Westliche Post of St. Louis*. Carl Schurz was a part owner of this newspaper. Pretorius employed Joseph Pulitzer, for whom this work in German American journalism helped launch one of the most storied careers in American journalism.[30]

**Louis Prang** fled to the United States in 1850 after the failed revolutions were put down. He settled in Boston where he was a well-known lithographer. Prang soon entered the political arena to protest an 1860 act of the Massachusetts legislature that restricted voting and holding office for two years by naturalized citizens. Prang is recognized as the father of the Christmas card and even has a 1975 commemorative U.S. postage stamp.[31]

**Maj. Gen. August Willich**, a Communist, was one of only a few really brilliant Union officers among the Forty-Eighters. Karl Marx referred to Willich as a "communist with a heart" (www.germanheritage. com). Willich was the son of a Napoleonic war veteran. He received a military education and was commissioned an officer in the Prussian Army. In 1846, he and other Marxist-leaning officers wrote letters of resignation so inflammatory that they were court-martialed. Willich was acquitted and resigned. He joined Franz Sigel, Carl Schurz, Frederick Hecker, and Louis Blenker in the 1848 revolt in Baden. He fled to the United States through Switzerland after the revolution failed.

*Maj. Gen. August Willich was a Communist and served as a Prussian officer before immigrating to the U.S. In 1871, he returned to Germany and attempted to serve during the Franco-Prussian War but was turned down due to age.* (Courtesy Library of Congress)

Willich was commissioned a lieutenant in the U.S. Army in 1861, eventually rising to the rank of major general. He saw extensive action in the western theater, mustering out in 1866. Willich returned to Germany during the Franco-Prussian War (1871) and "offered his services to the king he had tried once to overthrow, but was not accepted because of his advanced age."[32]

**Hans Kudlich** was a Sudeten German of Austrian nationality, educated in law and medicine. Revolution broke out in Vienna in October 1848 and Kudlich participated. He was soon accused of conspiring to assassinate a government minister. He fled to Baden and participated in the revolution there before fleeing to Switzerland and eventually settling in New Jersey and practicing medicine. In New Jersey, he wrote and spoke against slavery. Kudlich was tried *in absentia* in an Austrian court in 1854 and sentenced to death. In 1867, Emperor Franz Joseph pardoned Kudlich, who returned to Austria in 1872 to write his autobiography and various novels about the struggle for freedom. He went back to New Jersey in 1873 and died there in 1917.[33]

**Max von Webber** (or Weber) was a graduate of the German military academy and an officer in the Prussian Army until joining Franz Siegel's group of revolutionaries. After fleeing to the United States, Webber ran a German hotel in New York City. He was commissioned colonel in a New York unit in May 1861. He was promoted to brigadier general in April 1862. Webber saw action at Sharpsburg (Antietam) and Harpers Ferry. After the war, he worked in the Internal Revenue Department and served as the U.S. consul at Nantes.[34]

**Alexander Schimmelfennig** was a Prussian Army officer before siding with Blenker, Hecker, and Willich during the revolution in 1848. He fled to the United States. In 1861, he was commissioned colonel in the Seventy-fourth Pennsylvania and saw action at the Union defeat at Second Manassas. Schimmelfennig was promoted to brigadier general in November 1862 and fought at Chancellorsville and Gettysburg where he was severely wounded. He was relieved of command due to ill health and returned to Pennsylvania. He died there of tuberculosis in the fall of 1865.[35]

**Albin Francisco Schoepf** was a Hungarian graduate of the Vienna military academy and Prussian Army officer until he went to Hungary to fight in the revolution of 1848. He was exiled to Turkey, and he instructed and fought with the Ottoman Army. He immigrated to the United States and worked in various government jobs until he was commissioned brigadier general in the Army of Ohio First Brigade in September 1861.[36]

**Edward Degener** was one of numerous Forty-Eighters who held elective office in Germany before the revolution and America after he immigrated. According to the *Handbook of Texas Online*, Degener was "twice elected a member of the legislative body in Anhalt-Dessay and was a member of the German National Assembly" in 1848. He immigrated to the United States in 1850 and settled as a farmer in Sisterdale, Texas. During the war, the Confederate Army court-martialed Degener due to his devotion to the Union cause. After the war, he served in the Texas constitutional conventions in 1866 and again in 1868-69. He was elected to Congress and served one year after Texas was readmitted to the Union.[37]

**Julius Froebel** defies categorization or simple description other than he was a prolific writer and "opinion maker" in both the German and English language. Froebel was apparently a citizen of three nations at various times during his life. He was born in Germany in 1806, became a Swiss citizen, wrote revolutionary political pamphlets to Germany from the protection of Switzerland (many of which were suppressed), returned to Germany, and was elected to the German parliament. He was arrested in 1848 and condemned to death but pardoned before execution. Froebel traveled to America and became a correspondent for Horace Greeley at the *New York Tribune*, during which time he apparently became a U.S. citizen. He returned to Germany in 1857 for a brief time and resisted expulsion on the grounds of naturalization as a U.S. citizen. His German and English treatises focused on scientific as well as political topics.[38]

**August Siemering** is perhaps one of the most unusual Forty-Eighters in that he was conscripted into the Confederate Army and obtained the rank of lieutenant by the end of the war, according to the *Handbook of Texas Online*. Siemering emigrated from Germany after the revolution of 1848 and settled in Texas in 1851. He taught school in Sisterdale and Fredericksburg and published a German-language newspaper that was strongly abolitionist. His antislavery views were not well known in Texas because they were not published in English. After the way, Siemering's newspaper, the San Antonio *Freie Presse*

*Gen. Peter Osterhaus received military education in Berlin. He was forced to flee Germany after the 1848 revolution.* (Courtesy Library of Congress)

*für Texas,* became one of the leading Republican newspapers in the South.[39]

**Peter Osterhaus** was born in Germany in 1823 and graduated from military school in Berlin. He was forced to flee Germany after participating in the revolution. He settled in St. Louis and ran a bookstore. When the war broke out, he joined the U.S. Army; he was eventually promoted to the rank of brigadier general. He was appointed U.S. consul to France in 1866.[40]

### The Forty-Eighters Role in Electing Lincoln

The election of Lincoln in 1860 was like no other. Lincoln is the only president ever elected with less than forty percent of the popular vote. He garnered 39.9 percent and was truly the only regional candidate to be elected president. There was no Republican Party in the South, and Lincoln was not even on the ballot in most Southern states. Even if he had been on the ballot, it is unlikely that it would have mattered much. In his birth state of Kentucky, Lincoln finished fourth, with less than one percent of the vote. In Virginia, he received only 1.1 percent of the vote. (Imagine a presidential election today where the candidate who wins in the Electoral College gets only one percent of the vote in two or more states.) In California, a very small state at the time, Lincoln won a four-way race with less than one of every three votes. Nationwide, a solid majority, 60.1 percent voted against Lincoln.

With the swing of just a few thousand votes in states with heavy recent German immigration (Illinois, Indiana, and either Wisconsin or Michigan), Stephen Douglas would have carried those states and the election would have been thrown into the House of Representatives. The new Congress that was elected along with Lincoln in 1860 was seated in January and the new House would have elected the president. Back then, the president was not sworn in until March. The Republicans had lost their razor-thin majority in the House, and they would have been highly unlikely to prevent the House from electing either Douglas or Vice Pres. John C. Breckenridge as the sixteenth president. Lincoln would have been no better known than Samuel Tilden who lost to Rutherford B. Hayes by one electoral vote (185-184) in 1876; but a half-million Americans would not have lost their lives.

However, it didn't happen that way. Lincoln squeaked by in the electoral vote and became president. The question is, then, who put Lincoln over the top in the closely fought states of Illinois, Indiana, Iowa, Michigan, Minnesota, Ohio, and Wisconsin, all of which Lincoln won? Who took the leadership roles in Lincoln's campaign, and who took the credit for victory?

The scholarly literature provides a clear and startling answer to this question. As we seek this answer, perhaps it is instructive to note that virtually nothing has been published on this vital topic in the past two generations. It's almost as if an unseen guiding hand were attempting to sanitize the American consciousness of the importance of European thought and German American participation in this nation's greatest and bloodiest tragedy.

If there were such an unseen hand, it has done a marvelous job. The college textbook of a generation or more, *The Civil War and Reconstruction* (published in 1961 with a 1969 edition), written by Lincoln scholars J. G. Randall (University of Illinois) and David Donald (Johns Hopkins), fails even to mention the term "Forty-Eighters" in its 866 pages. Its few references of Carl Schurz don't even mention the campaigns of 1856 and 1860. Franz Siegel is mentioned only in his ignominious retreat at New Market when his command was attacked and chased away by Virginia Military Institute cadets. Hecker, the man greeted by the mayor of New York and a crowd of twenty thousand is not mentioned. Neither is Kapp, the man who became a Lincoln elector in New York only ten years off the boat. One must look beyond contemporary Lincoln scholars to find the whole truth.

By the first half of the twentieth century, there was a consensus among historians that German immigrants, primarily under the leadership of the radical Forty-Eighters put Lincoln over the top in six key states of the old northwest. Writing in the *Mississippi Valley Historical Review* in 1942, historian Andreas Dorpalen states: "It is generally recognized today that Lincoln could never have carried the northwest in 1860, and with it the country, without German support."[41]

Also in the *Mississippi Valley Historical Review,* Donnal V. Smith wrote in 1932, "that without the vote of the foreign-born, Lincoln cold not have carried the Northwest, and without the Northwest, or with its vote divided in any other way, he would have been defeated."[42]

Examining the election of 1860 in the *American Historical Review* less than a half-century after the war, historian W. E. Dodd noted the irony of the influence on American history that was wielded by foreigners. "The election of Lincoln and, as it turned out, the fate of the Union were thus determined not by native Americans but by voters who knew least of American history and institutions." Dodd says the election of 1860 "was won only on a narrow margin by the votes of the foreigners whom the railroads poured in great numbers into the contested region."[43]

What railroad was responsible for this great number of foreigners, especially recently immigrated Germans? Dodd says it was none other than the Illinois Central Railroad,[44] which just happened to be one of Lincoln's lucrative clients as DiLorenzo has pointed out.[45]

During the 1850s, the Illinois Central Railroad was financed and controlled by the same group of men in New York and Boston who controlled the Panama Railroad and the Pacific Mail Steamship Company that monopolized the only means of transit across the Isthmus of Panama. The Illinois Central rapidly sold to settlers from New England and Germany an immense tract of land in the middle of Illinois that the railroad had obtained from the federal government. "The land agent of the [Illinois Central] published a guide to foreigners which was widely circulated in Germany and which directed all newcomers to this region," according to Dodd. In 1856-57, it sold a million acres of land and likely accounted for most of the 411,000 new settlers in Illinois.[46] By 1860, there were 130,000 German-born immigrants in Chicago. Milwaukee was dubbed the "German Athens." There were large German communities also in St. Louis, Cincinnati, and New York.

In the election of 1860, one did not even have to be a citizen of the United States to vote in the states of Indiana, Michigan, Ohio, Minnesota, and Wisconsin. In order to accommodate the recent influx of German immigrants these states allowed foreign, white male property owners to vote merely on their declaration to become citizens and upon residency requirements that varied from only four months in Minnesota to thirty months in Michigan. In Ohio, foreign-born white males were allowed to vote with a one-year residency restriction and payment of a property tax.[47]

Forty-Eighters such as Carl Schurz and Frederich Hecker laid much of the groundwork of the Republican Party in the old northwest in the presidential campaign of the first Republican nominee, John C. Fremont, in 1856. They and other German immigrants campaigned for Fremont among the German communities in the West.[48]

By 1860, the Forty-Eighters controlled half the German-language newspapers in America. Lincoln personally took note of the influence of German-language newspapers, so much so that he purchased the German-language *Illinois Staatsanzeiger,* "press and all," before the general election campaign started.[49]

Historians viewed the Germans and Scandinavians in the northwest that year as "a group of voters that would be practically certain to vote as a unit."[50] Considering that the German population was at least five percent of the total in Indiana, Iowa, and Michigan; seven percent in Ohio and Illinois; and ten to fifteen percent in Minnesota and Wisconsin respectively, the Germans constituted a significant source of political support.[51]

Schurz, Frederich Kapp, and numerous other Forty-Eighters were delegates to the 1860 Republican Convention in Chicago. The reader will recall from previous reference that Schurz was also a member of the Republican National Committee, and he served on the important platform committee at the 1860 convention. Every one of the seven northwestern states had representatives of its foreign-born citizens in their delegations. After a great deal of debate and posturing among the German-led element, and after the convention adopted support for free homestead land, the German contingent threw its support to Lincoln, the eventual nominee. No sooner than Lincoln was officially notified of his nomination, "foreign-born leaders began an active campaign for his election."[52]

Based on census data and election results in 1860, Smith estimated the number of foreign-born votes in each of the seven northwestern states and compared this number to Lincoln's majority over Douglas. In each state, Lincoln's majority was less than the estimated foreign-born Republican vote, indicating that it was the German vote that swung the election.

## Table 1. The Effect of the German Vote on Lincoln's Election

| State, (electoral votes) | Estimated German vote for Lincoln | Lincoln's majority over Douglas | Results without the German vote for Lincoln |
|---|---|---|---|
| Illinois (11) | 45,300 | 12,000 | Lincoln loses Illinois by 33,300 |
| Indiana (13) | 26,000 | 24,000 | Lincoln loses Indiana by 2,000 |
| Iowa (4) | 21,000 | 15,300 | Lincoln loses Iowa by 5,700 |
| Michigan (6) | 33,400 | 23,400 | Lincoln loses Michigan by 10,000 |
| Minnesota (4) | 12,000 | 10,000 | Lincoln loses Minnesota by 2,000 |
| Ohio (23) | 65,900 | 44,300 | Lincoln loses Ohio by 21,600 |
| Wisconsin (5) | 56,000 | 21,000 | Lincoln loses Wisconsin by 35,000 |
| Totals (66) | 259,600 | 150,000 | |

Table generated from Donnal V. Smith, "The Influence of the Foreign-Born of the Northwest in the Election of 1860," *The Mississippi Valley Historical Review* 19, no. 2 (September 1932): 192-204.

Table 1 shows the effect of the German vote on the election of 1860. There were 303 electoral votes in the election of 1860. It took a majority of 152 to win. If one subtracts Illinois's 11 and Ohio's 23 electoral votes from the Lincoln column, the election would be thrown into the House. Thus, one can conclude that the German immigrants under the influence of the radical Forty-Eighters swung the election for Lincoln. This fact was the consensus views among American historians throughout the first half of the twentieth century. Smith estimates there were 259,000 German votes that went to Lincoln. At the Republican convention that nominated Lincoln, Carl Schurz told the audience that he spoke for 300,000 German American voters.[53]

## Conclusion

The historic record preserves a direct and significant connection between the failed revolutions in Europe in 1848 and the American Civil War. This fact is not taught in any high school or college textbooks because it muddles the simplistic, if not simple-minded, explanation that the war was all about slavery, one side was "right" and by necessity, the other side was "wrong." If the war was not all about slavery, then the moral superiority of the federal government over the states, and the North over the South, evaporates. If this were to happen, the nation would lose its racial scapegoat: the South. The game of occupying the morally superior position by the Lincoln scholars, the statists, the centralizers—they *are* "New Puritans"— would end if their boogie-man were to be exonerated, and they will do everything they can to ensure that this does not happen.

We do not know why Randall and Donald failed even to discuss the Forty-Eighters in their 866-page "bible" of Civil War college texts. The bibliography in their highly influential book lists one thousand sources but does not include the scholarly articles by Smith, Dodd, Dorpalen, or Wittke, all published prior to their own work.[54] Smith's article addresses the influence of foreign-born voters in the northwest in the election of 1860. Dodd's article deals with all aspects of the election of 1860 in that area. Dorpalen's article addresses the much larger issue of German American influence on the era of the Civil War. Wittke's article consists of a detailed analysis of the influence of the Forty-Eighters on American history in a broad context. None of these are referenced in Randall's and Donald's bibliography.

In spite of the deafening silence of the Lincoln scholars, the fact remains that thousands of revolutionaries fled for their lives and came to America in two or three years just after 1848. Their revolt collapsed in the Fatherland, but the revolutionary fervor of the Forty-Eighters was unabated, their passion to change the world unbroken and unfulfilled. They saw in America a new venue and a new platform from which to launch the world revolution they sought.

The cultural and educational differences between the Forty-Eighters and most Americans were profound. Most were well educated, many of them lawyers, doctors, former university professors, writers, office-holders in their homeland, and editors. A number of them were graduates of military academies in Europe. Some came from the landed aristocracy and forsook their birthright in favor of radicalism. As a group, they were some of the finest leaders in the world—persuasive, sophisticated, well traveled, well connected, multilingual, and in the know. They were also entirely secular, antichurch, and antireligion. Most were agnostics or atheists and despised and ridiculed the typical piety of Americans and simplicity of American life.

The political differences between the Forty-Eighters and other Americans were also startling. They were internationalists who believed in and participated in international politics. Borders were irrelevant to them. They corresponded with and debated or encouraged radicals all over Europe. Many Forty-Eighters were Marxists; some considered themselves communists. One of the Forty-Eighters was Marx's own brother-in-law. Unlike most Americans who wanted only to make a life for themselves in a limited community with a minimum of outside interference, the Forty-Eighters saw themselves as international agents of change, citizens of the world rather than New Englanders, or New Yorkers, or Southerners. They were also imperialists who believed that a democratic empire should impose its form of government on other peoples around the world. No doubt, they strongly disagreed with the idea that America is the friend of liberty around the world but custodian only of its own, as expressed by John Adams.

It is also true that the Forty-Eighters favored democracy. But the form of democracy they wanted was one without the limits on government that our Founding Fathers wisely erected. They wanted a powerful central government that would be unfettered by a federal system of shared power with the states. They sought to pull down the states and erect a single, central government in its place. Their real interest in democracy was more or less mob rule, in that the political majority would always have the authority to take virtually any action it wants, leaving the political minority with virtually no rights. In this regard, they were also antiprivate property, as they believed all interests and endeavors should be subordinated to the central government. The Forty-Eighters wanted an imperial, all-powerful democracy that could impose anything it wanted on its own citizens or on the citizens of other countries, as long as it was done in the name of the majority. With this philosophical support, it should surprise no one that the

American Civil War was the first total war in modern history, i.e.,
war waged by government against civilian populations. Nor should
it be surprising that the federal government would simultaneously
launch a war of ethnic cleansing—racial genocide against the Plains
Indians.

One other attribute about the Forty-Eighters must not be
forgotten. Each had direct experience in fomenting revolution and
the exercise of military action. They were all military veterans of the
revolutions of 1848. What they failed to do in Germany, they hoped
to accomplish in America.

The sudden appearance of thousands of revolutionaries on American
shores at a time of intensifying political debate was a significant
contributing factor that led to war and even influenced the advent
of total war. The Forty-Eighters immediately assumed positions of
leadership in established German communities all across the country,
particularly in the North. Some were authors who were well known to
German Americans. Many of the Forty-Eighters who were newspaper
editors and publishers were as familiar to German-Americans as they
were to Germans in Germany. The same is true for former university
professors and military leaders who fled to America.

The Forty-Eighters wasted no time asserting themselves in
leadership roles in existing German communities or participating in
the political debate and process in America. Many voted in states of
the old northwest before they were even citizens. And as historians
Smith and Dorpalen established, they actually swung the election
to Lincoln in 1860. In their newly elected president, they found
the champion who would crush the states and reorder the nation
in a manner that they heartily supported. True to their cause, they
rushed to arms at Lincoln's call. Although quite a number became
officers in the U.S. Army, and at least ten became general officers,
their actual contribution on the battlefield was modest.

As true internationalists, when their mission in America was
accomplished, some returned to their Fatherland after the war.
A few Forty-Eighters who managed to obtain elective office in
America only to return to Germany after the war, were subsequently
elected to offices in their original homeland. This unique link
and even partial interchangeability of the political leadership

between mid-nineteenth-century Germany and the United States is an overlooked yet pivotal factor in America's most devastating and costly conflict.

As Dodd pointed out, the fate of the Union was determined not by natives, "but by voters who knew the least of American history and institutions." Indeed the Union was "saved" by German-Americans under the leadership of Forty-Eighters who not only "knew the least" about American institutions, they despised them the most.[55] Crucial support for Lincoln and his war agenda came from noncitizens who had the least to lose if the whole effort blew up in their faces. In fact, many Forty-Eighters who lost the struggle to wrest power in Germany in 1848 stayed in America for only a few years; contributed to what they considered a revolution, the Civil War (actually it was a counterrevolution); and returned home to participate in the war of German unification and the Franco-German War in 1870-71.

The American Civil War was "a belated chapter of the German revolution of 1848," not the war of racial equality assumed by today's pop culture. The war was "a liquidation of a European, not merely of an American past."[56] The Forty-Eighters played the role of catalyst in radicalizing the Republican Party, securing Lincoln's nomination, electing him president of the United States, and waging war on the South. They were the *sine qua non* of the counterrevolution.

# CHAPTER FOUR

# Lincoln's Call for Troops: Six Governors Say "No"

*"Nobody has a more sacred obligation to obey the law than those who make the law."* —Sophocles

Lincoln's election was the first victory in presidential politics by a truly sectional party. There was no Republican Party in the South in 1860 nor did the Republicans need the South to get Lincoln elected. He carried every Northern state except New Jersey, and that was enough to win. He didn't even need California and Oregon where Lincoln eked out wins with only about a third of the highly divided popular vote in a four-man race.

Vice Pres. John C. Breckenridge, the nominee of the Southern Democrats polled much more solid numbers in the North and was much less of a sectional candidate than Lincoln, who was only on Southern ballots in Kentucky, Virginia, and Missouri. Judging from his distant fourth place finish in each of these states, Lincoln had virtually no support in the South and would have received only a few scattered votes if he had been on the ballot.

Historians have duly noted that Southerners believed Lincoln's election demonstrated Northern contempt for them.[1] Lincoln's minuscule popular vote in the three border and upper Southern states demonstrates that the opposite was equally true.

After the votes were counted and it became clear that Lincoln would be the sixteenth president, the nation watched the South and waited for events to unfold. During the "secession winter" of 1860-61, seven states in the lower South severed their ties with the United States and formed the Confederate States of America.

On November 23, 1860, shortly after Lincoln's election was apparent, former president Franklin Pierce of New Hampshire (1853-57) wrote that he "never desired to survive the wreck of the

Union." Pierce, who was the son of a Revolutionary War soldier, had close political ties to the South especially with Jefferson Davis who served as Pierce's secretary of war. "I do not desire to live to see the day when the flag of my country, with all its stars in their places, will not float at home and abroad." Referring to the anticipated secession of South Carolina that was to occur just two weeks later, Pierce said, "[The] paralyzing fact" is that "if I were in their places, after so many years of unrelenting aggression, I should probably be doing what they are doing."

In the same letter, Pierce reveals his thoughts about secession: "If our fathers were mistaken when they formed the Constitution, if time has proved it, the sooner we are apart the better." This letter was found in Pierce's papers in his own handwriting, unsigned and unaddressed, and bears the endorsement, "Copy of letter not sent."[2]


## The First Inaugural Speech

It may come as a surprise to most Americans that Lincoln's devotion to the Constitution ended wherever and whenever it diverged from his political agenda. We shall see later that during Lincoln's tenure he repeatedly violated clear, specific, unmistakable provisions of the Constitution numerous times without any hesitation.

A *partial* list of these violations includes the unilateral launching of a war without consent of Congress (violates Article I, Section 8, the powers of Congress); using the U.S. Army to topple and chase from office the lawful and legitimately elected government of Missouri;[3] the questioning, arrest, and imprisonment of nineteen members of the Maryland legislature on the way to a legislative session as well as the mayor of Baltimore;[4] the suspension of the writ of *habeas corpus* by executive decree without authorization of Congress; using the U.S. Army to arrest private citizens and to suppress dissident newspapers; military occupation of cities in so-called "loyal" states, such as Baltimore; using the U.S. Navy to blockade ports (Article I, Section 9 prohibits the preference of ports in one state over another); arbitrary banishment and removal of Jews by the army (Grant's General Order No. 11 which removed thirty Jewish families from Paducah, Kentucky); and waging the first war in modern times on civilian noncombatants.

Lincoln also promised in his inaugural address—just moments after swearing his oath before God and nation with one hand on the Bible—*"there will be no invasion, no using of force against or among the people anywhere."*

No invasion? No use of force anywhere?

Lincoln lied.

What's more, he was pressured by incoming Secretary of State William H. Seward, the former governor and U.S. senator from New York, just two days before his inauguration to delete "saber rattling" references in an earlier draft of the speech that promised the recapture of federal property in the seceded states. Seward even threatened that he would not take office in the cabinet without a more conciliatory tone. Lincoln rose before dawn on his inauguration day to make changes on what he was to say, but history records a different attitude in his heart.[5]

Lincoln also met with John Bell of Tennessee the week before his inauguration. Bell was the Constitutional Union Party candidate for president in 1860, and as a former speaker of the House and U.S. senator, he had enormous prestige especially in the upper Southern states (he carried Tennessee, Kentucky, and Virginia in the 1860 presidential election), which upon Lincoln's inauguration remained in the Union and hopeful that secession and war could be avoided.[6] Bell, a wealthy slave owner, also commanded respect in the North for his senate vote against the Kansas-Nebraska bill, the only senator from the South to cast a negative vote.

Tennesseans had already narrowly rejected early secession on February 9, 1861, by a vote of 69,772 to 57,708.[7] But at their meeting, Bell warned Lincoln that the use of force would drive his own state, and probably the rest of the states of the upper South, out of the Union.[8]

An example of the twenty-first-century disinformation that obscures the truth about the American Civil War was the information posted on the *Harper's Weekly* Web site for an unknown period under the online biography of John Bell. *Harper's* maintained that Tennessee voters "overwhelmingly rejected" a referendum on secession. A six-to-five margin can hardly be called overwhelming, especially when it failed to mention Tennessee's second secession vote that passed by greater than a two-to-one margin. After the *Harper's* Web master was alerted to the error by this author, the biography was removed.

What did Lincoln tell Bell? We don't know. Bell, however, remained a Southern Unionist for the moment. So Lincoln made the "no invasion—no using of force" pledge. Seward and Bell must have been relieved. And there is no telling what Lincoln would have said if Seward hadn't threatened what amounts to a rupture in the Republican Party and Bell hadn't admonished him about the states of the upper South.

Lincoln was just tuning up for other pronouncements. There was much more to come.

## Trouble at Fort Sumter

At 4:30 A.M., April 12, 1861, Confederate forces fired on Fort Sumter. The Federals inside the fort were notified in advance of the day and hour the bombardment was to commence. This was no sneak attack. It lasted thirty-four hours without a single fatality during the battle. One Union solider was accidentally killed after the battle and another later died from wounds.[9]

Traditional scholars, such as Richard Ketchum, say that the opening shots simply "ratified" decisions already made by Lincoln and Confederate president Jefferson Davis. That's not really the case at all. "Both men had made up their minds to fight rather than to yield, and each man had come to see Fort Sumter as the place for the showdown," states Ketchum in his marvelously illustrated *The Civil War.*[10]

This sort of language places the blame equally on both governments, something that Ketchum and all other pro-Northern, pro-nationalistic, pro-central government historians attempt to do.

Ketchum overlooks the fact that Confederate president Jefferson Davis wrote President-elect Lincoln on February 27, 1861, to express his "earnest desire to unite and bind together our respective countries by friendly ties." Davis attempted to send special envoys to Lincoln "for the purpose of establishing friendly relations between the Confederate States and the United States." Lincoln would have no part of it and refused to see the Confederate commissioners.

Lincoln scholars James Randall and David Donald overlook Davis's attempt to establish "friendly relations." They do no mention it in their book, *Civil War and Reconstruction.*

They also overlook the fact that the demands were all in one direction: Northern demands on the South. The South's only demand was peaceful separation. The South had no demands to collect taxes in the North, change governments in the North, meddle in the internal affairs of the Northern states, or change any of the customs or institutions in the North. The South, like an aggrieved or abused wife, simply wanted peaceful separation.

Ketchum was correct in one point. It was, indeed, peaceful separation that Lincoln, like an enraged and abusive husband, had made up his mind to fight about rather than yield to.

Lincoln watched with great apprehension as the Virginia sovereignty convention debated the issues. The convention convened February 13 (three weeks before Lincoln took office) and debate continued without any serious or immediate threat of secession. In fact, on April 4, the convention voted against an ordinance of secession. On April 8, in a final attempt to avert crisis, the convention voted to send three commissioners including Thomas Jefferson's grandson, George W. Randolph,[11] on a mission to confer directly with Lincoln. The commissioners reached Washington on April 12 at the very hour Fort Sumter was under bombardment. Lincoln refused to meet with them and sent word that he intended to reoccupy all forts in the South by force if necessary.[12]

### Lincoln's Proclamation for Troops, States of the Upper South Secede

On April 15, 1861, six weeks to the day after Lincoln uttered the "no invasion, no using of force" pledge, he issued a call for seventy-five thousand troops for a ninety-day duration to invade the South and put down what he considered insurrection. There was no corresponding announcement by Davis to invade the North, depose Lincoln, or interfere with the operation of the federal government among the states that chose to participate in it.

The call for troops stunned the "holdout" states of Virginia, Tennessee, North Carolina, Arkansas, and the "border" states of Kentucky, Missouri, and Maryland. There is no parallel in American history that is even close to an official request by the president of the United States to the duly elected governors of the states requesting they furnish troops to invade and conquer a group of states.

The governors of six of seven holdout and border states immediately refused to provide Lincoln with troops. Only in Maryland where the ability to resist the Lincoln government was the most impaired by geography and the presence of the U.S. Navy Academy, was there any semblance of support and even then the Maryland support was equivocal at best.

During the debate of the ratification of the U.S. Constitution, seventy years earlier, James Madison in "Federalist No. 46," addressed precisely the scenario of the use of force by the federal government against a state or a group of states. This issue was raised during the ratification debate in New York state, but Madison dismissed it as a "madness" that could never come to pass.

Federalist Paper No. 46 was written to the people of New York by Madison who urged their ratification of the Constitution. Madison raised the dialectic argument to support ratification that "ambitious encroachments of the federal government on the authority of the State governments" might lead to the federal government's use of arms to subdue a single state or combination of states. Madison dismissed the fear of a future federal Leviathan bent on the military subjugation of a state as a specious argument against ratification. He countered the argument with this rhetorical question: "But what degree of madness could ever drive the federal government to such an extremity?"

Ohio congressman Clement L. Vallandigham used precisely the same word in an open letter to the Cincinnati *Enquirer*. Vallandigham's letter in April 1861 stated his hope that the people are likely to have second thoughts about war that would "dissipate the present sudden and fleeting public madness, and will demand to know why thirty millions of people are butchering each other in civil war?"[13]

Excellent question.

Was Lincoln mad? Or just crazy like a fox? Did he have an inkling that he was about to launch the bloodiest war in the history of man up to that point? Most historians tend to think not, but we don't know for certain.

Most historians contend that Lincoln was shocked that the states of the lower South had actually seceded and genuinely thought that the Confederate government and its military units would scatter at the first application of Union force.

Lame-duck president James Buchanan certainly seemed to realize that any armed conflict between the North and South (or more precisely between the federal government and the South), once started, would be a long and bloody struggle.

In Buchanan's message to Congress, December 3, 1860, just days after Lincoln's election on November 6, and before any Southern state had seceded, he stated his unequivocal opposition to secession along with his view of the perpetuity of the Union. On these matters, he and Lincoln agreed, but on constitutional issues, they were as far apart as night and day.

As for federal authority to resist secession, and as to the wisdom of doing so, Buchanan warned that in a war to forcibly preserve the Union "a vast amount of blood and treasure would be expended," and that such a fratricidal conflict would render future reconciliation "impossible."[14]

Buchanan's biographer, Jean Baker, excoriates the fifteenth president for his view of the Constitution that the power to use military force to coerce a state is "not to be found among the enumerated powers granted to Congress or president."[15] Yet, Buchanan was correct that Articles I and II of the Constitution do not provide the president or Congress with authority to coerce a state with force of arms.

Maryland governor Thomas Holliday Hicks also sensed the same grave consequences and said so. In his April 24, 1861, message to the Maryland legislature, Governor Hicks expressed the hope that Maryland and the other border states could mediate between the two sides, thus preventing "the terrible evils of a prolonged civil war."[16]

Even in tiny Delaware, the secretary of state expressed an unwillingness to coerce the seceded states and warned against the "horrors of a civil war."[17]

Clearly there were leaders in the North, perhaps including Lincoln, who knew that the federal government was getting into a war that would be bloody, expensive, horrible, and prolonged. And if Lincoln knew, or at least suspected, that the struggle would be long and costly, he certainly didn't reveal that to the public in his request for troops for ninety days.

Southern reaction to his proclamation was as swift as it was predictable. In the words of one North Carolina newspaper, "As with the stroke of lightning [Lincoln's proclamation] made the North wholly North and the South wholly South."[18] But political support for war was immensely more complicated than that.

Unionists at the Virginia sovereignty convention were so flabbergasted they first thought that Lincoln's purported proclamation was a forgery or hoax. One antisecession convention delegate, future Confederate general Jubal Early, dismissed the proclamation as inauthentic because he could not believe Lincoln's secretary of state, Henry Seward, could be guilty of the blunders in the document. The next day, April 16, authenticity was confirmed and Virginia governor John Letcher indignantly refused to send the Virginia militia into Lincoln's service. His responsed to the War Department by saying the request for troops "will not be complied with." Letcher said, "You have chosen to inaugurate civil war, and having done so, we will meet it in a spirit as determined as the Administration has exhibited toward the South."[19]

Lincoln's call for volunteers to invade the South changed everything. Suddenly there was no more question of war, but rather a question of "which side" for the holdout states. The Virginia convention reversed course and voted to secede on April 17.[20]

Such was the Old Dominion state's haste to defend her rights that her secession prior to official action in Tennessee and North Carolina meant that Virginia was temporarily surrounded by "loyal" states to the north, to the west, and to the south.

Earlier, in Tennessee and North Carolina, voters had turned down the idea of a sovereignty convention. Tennesseans voted February 9 by a fairly narrow margin against a convention. North Carolinians had voted narrowly February 28 against a convention, 47,705 to 46,711.[21]

Arkansas convened a sovereignty convention in March the same day Lincoln took the oath of office in Washington. It took no decisive action and adjourned after two weeks, subject to call. Arkansas governor Henry M. Rector had been elected in 1860 as a Union candidate, stating his belief in the Union as long as states were not coerced.[22]

When Lincoln's request for troops reached Little Rock, Governor Rector, insulted by the proclamation, fired off a response.

*Virginia governor John Letcher responded to Lincoln's call for troops by informing the War Department that he would not comply with the request.* (Courtesy Library of Congress)

*Arkansas governor Henry M. Rector was elected as a Unionist in 1860. He was insulted by Lincoln's call for troops to coerce Southern states, considering it unlawful and untruthful.* (Courtesy Old Statehouse Museum Collection, Little Rock, Arkansas)

In answer to your requisition for troops from Arkansas to subjugate the Southern States, I have to that none will be furnished. The demand is only adding insult to injury. The people of this commonwealth are freemen, not slaves, and will defend, to the last extremity, their honor, lives and property against Northern mendacity and usurpation.[23]

The sovereignty convention reassembled in Little Rock, and on May 6, the attendees passed an ordinance of secession by a vote of 65 to 5.[24]

Tennessee's governor Isham G. Harris was a strong proponent of secession and had worked through the secession winter to gather political support to take the Volunteer State out of the Union.

*Tennessee governor Isham G. Harris strongly favored secession. In response to Lincoln's call for troops, he informed the War Department that "Tennessee will not furnish a single man."* (Courtesy Library of Congress)

When Lincoln's call for troops reached Nashville, Harris answered it without hesitation the same day.

Harris telegraphed Secretary of War Simon Cameron with the following terse response:

> Sir: Your dispatch of 15th instant informing me that Tennessee is called upon for two regiments of militia for immediate services, is received. Tennessee will not furnish a single man for purposes of coercion but 50,000 if necessary for the defense of our rights and those of our southern bretheren.[25]

Lincoln was surely aware that Tennessee had the largest white male population of any of the Southern states and that her loss to the cause of the Union would be significant. Randall and Donald refer to Governor Harris's response as "haughty."[26] Dr. Robert H. White, (Tennessee State historian) characterizes Harris's message in terms of "clarity, brevity, finality."[27]

Harris and the Tennessee General Assembly put the question on the ballot for a second time, the only state to conduct two statewide votes. On June 8, Tennesseans voted to secede by a margin of 102,172 to 47,238. An interesting footnote to the second secession vote in Tennessee is that there were three counties where the vote was literally unanimous in favor of secession, one of which was Lincoln County (named in honor of Revolutionary War officer Benjamin Lincoln), where voters approved secession 2,912 to 0.[28]

In North Carolina, Gov. John W. Ellis replied to Lincoln: "I can be no party to this wicked violation of the laws of the country and to this war upon the liberties of a free people. You can get no troops from North Carolina."[29]

Governor Ellis called the legislature into special session in order to summon a convention. The convention was convened and the ordinance of secession was passed without a dissenting vote.

The situation in the border states was more turbulent than those of the states in the upper South, but even here the governors of two states indignantly refused to provide troops to Lincoln, and the response from the third is obscure.

In Kentucky, Gov. Beriah Magoffin was content with having a somewhat Unionist legislature that proclaimed Kentucky's official "neutrality" as a means of staving off secession.[30] Nevertheless,

*Kentucky governor Beriah Magoffin emphatically stated that Kentucky would furnish no troops for the "wicked purpose" of coercing Southern states.* (Courtesy Library of Congress)

Governor Magoffin replied, "I say emphatically Kentucky will furnish no troops for the wicked purpose of subduing her sister Southern States."[31]

Magoffin's refusal was "greeted with approval even by the Union men in Kentucky" who preferred real neutrality in the coming conflict.[32] Interestingly, Lincoln scholars view Kentucky's vote of neutrality as evidence that the secession movement was stifled in the Bluegrass State, when in reality it was an act of sovereignty on the same legal and philosophical footing as secession. Lincoln was mindfull of Kentucky's strategic location and influence on the other border states. Numerous individuals have attributed to Lincoln the saying that he would like to have God on his side, but he must have Kentucky.[33]

In the case of Missouri, Gov. Claiborne Fox Jackson was strongly pro-Southern. With a population of more than one million whites, Missouri was called upon by Lincoln to furnish 3,123 men.

Governor Jackson replied to Secretary Cameron in words that his biographer Christopher Phillips calls "icily uncompromising." Jackson responded:

> Sir: Your requisition is illegal, unconstitutional and revolutionary; in its object inhuman & diabolical. Not one man will Missouri furnish to carry on any such unholy crusade against her Southern sisters.[34]

Jackson was toppled from power in May when a U.S. Army sortie crushed the state's militia near St. Louis. The attack ensured that Missouri remained under federal control, but the price it paid in public opinion was a sympathetic reaction toward the South.[35]

Later in the year, Kentucky and Missouri passed ordinances of secession and were formally admitted to the Confederate government and represented in the Congress in Richmond. There were shadow governments at various times on both sides in both states depending on the fortunes of war at any given moment. These facts are frequently ignored, glossed over, or reduced in importance to a footnote in the Lincoln-dominated mainstream history books.

Maryland was perhaps the most Southern sympathizing state

that remained functionally, and legally in the Union. Governor
Hicks's response to Lincoln's proclamation is not recorded in the
Maryland Archives. Hicks did, however, appoint officers for three
regiments "called for by the President from Maryland," but it is not
clear whether those regiments mustered for that purpose or whether
Hicks actually turned them over to Lincoln.[36]

What is clear is that in April 1861, Hicks feared Maryland would
become the primary battleground, and he desperately wanted to
"force the contending parties to transfer the field of battle from our
soil" by following a course of neutrality.[37]

*Maryland governor Thomas Holiday Hicks refused to consent to Lincoln's landing
New England troops at the U.S. Navy Academy in Annapolis.* (Courtesy Library
of Congress)

On April 19, Maryland became the first real site of bloodshed as Massachusetts militia units indiscriminately fired on armed Baltimore civilians who did not take kindly to their presence. Four militiamen and twelve civilians were killed in the melee.

Hicks, though he was a slave owner, is portrayed as a strong Unionist by the Lincoln scholars because he took at U.S. Senate seat as a Republican before the end of the war. Of course by then the U.S. Army had exercised a powerful and effective, if illegal, role in Maryland's elections.[38] However, in April 1861 while the fate of Washington hung in the balance, Hicks refused his consent for the federal government to land troops from New England at the Naval Academy as did the mayor of Annapolis. Lincoln landed the troops anyway.[39]

The early presence of Northern troops in Maryland, the military arrest and imprisonment of many members of the Maryland legislature and the mayor of Baltimore, and the intimidation of elections squelched any move that could have taken Maryland out of the Union.

There was strong dissent to Lincoln's call for troops even in his home state, Illinois, a fact that is generally tucked away in an inconspicuous cubbyhole of history—if it is told at all. Popular sentiment in southern Illinois (the so-called "Little Egypt" section of the state so named due to the confluence of the Mississippi and Ohio Rivers) was opposed to the use of force to coerce the Southern states, at least early on. An editorial in the Cairo *City Gazette* stated opposition to calling out the militia for any purpose other than "home defense" and its opposition to sending any troops out of state "for the purpose of prosecuting the unnecessary war inaugurated by the present administration."[40]

Public meetings on April 15 in Carbondale and Marion demanded recognition of Southern independence and even went so far as stating that if the border states of Kentucky and Missouri seceded that Little Egypt should attach itself to the Confederacy. Army volunteer quotas were over subscribed in many places in Illinois, except for the regiment assigned to Little Egypt where they went begging. There were reports of hundreds of men leaving Little Egypt heading south to enlist in the Confederate Army.[41]

Even in Lincoln's home town, the state capital at Springfield, the

Illinois legislature "wrangled" over a militia bill for a number of days until Sen. Stephen A. Douglas delivered a speech in which he declared there were no neutrals in this war, "only patriots or traitors."[42]

So we see in the proclamation calling for troops, Lincoln's ability and willingness to parse words, spin the facts, or fabricate lies from whole cloth in order to accomplish his agenda of war.

Lincoln's call for troops stated "the laws of the United States have been for some time past and now are opposed, and the execution thereof obstructed by combinations too powerful to be suppressed by the ordinary course of judicial proceedings, or by the powers vested in the marshals by law."

What judicial proceedings?

Lincoln made no attempt to determine the legality or illegality of secession (or his authority to resist it). There was no suit challenging its legality. Lincoln didn't even ask his own attorney general for an opinion on the matter. Nor did he offer any legislation to the Congress. And why did he not?

He had good reason not to ask, because in doing so, it is entirely possible that the Supreme Court would have opposed Lincoln and agreed with the rights of states. Any actual court case would have likely involved questions as to whether the federal government has the right to invade a state or states for any reason. Quite to the contrary, the federal government has an express *constitutional duty* to protect each state from invasion (Article IV, Section 4). The federal government has no authority to depose lawfully elected state governments and rule by military government or martial law. Lincoln also would have had to answer whether there is constitutional authority for a president—on his sole initiative—to declare war without the consent of Congress. Of course, he has none, as the Constitution thankfully reserves this power to Congress (Article I, Section 8). Lincoln knew better. He was a successful attorney and knew better than most when he had no case.

If Lincoln thought he had had a case against secession, he would have had his attorney general file a suit in the Supreme Court to disband the sovereignty conventions meeting in Richmond (right under the federal government's nose) and Little Rock. If Lincoln thought these conventions were illegal, he would have had a duty to oppose them. Lincoln's silence on these two conventions speaks volumes.

Lincoln's proclamation also included a call for a special session of

Congress to convene July 4, 1861, giving him eleven weeks to get the war started and render moot any real debate. He missed that schedule by a couple of weeks, but by then, there was a Confederate Army between Richmond and Washington. Lincoln had all the excuse he needed to keep his men in service. Once again, we see Lincoln twisting words and manipulating events to make his illegal actions sound and seem legitimate, at least on the surface, and to evade accountability.

Even the Lincoln scholars begrudgingly acknowledge all this. "Government norms were abandoned," Randall and Donald confess. "War powers overbore the rule of law, and extralegal procedures were instituted." His call for troops "started the war regime as truly as if a declaration of war had been passed by Congress;" of course, Congress had not.[43] Lincoln "justified violating one law in order to support the larger, more significant purpose of preserving the Union."[44]

Lincoln acted illegally, trampled the Constitution, made a mockery of the rule of law, threw off the jurisdiction of the courts, set himself up as a virtual military dictator, and lied to the public. And that's not an assessment of Southerners. Rather, this was the assessment of Lincoln's contemporaries including Northern members of Congress, Gov. Horatio Seymour the sitting governor of New York at the time, former president Franklin Pierce of New Hampshire, and Chief Justice Roger Taney. Even Professor Randall, who has been called the preeminent Lincoln scholar of the second half of the twentieth century, concedes that military rule usurped civilian authority.

And for this we give him a national holiday.

Most histories point to two waves of secession, but there were actually three. First, the secession winter of 1860-61 during which the seven states of the lower South passed ordinances of secession prior to Lincoln's inauguration. Second, the four states of the upper South seceded in the spring of 1861 after Lincoln announced that he would invade. Third, the border state secessions in the fall of 1861.

We know now that the "fix" was in, in regards to the seven secessions in the first wave. Just after Lincoln's election political leaders in the deep South held a conference in Jackson, Mississippi. Mississippi was assured by Florida and perhaps other Gulf States that they would follow if she seceded. Jefferson Davis, then senator from Mississippi, cautioned against secession. Ignoring Davis's advice, Mississippi governor J. J. Pettus assured the South Carolina delegation that if the

Palmetto state seceded that Mississippi would go with her, knowing that other states were committed to follow.[45] Thus the dominos were set for South Carolina to act. And Lincoln's call for troops prompted the second wave, the upper South, in the spring of 1861.

The third wave of secession consisted of Missouri (October 31) and Kentucky (November 20); the states passed secession ordinances with pro-Confederate vestiges of state government more or less on the lamb. Pro-Lincoln historians dismiss them as *ultra vires*. While it is true that these ordinances were based on debatable authority, it was no less so than Maryland's ostensible loyalty to the Union where actual coercion and intimidation by the U.S. Army ensured that Maryland would not secede.[46]

No one seriously disputes that true, unimpeded state government ceased to function in all three border states after the shooting started. Lincoln occupied and subdued all three to the extent that he had the resources to accomplish it. His occupation and subjugation of Maryland was the most complete. His attempt to occupy and subdue Kentucky and Missouri was much more hit or miss.

There were two other secessions that had no great political or military importance and are mentioned here in an effort to complete the picture that so many history books written by the Lincoln scholars fail to do. The Arizona Territory passed a secession ordinance in Tucson on March 23 following its eastern neighbor Texas, for among other reasons, the U.S. Post Office withdrew mail service to the Southwest.

October 28, the Cherokee Nation (present-day Oklahoma) declared its independence from the federal government and its affiliation with the Confederacy. The Cherokees' declaration says that the secession of the Southern states was nothing more than asserting the right of "altering their form of government," the same right in the Declaration of Independence upon which the "self-government" of the Northern states is founded (Declaration by the People of the Cherokee Nation, 1861). However, unlike sparsely populated and isolated Arizona, the Cherokees and other tribes mustered several thousand troops in the butternut and gray uniform including several regiments of the Cherokee Mounted Rifles commanded by Brig. Gen. Stand Watie, a Cherokee chief.[47]

Both the Arizona Territory and the Cherokee Nation sent delegates who were seated at the Confederate Congress but were not actual members.

## Congress is Called into Special Session

Some of the most unfounded, unsupportable, and deliberately false representations made by any U.S. president at any time were the assertions Lincoln made in his message to the special session of Congress on July 4, 1861.

These assertions include, among other things, the following fabrications:

- That the states were never outside the Union or existed prior to the Union;
- That the Paris Peace Treaty of 1783 didn't declare the former Colonies "free and independent States"—or, the treaty used those words but, somehow, didn't literally mean it;
- That the Southern states were attempting to "destroy the Union itself," (this is a pernicious theme that follows from Lincoln's inaugural address that he will get much more mileage from in his speech at Gettysburg, twenty-seven months hence);
- That the use of coercive force against the South is the federal government's "indispensable means" of upholding its constitutional duty of guaranteeing a republican form of government to the states.
- And then there is the granddaddy of all of Lincoln's lies: That the federal government "*created*" the states, not the other way around.[48]

These are such hideous misstatements and outrageous lies, it almost makes one wonder if Lincoln were delusional. Or, in the weeks following Fort Sumter, perhaps it merely reflected desperation. Perhaps he thought that all subsequent generations of Americans and others around the world interested in the history of self-government were going to be dim witted.

In any case, it can never be overlooked that Lincoln was a sophisticated, successful trial lawyer who, according to Thomas DiLorenzo, was "one of the top attorneys in the Midwest," and his clients included the Illinois Central Railroad, which was "then the largest railroad in the world."[49] Whatever was on Lincoln's mind, and why he said what he said, the image of an ignorant, backwoods, aw-shucks lawyer most certainly *does not* apply.

Lincoln was a well-paid if not wealthy and well-connected

trial lawyer and former member of Congress, who married into a prominent family. He worked hard and rose to the status of the politically privileged and socioeconomic elite. The image of Lincoln the humble rail-splitter is a myth perpetuated by modern-day Lincoln apologists, believers, and state worshipers like Mario Cuomo.

Ask yourself this question: *Whoever got elected president of the United States without being able to outsmart, out-maneuver, and out-think some other pretty bright opponents?* And Lincoln is near the top of the class in these particular attributes.

Abraham Lincoln often referred to himself in the third person as the "Chief Magistrate." The sixteenth president had good reason for everything he said and did, just like every modern President.

Because these lies are so stupendous, take utterance from no less than the president of the United States—and in large part form the rationale for the launching of the bloodiest war in history at that time—they deserve the detailed attention of history.

### Lincoln's Deceptions Examined
The spectacular falsehoods in Lincoln's inaugural address call for troops and for a special session of Congress to ignore the Declaration of Independence, the history of the War for Independence, international treaty, the Articles of Confederation, the logic and arguments of *The Federalist Papers*, the ratification conventions for the U.S. Constitution in the thirteen states, the U.S. Constitution itself, the constitutions of those states, and the circumstances surrounding the first election for president, the seating of the first Congress, and U.S. Supreme Court decisions.

His sweeping misrepresentation of every foundational document, every source of authority, every historical debate, every applicable court decision, and all the institutions established by the republic subverted the rule of law that the Founding Fathers fought to establish.

Lincoln was a truly counterrevolutionary force in American political history. His claim stated in his first inaugural address that secession was unlawful and the ordinances of secession passed by thirteen states were "legally void" must be addressed.

CHAPTER FIVE

# Secession, the Constitution, and Law

*"The principle for which we contend is bound to reassert itself, though it may
be at another time and in another form."*

—Jefferson Davis, address to the
Mississippi legislature, 1881

## The "Legal Fiction" of *Texas* v. *White*

The Supreme Court case the Lincoln scholars cite in reference to
secession is *Texas* v. *White*, which was decided on a 5-3 vote by the
Supreme Court in 1869. All five Lincoln appointees voted as the
majority, and the three non-Lincoln appointees dissented.

The argument that secession is not a legal power to be exercised
by the states rests on this single case. The Lincoln scholars contend
that it stands as authoritative proof that secession was not legal, thus
the exercise of it by the Southern states was illegal, illegitimate,
unconstitutional, and, hence, treason. Their ethos is that the federal
government was absolved from the wrongs it inflicted on the nation
because it was fighting to reverse the illegal acts of the Southern
states. As Randall and Donald state, "The main point of the case
was that Texas continued to remain a state in the Union despite the
illegal transactions pertaining to secession."[1]

If this case deserves the legitimacy and reverence the Lincoln
scholars and statists invest in it, then the argument regarding the
legality of secession must be decided in the negative. If, however,
this case does not deserve the place in history that the Lincoln
scholars contend, then the issue of secession must be settled on other
Supreme Court rulings and legal doctrines, constitutional arguments,
and the larger historical context. This and the succeeding chapter
of this book establish why historians must discard *Texas* v. *White*
from the debate on secession and proposes other legal doctrines,

119

constitutional principles, and historical events to demonstrate the lawful, legal, and constitutional basis for the act of secession.

Having won the war and the Supreme Court firmly in the control of Lincoln's unprecedented five appointees, the party of Lincoln was in position to provide legal cover for the counterrevolution thus completed. *Texas* v. *White* is not simply a definitive case about secession, Lincoln scholars notwithstanding. Rather, it is the predictable response by the courts of the government that won the war. The winners were right; the winners obeyed the law; it was the losers who violated the law. One could not expect the courts of the government that won the war to rule any differently. They rewrote the common law to reflect their views of an all-powerful national government whose authority was no longer limited by the consent of the governed.

The Supreme Court ruled, "The Constitution, in all its provisions, looks to an indestructible Union, composed of indestructible States."[2] This ruling is illogical, historically inaccurate, constitutionally flawed, and corrupted with a fundamental conflict of interest and prejudicial behavior on the part of Chief Justice Salmon P. Chase, who wrote the court's decision. Furthermore, the legal issue between Texas, White, and the other defendants was moot. The case was heard in order for Chase, a conniving, active politician, even when he was chief justice, to seize an opportunity to rule on secession even though it had nothing to do with the legal issues in the case, which centered on Texas's attempt to get back bonds it had paid to the defendants. Point of fact, there were no legal issues raised by the attorneys on either side in this case for or against secession. Chase made it into a secession case anyway. After his death, the part of his ruling dealing with the bonds was reversed in another Supreme Court ruling (*Morgan* v. *U.S.*, 1885).

Nothing about this case can be understood in its proper context without an understanding of Chase. Chase's lead biographer, historian John Niven, describes a chief justice who was a politician on the court with presidential ambitions. He worked behind the scenes to obtain the Republican nomination for president in 1868, and then for the Democrat nomination in 1872.

Chase frequently spoke to and corresponded with President Johnson and members of Congress on matters of policy.[3] He traveled

*Salmon P. Chase was Lincoln's secretary of treasury and was appointed chief justice of the Supreme Court in 1865. While on the bench, Chase worked behind the scenes to obtain the Republican nomination for president in 1868 and the Democratic nomination in 1872.* (Courtesy Library of Congress)

for the purpose of observing conditions in the postwar South, observations that would affect his thinking about cases that would likely come before his court. He spoke publically on the political issues of the day.[4] Niven describes Chase's dissent in the so-called test oath cases: "His political antennae were vibrating as he judged the temper of Congress and the activities of Johnson . . . show[ing] a wavering of principle in the interest of expediency."[5]

What's more, in *Texas* v. *White*, Chase made prior "public comments" about the status of wartime and postwar government in the state, which was the whole point of the court's ruling.[6]

In this context, we see that Chase was clearly a scheming, unprincipled politician on the bench, who had improper and prejudicial contact regarding policy matters that were in the hands of the executive and legislative branches of government. He made improper firsthand observations to form his own opinions about matters that would find their way to his court, and he injected his own political calculus into his decisions on the bench. Chase appeared to be more interested in inserting his own political views into the legal issues brought to the highest court in the land than he did in providing an impartial tribunal in which justice would be done.

In spite of the discredit of this decision, let us look at the background of *Texas* v. *White* and systematically work through the historic and legal issues. The case arose as a dispute over the ownership of U.S. Treasury bearer bonds. The numbered bonds were issued to the State of Texas in 1851 for settlement of its western boundary. Texas had ceded to the United States government an area that included the eastern half of New Mexico, the panhandle of Oklahoma, much of eastern Colorado, part of western Kansas, and a small sliver of southeastern Wyoming, fixing the western boundary of Texas as it exists today.

Texas received the bonds into its treasury, and its legislature passed an act requiring the endorsement of the governor for the transfer of the bonds to any third party. After Texas seceded in 1861, its legislature repealed the earlier requirement of the governor's endorsement. The bonds matured on December 31, 1864, a date that no one envisioned would be during war. Some of the bonds were negotiated by Texas prior to the war and circulated among various owners with the endorsements of various Texas governors.

In 1862, the U.S. Treasury Department, not wanting to pay any of the bonds to a seceded state, hatched a clever catch-22 scheme to avoid its lawful financial obligations of the bonds. The scheme was to honor Texas's original, presecession statutory mandate for endorsement by the governor as if it were a requirement binding on the U.S. Treasury. The postsecession repeal of the endorsement requirement was not viewed by the treasury department as legitimate because it was passed by a "rebel" legislature. Even if a bond were subsequently endorsed, the endorsement would be by a "rebel" governor, thus, it too would not be honored. Because Texas was in rebellion during the war, neither its "rebel" governor nor its "rebel" legislature could cure the problem of endorsement. This was the contorted logic the treasury department devised in order to renounce its obligation to pay the bearer bonds under any circumstances that it thought might benefit Texas, or those to whom Texas sold the bonds.

In early 1865, Texas negotiated its remaining bonds with George W. White and John Chiles who were to deliver medicine to the state. By that time, the bonds had matured and were payable to any bearer who presented them to the U.S. Treasury. The war ended shortly thereafter without the delivery of any goods, and the provisional government of Texas sought to recover the bonds by filing an original bill in the U.S. Supreme Court, February 15, 1867. Texas asked for an injunction against White and Chiles to stop them from redeeming the bonds at the U.S. Treasury. The next day, February 16, 1867, the defendants presented the bonds to the treasury department and the bonds were paid.

Part of the legal issue before the Supreme Court was one of jurisdiction. Article III, Section 2 of the Constitution gives the Supreme Court original jurisdiction over all cases in which a state is a party. Was Texas a state in 1867 when it filed suit? Chase and the other four Lincoln appointees said Texas was indeed a state—"indestructible," they concluded. If they had concluded that Texas was not a state, they would have been unable to take the case and therefore deprived of the opportunity to use it for their own purposes.

And what was the court's ulterior purpose? It was to correct a position they had taken during that same court term in the *Lane County*

v. *Oregon* case (see the following section). Chase wrote both opinions. In the *Lane County* case, he wrote that the states "might continue to exist" even if outside the union. That would never do because if states could exist outside the union, they would be "indestructible," but the union would not. The Chase court ruled on *Texas* v. *White* in order to flip-flop on the issue of indestructibility of states, for without doing so they upended Lincoln's entire rationale of conducting this bloody and brutal war, namely to preserve the union.

One of the three dissenters on the court saw through this make-believe justice and called Chase's opinion "legal fiction."Associate Justice Robert Cooper Grier, a Pennsylvanian who was appointed to the court by President Polk in 1846 (after future president James Buchanan refused appointment), noted that the Reconstruction Acts of Congress placed Texas under the "military authorities of the United States" rather than a domestically elected civilian government. His dissenting opinion rings with stinging rhetoric. The question as to whether Texas was a state in 1867 should be decided as "political fact, not as legal fiction," Grier wrote.

> Is she not now held and governed as a conquered province by military force? . . .I am not disposed to join in any essay to prove Texas to be a state of the Union when Congress have decided that she is not. It is a question of fact, I repeat, and of fact only. Politically, Texas is not a state in this Union. Whether rightfully out of it or not is a question not before the court.[7]

Chase's opinion of the court in *Texas* v. *White* reveals how bizarre the logic, to think that the Constitution is perpetual and the Union of the states indissoluble, words not found in the Constitution itself. In fact, Chase supports his opinion with arguments that are entirely outside of, separate from, and prior to the adoption of the Constitution.

His opinion recited the same argument offered by Lincoln. The Articles of Confederation declared the Union to "be perpetual." The articles were replaced by the Constitution with the intention of forming "a more perfect Union." Chase asks, "What can be indissoluble if a perpetual Union, made more perfect, is not?"[8]

Chase asks a leading question that must be answered with another question. If the Articles of Confederation were truly perpetual,

*President Polk appointed Justice Robert Cooper Grier, from Pennsylvania, to the Supreme Court. Grier's dissent in* Texas v. White *called the ruling "legal fiction." He believed Texas was not a state in 1868 because it was "held and governed as a conquered province."* (Courtesy Library of Congress)

why were they replaced? Certainly, no history or legal scholar has ever argued that the Constitution is invalid because it replaced a "perpetual" union that already existed under the Articles of Confederation. If the adoption of the Constitution proves anything, it proves that even "perpetual" political arrangements and obligations can be altered or abolished by the people of the states—precisely what the Founding Fathers believed.

Chase further complicates his intricate theory about the nature of the Union by describing statehood in terms that no one had ever considered before. Historically, enabling legislation admitted states to the Union "on an equal footing with the original states in all respects whatsoever." (More on the equal footing doctrine in a later section.) Each new state as a separate, distinct political entity entered into the existing federation created by the older states. But the process of statehood that Chase describes in his opinion is one of "incorporation," an amalgamation into a larger body politic that "was final." Chase said the union Texas was admitted to "was as complete, as perpetual, and as indissoluble as the union between the original States. There was no place for reconsideration, or revocation, except through revolution, or through consent of the States."[9]

Chase's opinion reveals more inconsistencies. First, he acknowledges the right to secede equates to the right of revolution (the right of the people to alter, reform, or abolish government). Thus, he apparently leaves ajar the door to secession. Further, he adds another means by which states might secede, i.e., by consent of the other states. There is nothing in the Constitution about the consent of other states as a prerequisite for secession. What Chase could have meant by this is further evidence that his position is not supported by logic. For example, what level of consent would be needed for a state to secede, would it be by a three-fourths consent (the same super-majority needed to ratify the Constitution in the first place), or unanimous consent (required under the Articles of Confederation in order to levy taxes)? Is it the consent of the legislatures of the states, or the consent of Congress, or perhaps just the Senate as each state has equal representation therein?

Chase is a slow learner. His ruling left open all these caveats without providing specifics or limits, just as the Constitution had done seventy-nine years earlier.

Perhaps the most damning fact about *Texas* v. *White* relates to the direct conflict of interest on the part of the chief justice. If Chase had been a man of integrity, he would have recused himself from this case. That is a big "if" because Chase twice schemed during his tenure on the court to obtain the nomination for president (1868 and 1872).

Chase was the secretary of treasury who decided in 1862 that the federal government wasn't going to pay the bearer bonds held by Texas or others. He was the one who devised the catch-22 in order to avoid paying them, as discussed above. Chief Justice Chase even recorded in his opinion the position taken against the nonendorsed bonds by Secretary Chase: "The Secretary of the Treasury acted on this information, and refused in general to pay bonds that had not been indorsed [*sic*]."[10]

Chase, as secretary of treasury, "acted" on the information and committed his department of the government to specific position. *He was a party to this controversy—virtually a witness, and a biased one at that!* He violated the most fundamental element of justice, an impartial tribunal. Without an impartial tribunal, a court where the judges have no connection to the case and no allegiance to the parties, all that is left is a procedurally correct kangaroo court (and that's assuming procedures are followed). He should have recused himself, but he did not. His motivation in failing to do so is so obvious it requires no further discussion. Ironically, Chase's stand that the endorsement of the governor of Texas was binding on future holders of the notes was reversed in another bond case, *Morgan* v. *U.S*, 1885.

*Texas* v. *White* represents the low point of American jurisprudence, particularly as it pertains to the actual conduct of a chief justice. It is an important case because it set the stage for the coming federal Leviathan we have today. It established in legal framework the perpetuity and indivisibility of the federal government.

Chase took a legal blank canvas in *Texas* v. *White*, a two-year-old moot case, and painted his own political picture, a transformational moment in American jurisprudence. He failed to recuse himself even as he quoted from policies that he, himself, formulated as secretary of the treasury. He made improper public comments on the case during the period he was scheming for the presidency. He failed to provide an impartial tribunal. And, he read into the Constitution a history, background, and purpose unsupported by fact, logic, or any of his predecessors on the court. Yet, in *Texas* v. *White,* Chase could not find a single precedent-setting case to overturn, or a single court doctrine to reverse. For these and other reasons, we shall discard *Texas* v. *White* from the historic debate on whether secession is a lawful and constitutional power of the states and move on to more productive material.

### Other Decisions by the Chase Court
*Lane County* v. *Oregon,* 1868

The Chase court handed down other bizarre rulings that deserve attention. Most of them regard property or contract cases. It seems as if from 1868 until Chase's death in 1873, the Supreme Court, under his leadership, grew more bold and arrogant.

In the same term the court ruled on *Texas* v. *White,* it also ruled on *Lane County* v. *Oregon.* The controversy in the Lane County case was whether the county had to pay its tax levy to the Oregon treasurer in gold and silver coin as required by state law or in United States notes (paper money), which was the medium in which taxes were collected after 1863. Lane County insisted it should be allowed to pay the state tax levy in paper money; the Oregon treasurer demanded gold or silver. In attempting to recover money previously paid in gold, Lane County lost at the trial level, upon appeal to the Oregon Supreme Court, and at the U.S. Supreme Court.

The interesting part of this case is the Supreme Court's twist on the relationship between the states and the United States. It ruled:

> The states disunited might continue to exist. . . . Both the states and the United States existed before the Constitution. The people, through that instrument, established a more perfect union by substituting a national government, acting, with ample power, directly upon the citizens, instead of the Confederate government [under the Articles of Confederation], which acted with powers, greatly restricted, only upon the States.[11]

This is factual and historic half-truth. Clearly, the states existed prior to the Constitution; they were the sole and exclusive parties that wrote and adopted it. If, as Chase insists (he wrote this opinion), the United States government existed before the Constitution, why was it not a party to the ratification process? If there already were a supreme union between the states, why would Article VII of the Constitution say that it would operate only in the states that ratified it? If there were a union of states, why wouldn't it operate in all of them once the requisite nine states approved? There simply is no logic that supports this ruling.

There is another problem of fact and reason with the Lane County ruling. Under the Articles of Confederation, there was no national judiciary. How could the judicial branch of government interpret history in such a way as to find authority in a compact among the states (the Articles of Confederation) that had been superseded by the Constitution? Furthermore, how could the court find authority in the Articles of Confederation that was annulled prior to the court's very existence? Again, there is no logic to support the Court's stance on the relationship between the states and the federal government.

*Hickman v. Jones,* 1869

This case originated in Alabama as a case of treason against the Confederate States by Mr. Hickman. He was tried and found guilty. The case was heard by the Supreme Court due to a controversy regarding instructions to the jury at Mr. Hickman's criminal trial.

The historically important part of this case is, once again, the court's ruling on the relationship between the states and the national government. Part of the ruling stated:

> The rebellion out of which the war grew was without any legal sanction. In the eyes of the law, it had the same properties as if it had been the insurrection of a county or smaller municipal territory against the State to which it belonged. . . .
>
> Nor was there a rebel government de facto in such a sense as to give any legal efficacy to its acts. It was not recognized by the National, or by any foreign government. It was not at any time in possession of the capital of the nation. It did not for a moment displace the rightful government.[12]

It did not displace the rightful government, the U.S. government? The Chase court cleverly deflects the real question of secession as political divorce and replaces it with the inference that if the

Confederacy had won, the United States would no longer exist. This is entirely false, as there was no demand at any time, no political or military objective by the Confederacy to end or break up the United States. The Confederates simply wanted to go in peace.

*White v. Hart*, 1871

Perhaps the most self-contradictory ruling by the Chase court was written by Justice Noah Haynes Swayne, the first of Lincoln's five appointees to the Supreme Court. The case arose in Georgia regarding payment of a promissory note, the consideration for which was a slave, or was alleged to have been a slave. In stating the facts of the circumstances of the case, Swayne made comments about the condition of the State of Georgia, which is not only at odds with *Texas v. White* and *Lane County v. Oregon,* but also with his own words. He wrote,

> From the close of the rebellion until Georgia was restored to her normal relations and functions in the Union, she was governed under the laws of the United States known as the Reconstruction Acts. Under these laws her present constitution was framed, adopted, and submitted to Congress [for readmission].[13]

In other words, Justice Swayne admits that Georgia was out of the Union! And if she had been out of the Union, it was secession that removed her from the Union. What was there to be "restored" except statehood? If Georgia was a state at the time Swayne describes, why would her "normal relations and functions *in the Union*" have to be restored? Was Georgia "in the Union" while she was waiting to be "restored" to the Union or not? If she was "in the Union," why was she not governed under her own laws and her own republican form of government rather than under the military government provided for in the Reconstruction Acts? Swayne is perhaps more accurate than he intended when he points out that even Georgia's Constitution at that time had been dictated to the legislature by the military authorities governing her. Why was her dictated-to constitution submitted to Congress if she had never left the Union? Was Texas an "indestructible State" when Georgia was not?

No. This is where Swayne contradicts himself. Regarding the relationship of States to the national government, Swayne writes:

*Justice Noah Swayne was the first of five Lincoln appointees to the Supreme Court. He wrote in* Daniels v. Tearey, *1880, that the issue of secession was "settled by the arbitrament of arms," rather than law.* (Courtesy Library of Congress)

> The National Constitution was, as its preamble recites, ordained and established by the people of the United States. It created not a confederacy of States, but a government of individuals. It assumed that the government and the Union which it created, and the States which were incorporated into the Union, would be indestructible and perpetual; and as far as human means could accomplish such a work, it intended to make them so.[14]

Apparently Georgia was just as indestructible as Texas, just as "in the Union" as Texas, just as occupied by the U.S. Army as Texas, and just as "governed as a conquered province" as Texas (paraphrasing Justice Grier in *Texas* v. *White*).

It was hard for the Lincoln court appointees to get the story straight when they kept rewriting it, just as it is hard for the Lincoln scholars today to get it right every time they rewrite history. There are too many versions to remember. Georgia was out of the Union, but in the Union. Georgia lost its "perpetual" statehood, which Congress "restored." Georgia was an "indestructible state," but governed as a "conquered province." Georgia was a "perpetual" state, but which time: When it ratified the Constitution in 1788, or when Congress readmitted it in 1870? Taken together with the Lane County case, the states wrote and adopted the Constitution, which created the United States, but the United States existed before the states created it. It's enough to make one's head swim.

Swayne had a tendency to reveal much more than he likely intended. He wrote the opinion of the court in *Daniels* v. *Tearney*, 1880. He said the issue of whether secession was legal "has been settled by the arbitrament of arms and the repeated adjudications of this court."[15] For once, the whole truth. The secession issue was settled by force of arms, not the rule of law.

### Secession "Overturned" the National Authority in Virginia

Tucked away in an extremely important Supreme Court case on war powers is the court's inadvertent acknowledgment that the action by the Virginia Sovereignty Convention "overturned" federal government jurisdiction. This fact is one that the Lincoln scholars never discuss, for obvious reasons.

In *Ex Parte Milligan* (1866), the court ruled that military tribunals are unconstitutional when civilian courts remain in operation, even during times of war. The case arose when Lambdin P. Milligan, a civilian who never entered military service, was arrested in his home in Indiana on October 5, 1864, by order of Gen. Alvin P. Hovey. Ironically, Hovey had served on the Indiana Supreme Court before the war and would serve in Congress and as governor of Indiana after the war.[16]

Milligan, a twenty-year resident of Indiana accused of planning to steal Union weapons and fight against the Indiana government, was tried before a military commission in Indianapolis under Hovey's order and sentenced to death even though a federal grand jury had refused to indict him for any crime. Milligan's attorney filed for a writ of *habeas corpus,* claiming that his client's imprisonment was unlawful. The Lincoln administration claimed Milligan was a prisoner of war and was not entitled to any protection of the Constitution. This was tantamount to a self-declaration that the president, as commander in chief, is a military dictator. Thankfully, the Chase court rejected such dangerous reasoning and found there was no basis for military dictatorship-like rule under the Constitution.

The question before the Supreme Court in *Milligan* was whether Hovey's military tribunal had the legal power to arrest, try, and punish a civilian. The court found that it did not and ruled that the "birthright of every American" accused of a crime is to be tried according to law in civilian courts as long as those courts are open and in normal operation. The ruling noted that the federal courts in Indiana met soon after Milligan's arrest and those courts "needed no bayonets to protect it, and required no military aid to execute its judgments."[17]

The court found that "there are occasions when martial rule can be properly applied," such as "foreign invasion or civil war," provided that the geographic area of martial law is limited to the theatre of active military operations where civilian authority has been displaced. The court also said the duration of martial law cannot extend beyond the time needed to reinstate the civilian courts after combat is ended.[18]

The ruling draws a comparison and contrast between Indiana and Virginia during the war years:

> Martial rule can never exist where the courts are open and in the proper and unobstructed exercise of their jurisdiction. It is also confined to the locality of actual war. Because during the late Rebellion, it could have been enforced in Virginia, where the national authority was overturned and the courts driven out, it does not follow that is should obtain in Indiana, where that authority was never disputed and justice was always administered.[19]

What was it that made Virginia different than Indiana? How was it that "the national authority was overturned and the courts driven out" of Virginia? It was secession, of course. Virginia convened a convention in 1861 with the same authority that the original constitutional convention had in 1788. The 1861 convention rescinded the 1788 ratification of the Constitution and thereby "overturned" the national authority.

Notice that the court did not say that national government was "overthrown" by Virginia, rather is was "overturned." To "overthrow" a government is to defeat or to conquer it. The word "overthrow" suggests the use of illegal means to accomplish the defeat. The Russian Revolution overthrew the Romanov dynasty, and then the Bolsheviks killed the czar and his family. But Virginia was defeated and conquered by the federal government, not the other way around. Indeed, an overthrow occurred in Virginia. The federal government overthrew the duly elected state government.

The word "overturn" is used when the Supreme Court reverses a ruling. It connotes a change brought about by legal means. The *Brown* v. *Board of Education* ruling in 1954 overturned the separate but equal doctrine, reversing earlier rulings. Why would the Supreme Court apply the word "overturned" to Virginia's secession unless they believed there was an authority that was subject to being "overturned" (reversed) by secession?

Therefore, by the Supreme Court's own words, secession did, in fact, overturn national authority in Virginia. The federal courts were "driven out." Lincoln's whole point of invading the states was to reassert by force of arms the federal authority that had been legally and peacefully abolished (overturned).

It is doubtful that the Supreme Court in 1866 fully appreciated the words they chose in *Milligan*, because those words reveal an inadvertent admission that the court likely did not intend to make.

Unlike the spoken word, which can always be disputed, written words have permanence. For all time, *Milligan* implies that it was secession that "overturned" the national government in Virginia. In 1866, when this case was decided, the court was unencumbered with the doctrine of "indestructible" states (*Texas* v. *White*, 1869), the Union of states existing before the states created it (*Lane County* v. *Oregon*, 1868), or states that were simultaneously "perpetual" and out of the Union until Congress "restored" them (*White* v. *Hart*, 1871).

### The Unmistakability Doctrine

Nowhere are Lincoln's specious theories about state sovereignty, the relationship between the national and state governments, and his authority as president more powerfully contradicted and repudiated than in the findings of the United States Supreme Court. From the founding of the republic even to cases as recent as 1996, there are principles applied that run counter to everything Lincoln stood for. Another great irony is that as one of the leading lawyers in the country, Lincoln held the judicial branch in such disdain and contempt on the fleeting basis of political whim.

One of the doctrines adopted by the Supreme Court in 1810 under Chief Justice John Marshall is known as the unmistakability doctrine. (Serving from 1801 to 1835, Marshall is the longest serving chief justice.)

The doctrine of unmistakability applies to contracts between the federal government (and federal agencies, or state governments) and private parties. Simply stated, it holds that the federal and state governments cannot contract away or otherwise surrender attributes of sovereignty except in unmistakable terms.[20] More recent amplification of this doctrine holds that the transfer of governmental sovereignty cannot be inferred "from silence" in a contract. The only way an attribute of sovereignty can be contracted away by the federal or state governments is for it to be "specifically surrendered in terms which admit of no other reasonable interpretation."[21] In *Stone* v. *Mississippi*, 1879, the court established the long-standing doctrine that a government "may not, in any event, contract to surrender certain reserved powers," as repeated in *United States* v. *Winstar Corporation*, 1996.[22]

Even during Lincoln's sojourn in the White House, the Supreme Court ruled that neither the right of taxation "nor any other power of sovereignty, will be held . . . to have been surrendered, unless such surrender has been expressed in terms too plain to be mistaken."[23]

Furthermore, in 1908 the Supreme Court ruled that a governmental agent's authority to make surrenders of sovereignty must appear in express terms in a contract in order for the surrender to be valid.[24]

In 1986, the Supreme Court upheld these previous cases by ruling that the canon of contract construction is such that surrenders of sovereign authority must appear in "unmistakable" terms.[25] Furthermore, in 1987, the Supreme Court again upheld the principle that attributes of sovereignty cannot be surrendered from silence. The court also noted the likelihood that there are some sovereign powers that cannot be waived at all.[26]

Unmistakability has even been applied and upheld in a case involving a contract controversy regarding the space shuttle.[27] As recent as 1996, the court applied the unmistakability doctrine in sorting out the 1980s savings and loan bailout fiasco (see *Winstar* decision).

Another Supreme Court case that is not considered part of the unmistakability cases *per se*, but is germane to the issue of the grant of power under the Constitution, is the 1816 case *Martin* v. *Hunter's Lessee*. In this case, the court found that the federal government "can claim no powers which are not granted to it by the Constitution, and the powers actually granted, must be such as are expressly given, or given by necessary implication."[28]

So we see that from the early years of the republic to the twenty-first century, the Supreme Court has held that surrender of sovereignty by contractual agreement cannot occur unless the terms are specifically written in the contract; are "too plain to be mistaken" or "admit of no other reasonable interpretation"; and the agent's authority to surrender authority appears in express terms. Then there are some sovereign powers, reserved powers, that the federal and state governments cannot surrender under any circumstances.

Let's stop a moment to think. A contract is nothing more than a legally binding agreement between parties. In the larger context, an agreement can be a political compact between or among states.

How then, does the unmistakability doctrine apply to state

sovereignty and the question of secession? The applicability lies in extending the principle from a government-to-private-party relationship to a government-to-government relationship.

If states can only contract away or surrender sovereignty in dealings with private parties in *unmistakable terms*, how could states do so in an agreement with other states to form the federal government to begin with, i.e., the Constitution?

If states cannot surrender sovereignty *by silence* in agreements with private parties, how could states surrender sovereignty *by silence* in the Constitution? Search the Constitution for the words "sovereign" or "sovereignty." See for yourself if the government erected under its auspices was explicitly made sovereign, or if any of the states forming this government explicitly abandoned their own sovereignty to it.

If the federal government can claim "no power" to be exercised over the states unless it is "actually granted" in the Constitution, and "expressly given," how is it that the use of violence to "preserve the union" can be claimed to be legal by anyone?

If states cannot transfer sovereignty in dealings with private parties unless the terms of the transfer is in language "too plain to be mistaken" and the agent's authority to make such a transfer appears in express terms, how then can states transfer sovereign power in their organic documents or abridge any other rights and prerogatives, by inference and assumption?

If states may not surrender reserved powers *in any event*, and the right to secede *is* a reserved power, what answer must one conclude? That when one applies the doctrine of unmistakability to the question of secession, that secession is a lawful and legitimate power to be exercised by the states.

Under this current doctrine of the Supreme Court, beginning in 1810, if extended and applied to government-to-government relationships (a doctrine that was in place as a settled issue in the law at the time Lincoln practiced law and was upheld by the Supreme Court while he was president), there is no question that the states were well within their sovereign rights to secede. The only open question is whether states could have surrendered their *reserved power* to secede, even if they had desired to do so, without crafting language in the Constitution explicitly surrendering it.

Clearly, the Constitution is silent on the right to secede; therefore, secession is one of the powers reserved to the states under the

Tenth Amendment. And it is silent on the issue of sovereignty *per se*, though the states expressly shared or delegated numerous attributes of sovereignty to the federal government yet retained all residual attributes of sovereignty. Moreover, there is Lincoln's own admission in his first inaugural address that he had no authority to "fix the terms for the separation of States" because the Constitution is silent on state and national sovereignty, silent on perpetuity, silent on indivisibility, silent on complete dissolution, silent on secession, and silent on the consequences thereof. These issues were left for future generations.

If one goes back to the enabling act that called for the convention of 1787, one finds that it, too, is silent on the whole issue of sovereignty. If anything, the Philadelphia Convention greatly overstepped its authority by scrapping the Articles of Confederation and writing an entirely new document, the Constitution. The Congress under the Articles of Confederation authorized the Philadelphia Convention for the "sole and express purpose of revising the Articles of Confederation." Certainly, there was nothing that even implied a planned surrender of sovereign authority to the Constitution in language "too plain to be mistaken." The Constitution was barely ratified in several states for fear of creating precisely the entity that Lincoln remolded into Leviathan two generations later.

There was no express authorization by any legislature of the states or any ratification convention of the states overtly to transfer sovereignty, nor was there any express language for them to do so. In fact, New York ratified the Constitution with the specific condition that such ratification could be rescinded, i.e., "that the Powers of Government may be reassumed by the People, whensoever it shall become necessary to their Happiness." If the people of New York retained the power to reassume government whenever their "happiness" dictates, then the government erected upon those powers cannot be permanent or perpetual. Neither can it be said that the people conveyed sovereignty to such a government.

Finally, the argument as to whether the states had unmistakably transferred their authority to the central government by the act of ratifying the Constitution was no argument at all. The president of the United States in 1860, James Buchanan, knew well the application of the principle of unmistakability to this issue and believed that no transfer of sovereignty had taken place. Like Lincoln, Buchanan was an imminent attorney, but unlike Lincoln, he actually believed in the rule of law. On Christmas Eve 1860, with South Carolina's secession a *fait accompli,* Buchanan stated that there was never an unmistakable grant of sovereignty by South Carolina to the United States, and he also knew there was no authority in the Constitution to coerce her back into the Union.

As legal historian John Remington Graham has pointed out, Buchanan fully appreciated the historical fact that it was the individual and sovereign states that made and adopted the Constitution each in its own separate convention. None of the states surrendered their sovereignty. From a historical perspective, Buchanan's beliefs on the matter represented mainstream views among the first fifteen presidents. About South Carolina's sovereignty, and her right to make all decisions of union or secession, he said, "She did not part with her sovereignty in adopting the Constitution. . . . Nothing but a clear, express grant can alienate it."[28A]

Buchanan knew well that there was never any express grant of sovereignty from any individual state to the United States government. Absent such express grant, he knew South Carolina was acting in a legally acceptable manner and that he had no authority to invade any state or topple any state government. Lincoln knew this too, but instead of avoiding war, he intended to provoke it.

Thus, the application of the unmistakability doctrine to the coercive relationship between the federal government and the states, as Lincoln saw it, fails all tests established and upheld by the Supreme Court under the leadership of no less than five chief justices appointed by presidents from John Adams to Ronald Reagan spanning 195 years.

### The Legislative Entrenchment Doctrine

Legislative entrenchment is another current Supreme Court doctrine supporting the legality of secession that was also the law of the land in Lincoln's day. But it is much older than America's constitutional traditions. The doctrine is simple: One legislature may not bind a future legislature by a simple act. The principle is based on English common law's recognition of Parliament as the sovereign with "no superior on earth." If a prior Parliament had the authority to bind a subsequent Parliament by a simple act (law), then the prior body would have been superior to the present one.

William Blackstone wrote of this doctrine in his *Commentaries on the Laws of England,* the first of four volumes was published in1769. His words continue to be quoted in contemporary scholarly literature as well as Supreme Court opinions, such as in Justice David Souter's opinion in *United States* v. *Winstar Corporation,* 1996:

> One legislature cannot bind subsequent legislatures. It is a principle expressed long ago by Blackstone: "Acts of parliament derogatory from the power of subsequent parliaments bind not . . . Because the legislature, being in truth the sovereign power, is always of equal, always of absolute authority: It acknowledges no superior upon earth, which the prior legislature must have been if it's ordinances could bind the present parliament."[29]

In his eighteenth-century writings, Blackstone credits the Roman Republic in the first century B.C. with the genesis of the principle against legislative entrenchment.

> And upon the same principle Cicero, in his letters to Atticus, treats with a proper contempt these restraining clauses which endeavor to tie up the hands of succeeding legislatures. "When you repeal the law itself, says he, you at the same time repeal the prohibitory clause which guards against such repeal."[30]

Most legal scholars insist that in the American constitutional system, legislatures do not now, nor have they ever had, authority to entrench. Only a few scholars hold a contrary view. Michael B. Rappaport and John McGinnis argue that the Framers use of the term "legislative power" in Article I of the Constitution (powers of Congress) "excluded the authority to entrench." Moreover, they insist that even the legislatures of the original thirteen states that created and ratified the Constitution "did not possess this authority [to entrench]."[31]

In American jurisprudence, legislative entrenchment finds its origin in the same 1810 *Fletcher* v. *Peck* Supreme Court ruling that was the source of unmistakability. Chief Justice John Marshall wrote in the court's opinion:

One legislature is competent to repeal any act which a former legislature was competent to pass; and that one legislature cannot abridge the powers of a succeeding legislature. . . . The correctness of this principle, so far as respects general legislation can never be controverted.[32]

In 1853, Chief Justice Roger Taney expounded on the principle of entrenchment when he wrote the court's opinion:

The powers of sovereignty confided by the legislative body of a state are undoubtedly a trust committed to them, to be executed to the best of the judgment for the public good; and no one Legislature can, by its own act, disarm their successors of any of the powers or rights of sovereignty confided by the people to the legislative body.[33]

In an 1879 case regarding an act of the Ohio legislature that moved the Mahoning County seat from its "permanent" location in Canfield to Youngstown, the Supreme Court found that the principle against legislative entrenchment applied.

The legislative power of a State, except so far as restrained by its own constitution, is at all times absolute with respect to all offices within its reach. It may at pleasure create or abolish them, or modify their duties. It may also shorten or lengthen the term of service. And it may increase or diminish the salary or change the mode of compensation.[34]

The court rejected the arguments by the plaintiffs' attorney, James A. Garfield, who would be elected president thirteen months later.

So pervasive is this doctrine against entrenchment, as noted by University of Chicago law professors Eric A. Posner and Adrian Vermeule, that "the academic literature takes the rule as a given, universally assuming that legislative entrenchment is constitutionally or normatively objectionable." This doctrine is the standard taught in law texts across the country.[35]

One of the theories supporting the doctrine against entrenchment is the agency theory attributed to Julian N. Eule. Under this theory, the Constitution establishes an agency relationship between Congress and the citizenry, which entrenchment violates. The key assumption is that each Congress serves the public's agent only until the next election when a succeeding Congress will become the agent. Posner and Vermeule disagree with this theory and use most of their forty-page article in the 2002 *Yale Law Journal* to argue that the doctrine is not constitutionally objectionable and should be discarded.[36]

Much of their argument for dropping the rule against entrenchment centers on several exceptions they cite that, they argue, establish forms of entrenchment without creating constitutional objections. These include: 1) The Senate's filibuster and cloture rule (Senate Rule XXII) to cut off debate; 2) the budget sequestration provisions of the Gramm-Rudman deficit control law; 3) numerous interpretative rules codified in the Dictionary Act by Congress and aimed at the federal courts; 4) hybrid entrenchments such as the Alaska Natural Gas Transportation Act, which barred consideration by either House of Congress of certain aspects of energy policy; 5) government contracts that contain breach of contract provisions; and 6) treaties with other nations.[37] None of the exceptions noted by the authors contain blatant, unequivocal entrenchments, i.e., unrepealable limitations, with perhaps the exception of treaties. (Of course, history teaches that treaties between nations are binding only until they are renounced, broken, or renegotiated.) Catherine Fisk and Erwin Chemerinsky agree that Senate Rule XXII is an entrenchment of Senate rules, and they find that it is unconstitutional because it "frustrates" the will of the majority in future Senates and thus "violates the democratic principles of representation and accountability." Embedded in the rule are restrictions that "[bind] future Senates and [make] repeal or revision of the rule extremely difficult" and constitutionally objectionable.[38]

Rappaport and McGinnis reject the arguments about exceptions to entrenchment posed by Posner and Vermeule. They content that entrenchment obscures the difference between constitutional and legislative limitations, and "the distinction between constitutional and ordinary legislation is fundamental in our system, and entrenchment flouts that distinction." They warn that if Congress could legitimately exercise entrenchment, "the legislative power [of] Congress . . . would simply be enormous."[39]

Would one consider the following scenarios consistent with American constitutional traditions, or even self-government? What if Congress passed a law that taxed all estates at one hundred percent, complete confiscation, and enacted a "no-repeal" provision so that no future Congress would have the authority to repeal the law? Or in the name of fuel economy and environmental protection, what if Congress passed an unrepealable law to ban any personal motor vehicle transportation with more than four seats from the interstate highway system, making it functionally impossible for any family with more than two children to travel?

Such power would be enormous. Fisk and Chemerinsky agree that entrenchment is constitutionally objectionable. They say entrenchment "frustrates the accountability necessary for effective democratic rule."[40]

The father of the Constitution, James Madison, had plainspoken objections to entrenchment. In 1790, he supported legislation to move temporarily the nation's capital from New York to Philadelphia while Washington, D.C. was undergoing preparations to become the permanent capital. Some feared that once the capital was placed in Philadelphia, even on a temporary basis, the city would somehow find political support to keep it there. Madison answered his critics with a lecture on legislative entrenchment:

> But what more can we do than pass a law for the purpose [of making Washington the future capital]? It is not in our power to guard against a repeal. Our acts are not like those of the Medes and Persians, unalterable. A repeal is a thing against which no provision can be made. If that is an objection, it holds good against any law that can be passed.[41]

Madison further revealed his bias against the authority to entrench in the language of the Virginia Statute for Religious Freedom, which he introduced:

> And though we know this assembly elected by the people for ordinary purposes of legislation only, have no power to restrain the acts of

succeeding assemblies, constituted with powers equal to our own, and that therefore to declare this act irrevocable would be of no effect in law; yet we are free to declare and do declare, that the rights hereby asserted are of the natural rights of mankind, and that if any act shall be hereafter passed to repeal the present, or to narrow its operation, such act will be an infringement of natural right.[42]

Law professor H. Newcomb Morse argues that Madison was biased in favor of each individual state being the sole and final arbiter of whether another state has violated, and thereby dissolved, the compact (Constitution). Madison believed "a breach by any one article by any one party, leaves all other parties at liberty to consider the whole convention as dissolved."[43] Since only a given state has the right to ascertain whether other states have broken the compact, one must conclude that the father of the Constitution believed that the legal authority to leave the union of States was not entrenched against the states.

In addition, Jefferson had objections to entrenchment. His declaration was that "the Earth belongs always to the living generation," that "the Constitution and the laws of their predecessors are extinguished then, in their natural course, with those whose will gave them being."[44]

Whether Posner's and Vermeule's arguments for dropping the rule against entrenchment or their list of exceptions are persuasive, they readily acknowledge the long standing tradition and Supreme Court doctrine against legislative entrenchment. Interestingly, they did not include secession of the Southern states (or an argument against their legal ability to do so) in their list of exceptions to the entrenchment rule. In private correspondence, Posner indicated that he and Vermeule simply did not think about it, nor did Fisk, Chemerinsky, Rappaport, or McGinnis. But the Founding Fathers did, and they discussed the issue of entrenchment at the Philadelphia Convention of 1787 when they authored the Constitution and afterwards during the debate over ratification.

Virginia delegate George Mason opposed referring the Constitution to state legislatures for ratification for the very reason of the principle of entrenchment. Mason disfavored the direct involvement of the state legislatures "because succeeding Legislatures having equal authority could undo the acts of their predecessors; and the National

Government would stand in each State on the weak and tottering foundation of an Act of Assembly." Thus, the Philadelphia Convention chose ratification by the people through conventions in each state in an attempt to evade the issue of entrenchment.[45] Of course, there was no mandate requiring the legislatures of the states to respond to the request to ratify the Constitution by enabling a convention empowered to do so or to respond at all, although all states did so in due course. Nor could there have been such a demand on the states because it would have been repugnant to their sovereignty.

Historian Kenneth Stampp explains that having single-purpose conventions ratify the Constitution avoids the problem of relying on acts of state legislatures, which meet every year or every biennium and might be tempted to repeal such prior act. However, Stampp recognizes that it does not avoid the conceptual problem of the principle against entrenchment.

> Of course, the logic of this argument leads to the conclusion that succeeding state conventions, having equal authority, could undo the work of their predecessors—precisely what the secessionists of 1860-1861 believed.[46]

The agency theory recognizes the relationship between the citizenry—the true sovereigns—and elected officials in the legislative branch who exercise power on their behalf. It follows that the citizenry has the ultimate competency to alter, reform, or abolish the forms of government that fail to serve them.

When the citizenry of the states created the federal government, as they did by ratification conventions in the states in 1787-90, they had the right to convene a subsequent convention with the same authority as the first (if the citizenry retains their sovereignty). The establishment of the federal government cannot be inadvertently or accidentally entrenched against the interests of the people. If it can be entrenched at all (which is doubtful if the people of the states retain sovereignty), it would have to be done purposefully, willfully, knowingly, and explicitly. But there is nothing in either the ratification debate or the Constitution itself that even hints that such an entrenchment was intended, much less accomplished. The Founding Fathers were worried enough about obtaining support for ratification without opening additional arguments against it.

The rule of legislative entrenchment relates to the issue of the secession of Virginia, North Carolina, South Carolina, Georgia (part of the thirteen original states to ratify the Constitution) in terms of the means by which these states adopted ordinances of secession.

Consider the chain of events. In 1787-90, the legislatures of the thirteen original states passed statutes to select convention delegates who would convene when and where provided by the statute and empowered with the authority to ratify or reject the Constitution. Eventually the states did ratify. However, North Carolina and Rhode Island were so deliberate in the process that Washington was elected president, sworn in, and the first Congress met and adjourned before either state ratified the Constitution and participated in government alongside the other eleven.

Subsequently, in December 1860, the South Carolina legislature passed an act that called for selection of another convention with the same authority as the original one in 1788. The 1860 convention passed an ordinance of secession that simply rescinded the ratification of the Constitution by the 1788 convention. Thus, the political ties to the United States were severed by South Carolina.

This view is clearly validated from no less an authoritative source than James Madison as he participated in the ratification debate. In an attempt to calm fears at the Virginia ratifying convention, Madison posed the rhetorical question as to who are the parties to the Constitution? His answer was that the people of the thirteen sovereignties are the parties to the Constitution, not the people of the aggregate whole.[47] His arguments won the day, calmed fears, and Virginia ratified, but its ratification was conditional, as was the ratifications of six other states.

Similar fears and discussions were expressed at other ratifying conventions. At the Pennsylvania convention, delegate John Smilie asserted that if the people of Pennsylvania change their minds at a future date, they would have every right to assemble another convention and overturn the ratification.[48] Indeed, the doctrine against entrenchment is so ingrained in our constitutional traditions that legal scholars Fisk and Chemerinsky wrote that if entrenchment were permissible it would lead to the "systematic malfunctioning" of the American legal system.[49]

## The Law of the Land in 1860 and Today

Beyond the application of the principle against entrenchment, there is the obvious question as to whether South Carolina (and the other Southern states) had a legal right to secede under the law of the land at the time.

If one believes the rulings of the U.S. Supreme Court represent the obligatory and final interpretation of the law of the land, then one cannot help but answer, yes, South Carolina indeed had the legal right to do what she did. See Figure 1.

### Figure 1. Supreme Court Rulings on Legislative Entrenchment

| Case | Opinion |
| --- | --- |
| *Fletcher* v. *Peck,* 1810 | "One Legislature is competent to repeal any act which a former Legislature was competent to pass." |
| *Ohio Life* v. *Debolt,* 1853 | "No one Legislature can, by its own act, disarm their successors." |
| *Boyd* v. *Alabama,* 1877 | "We are not prepared to admit that it is competent for one legislature . . . to restrain the powers of a subsequent legislature to legislate." |
| *Boston Beer Co.* v. *Commonwealth of Massachusetts,* 1878 | "The hand of the legislature cannot be stayed" (from repeal of prior laws). |
| *Fertilizing Co.* v. *Hyde Park,* 1878 | Legislature has power to repeal previous acts. |
| *Newton* v. *Mahoning County,* 1879 | Legislatures "may at pleasure create or abolish" statutes. |
| *Stone* v. *Mississippi,* 1880 | Legislatures "cannot give away nor sell the discretion of those that are to come after them." |
| *Butchers' Union Slaughterhouse and Livestock Company* v. *Crescent City Livestock Landing and Slaughterhouse Company,* 1884 | One legislature cannot "restrain the power of a subsequent legislature." |

| *Douglas* v. *Kentucky*, 1897 | Legislatures have the power to repeal prior statutes and grants. The absence of such power would be "destructive of the main pillars of government." |
| --- | --- |
| *Connecticut Mutual Life Insurance Co.* v. *Spratley*, 1899 | "Every succeeding legislature possesses the same jurisdiction and power with respect to them as its predecessors. The later have the same power of repeal and modification which the former had of enactment, neither more nor less." |
| *Reichelderfer* v. *Quinn*, 1932 | "The will of a particular Congress . . . does not impose itself upon those to follow in succeeding years." |
| *U.S.* v. *Winstar Corp.*, 1996 | "One legislature cannot bind subsequent legislatures." |

Chief Justice Marshall wrote in 1810, "one legislature is competent to repeal any act which a former legislature was competent to pass; and that one legislature cannot abridge the powers of a succeeding legislature."[50] And again in 1853 by Chief Justice Taney, Marshall's successor wrote, "no one Legislature can, by its own act, disarm their successors of any of the powers or rights of sovereignty confided by the people to the legislative body."[51] In 1899, in *Connecticut Mutual Life Insurance Co.* v. *Spratley*, the Supreme Court reaffirmed the *Newton v. Mahoning County* decision and reapplied the word "evil" to describe entrenchment.

> Every succeeding legislature possesses the same jurisdiction and power with respect to them as its predecessors. The latter have the same power of repeal and modification which the former had of enactment, neither more nor less . . . It is vital to the public welfare that each one should be able at all times to do whatever the varying circumstances and present exigencies touching the subject may require. A different result would be fraught with evil.[52]

In the *Connecticut Mutual Life* case, the court declares that "the same principle" against entrenchment is found in *Fertilizing Co.* v. *Hyde Park* (1878), *Butchers' Union Slaughterhouse and Livestock Company* v. *Crescent City Livestock Landing and Slaughterhouse Company* (1884), *Boyd* v. *Alabama* (1897), and *Douglas* v. *Kentucky* (1897). A few decades thereafter in *Reichelderfer* v. *Quinn* (1932), the court declared that "the will of a particular Congress . . . does not impose itself upon those to follow in succeeding years."[53]

Since there was never any challenge based on law or history as to the authority of the South Carolina legislature to establish a convention in 1788, there can be no question of its authority to convene another convention with the same authority as the first. To question the legitimacy of South Carolina's second convention is to question the first. Both were enabled by the legislature, and both had popular support from the people on whose behalf they acted. If its 1788 ratification of the Constitution was *ultra vires* (without authority), then it was never legally a state in the Union from the start, and its attempt to leave the Union in 1860 would have been nonsense.

It was the law of the land from the time Lincoln was one year old; it was the law of the land when he practiced law; it was the law of the land when he became president and invaded the South; and it remains the law of the land into the twenty-first century. Indeed, even a conservative, limited reading of Marshall's words raises a serious doubt as to whether the South Carolina legislature could have "entrenched" the question of ratification of the U.S. Constitution even if it wanted to, thus making it impossible for any subsequent legislature or convention to address it.

If one argues that the legislatures of the Southern states were estopped from calling another convention, one must answer the question about whether the people themselves retained the authority to do so. Even today, the people of the states remain the sole and exclusive political entity with the authority to amend the Constitution. Just as Madison stated in the Virginia convention, it is the people of the various states, not the people as composing one great body. How can a political entity clothed with the authority to amend, fail to be the sovereignty that has power to enact or terminate? If this authority does not remain with the people, then this power has been entrenched against the citizens, who would not have the authority to replace the Constitution with a new one, should they so choose. Moreover, if the people are not sovereign and no longer have the authority to assemble another convention to rewrite or replace the Constitution, then one must explain who the sovereign is and how was it that the people were divested of their birthright?

The answer is quite simple, according to Fisk and Chemerinksy. Depriving any legislature from the same jurisdiction and power of its predecessors is unconstitutional and violates the law of the land that has been decided over and over by the Supreme Court.[54] And the history of this principle is traced to the common law of England and even all the way back to the Roman Republic before the birth of Christ. It is an essential element to representative government.

What sort of power was exercised in 1788-90 with the authority to propose, adopt, or even reject the Constitution? It was the sort of power described by the Supreme Court's ruling in *U.S.* v. *Ballin* in 1892. The question in this case was whether a particular law had properly passed the U.S. House of Representatives. Specifically, was the current House rule that established the requirement for a quorum valid? The court ruled, "The power to make rules is not one which once exercised is exhausted. It is a continuous power, always subject to be exercised by the House, and, within the limitations suggested, absolute and beyond the challenge of any other body or tribunal."[55]

In like manner, the power to make, modify, or repeal law is a legislative matter. It is not a power that is "exhausted" once used, but rather it is a "continuous power." If our constitutional traditions allowed future legislatures to be disarmed as a result of the exercise of power by their predecessors, the future would indeed be "fraught with evil."

### The Equality of States, or Equal Footing Doctrine

What about the Southern states that were not participants in the ratification of the Constitution because they had not yet come into existence? Did they also have a right to secede? We will see that under the Supreme Court's doctrine of equal footing, all states share in the same powers and attributes of sovereignty with the original thirteen.

The first two states admitted to the United States under the Constitution were Vermont (1791) and Kentucky (1792). The act of admission for these states declares that the state is admitted "as a new and entire member of the United States of America." There were no terms or conditions exacted from either. When the third new state, Tennessee, was admitted in 1796, it was declared to be "one of the

United States of America" and admitted "on an equal footing with the original states in all respects whatsoever," phraseology that has been used ever since in admitting other states.[56]

Two landmark cases decided in the court's 1845 term address this issue. One case arose in Alabama (*Pollard* v. *Hagan*), the other in Louisiana (*Permoli* v. *First Municipality of New Orleans*).

In the *Pollard* v. *Hagan* case, the court dealt with the issue of the vesting of title to navigable waterways, which right transferred from the federal government to the state upon admission as a state. The territory that became the state of Alabama was originally part of Georgia. In 1802, Georgia ceded this territory to the United States by a deed of cession, which included the stipulation that said territory should form a state to be admitted "on the same conditions and restrictions, with the same privileges, and in the same manner" as other states.

The court found, "When Alabama was admitted to the union, on an equal footing with the original states, she succeeded to all the rights of sovereignty, jurisdiction, and eminent domain which Georgia possessed at the date of the cession." The court further explained that when new states are admitted to the union their municipal sovereignty is complete, "and they, and the original states, will be upon an equal footing, in all respects whatever."[57]

The *Permoli* case rose from controversy over funeral and burial restrictions in a municipal ordinance in New Orleans. For reasons of public health, due to nearby swampiness, bodies were not allowed to be presented at funerals in a particular Catholic church for fear of the spread of disease. The citizens who filed the suit seeking to overturn the ordinance argued that the religious liberty provisions of the Ordinance of 1787 extend to Louisiana. The municipality's argument compared the condition and status of Louisiana to that of Massachusetts, one of the original states. The argument it presented was that once Louisiana was admitted to the union of states, she became "Massachusetts's equal," and that if Congress had no authority to extend the Ordinance of 1787 over Massachusetts, it had no authority to extend it over Louisiana. "What Massachusetts may do, Louisiana may do. What Congress may not forbid Massachusetts to do, it may not forbid Louisiana to do," was the argument to the court. A corollary argument asserted that there "is and must be, from a constitutional necessity, a perfect and unchangeable equality among the states." The court agreed with these arguments and found that Louisiana and, by extension, all states are admitted "on an equal footing with the original states in all respects whatever."[58]

In an 1883 case, *Escanaba and Lake Michigan Transport Co.* v. *City of Chicago,* the court upheld both *Pollard* and *Permoli.* The court found that upon statehood, Illinois "at once became entitled to and possessed of all the rights of dominion and sovereignty which belonged to the original states. She was admitted, and could be admitted, only on the same footing with them. . . . Equality of constitutional right and power is the condition of all the states of the Union, old and new."[59]

In an 1888 case from Oregon, the Supreme Court upheld *Pollard, Permoli,* and *Escanaba* (*Willamette Iron Bridge Co.* v. *Hatch*). In 1892, the court again applied the equal footing doctrine to a case from Texas. It found that Texas "was admitted into the Union on an equal footing with the original states in all respects whatever."[60]

In a 1911 case from Oklahoma, the court found that the Union:

> Was and is a union of states, equal in power, dignity, and authority, each competent to exert that residuum of sovereignty not delegated to the United States by the Constitution itself. To maintain otherwise would be to say that the Union, through the power of Congress to admit new states, might come to be a union of states unequal in power, as including states whose powers were restricted only by the Constitution, with others whose powers had been further restricted by an act of Congress accepted as a condition of admission.[61]

The court further determined that no state "may be deprived of any power constitutionally possessed by other states, as states, by reason of the terms in which the acts admitting them to the Union have been framed."[62]

Equal footing was upheld again by the Supreme Court in another Oklahoma case in 1914 (*McCabe* v. *Atchison, Topeka & Santa Fe Railway Co.*). It was applied to and upheld in a 1973 Arizona case (*Bonelli Cattle Co.* v. *Arizona*), which was subsequently modified by (but equal footing was nevertheless upheld) in a 1977 Oregon case (*State Land Board* v. *Corvallis Sand & Gravel Co.*).

So we see that all the other Southern states that seceded in 1861 had the entire complement of rights, privileges, and sovereignty that were enjoyed by South Carolina, Georgia, Virginia, and North Carolina and the original thirteen states. What Massachusetts may do, Arkansas may do, or Kentucky, or Texas. What Congress may not forbid Massachusetts to do, it may not forbid Mississippi to do, or Tennessee, or Missouri.

If all the states are equal, do any states or combination of states have the legal or moral authority to destroy another state and replace its lawfully elected government with one imposed by military occupation? If so, which states have such authority? How did they get it? When and under what circumstances is the application of military force warranted among the states?

Lincoln's answer to this question haunts American history and takes a fearsome toll on current foreign policy. Lincoln's answer was, of course, the side with the most bayonets makes the rules. He clearly has supporters among the elite establishment state-worshipers even today. The smell of gun power wafts across our history.

Princeton professor James M. McPherson writes in his highly acclaimed *Battle Cry of Freedom* (1988) as if he is ignorant of the doctrine of equality of the states. Perhaps he is. In dismissing the legal basis for secession, he writes that the Southern argument supporting secession was that states ratified the Constitution by convention, therefore "a state could reassert total sovereignty in the same manner," i.e., convene a convention with the same authority as the first. But, McPherson sees a "slight problem" with this theory in regards to the seven states that entered the union after ratification of the Constitution (Mississippi, Florida, Alabama, Louisiana, Texas, Arkansas, and Tennessee). Those states, McPherson asserts, have "the appearance of being creatures rather than creators of the Union."[63]

Naturally, a historic work that provides intellectual legitimacy to the emergence of the dominant welfare/warfare/surveillance state under the banner of self-anointed deliverer of racial justice for all will generate rave reviews by the mainstream press. The *New York Times* said McPherson's work "may actually be the best [Civil War book] ever published." The *Los Angeles Times* claimed, "Surely . . . of the 50,000 books written on the Civil War," (an estimate that is likely low by at least an order of magnitude) that McPherson's book is "the finest compression of that national paroxysm ever fitted between two covers." Not to be outdone, the *Washington Post* goes full throttle with hyperbole: *Battle Cry of Freedom* is "the finest single volume on the war and its background."[64]

So how could an eminent historian of the best and finest Civil War book ever written dismiss the legal basis for secession in seven states in less than one paragraph of a 300,000-word book without ever informing his readers that such a basis exists and that that basis originated with the U.S. Supreme Court?

McPherson's position is that the states admitted after ratification of the Constitution appear to be creatures rather than creators of the Union. In taking this position, he places himself at variance to history and the common law of the land. The Supreme Court has repeatedly upheld equality of and among the states. It was the law of the land when Lincoln took his oath as a practicing attorney in Illinois, and it was the law of the land when he took the oath of office as president and swore to uphold the Constitution (which includes upholding the common law established by the judicial branch pursuant to the Constitution). The court still applies the equality of states doctrine in the twenty-first century.

In fairness to McPherson, his view that seven seceding states of the union that joined after ratification of the Constitution have the "appearance of being creatures rather than creators" of it, has supporters foreign and domestic, contemporary and historic. One historically prominent German wrote, "It was not these states that had formed the Union, on the contrary it was the Union which formed a great part of such so-called states." As a result, I believe there can be no question of any original sovereignty of the overwhelming part of the states that joined the union after ratification of the Constitution, which is the same position McPherson holds. The quotes that align perfectly with McPherson's view are found in the second volume of *Mein Kampf* (*My Struggle*), the book Adolph Hitler dictated to Rudolph Hess while the two men were serving time in Landsburg prison for treason.[65]

Another supporter of McPherson's views is historian Jean H. Baker. In her 2004 biography of Pres. James Buchanan, Baker mentions the term "equality of states," but inexplicably, she gets it horribly wrong.

Ignoring the fact that the terminology Baker uses (equality of states) came from the written decisions of the U.S. Supreme Court, she says in an unattributed passage that it was nothing more than a "Southern slogan" regarding the equality of property in man with other forms of property. "A Southern slogan of the time, 'the equality of states' held that property in slaves must be on the same footing as all other property, from gold to horses, from pianos to mattresses."[66] Baker commits an egregious double error by deliberately misidentifying the term and then stating that the term has a meaning other than its true, historic, legal meaning.

The common thread to both Baker's errant representation and McPherson's omission of the equality of states doctrine is that each result produces a false positive in the test of legality of secession—no real surprise here. In statistics, this sort of error is called a type 1 error. A type 1 error is said to occur when one rejects a hypothesis that is true. In this case, both historians suppress information that could be viewed as objective information supporting the Southern position that secession was legal. Baker's error is more understandable as she takes the vanguard, Machiavellian position that the law is not very important anyway. She writes that Lincoln "was justified violating one law [or many] in order to support the larger, more significant purpose of preserving the Union."[67]

McPherson is just a contemporary example of a much larger problem. Lincoln scholars James G. Randall and David Donald's *Civil War and Reconstruction*, a textbook used in innumerable college Civil War history classes for decades, fails to mention a word about equality of states. Two or more generations of Americans who actually studied history in college were not provided the relevant, supporting historical facts about secession.

If we take McPherson's dismissive attitude about established common law and the history of the establishment of states, and we add Baker's error, we are led to the worship of a starkly authoritarian central state where the national government has the power to do almost anything that it can justify in the name of democracy. It transforms the office of president from the benign "chief magistrate" (that most of the first fifteen occupants of that office considered themselves to be) to the CEO of USA, Inc., a virtual subsidiary of the fusion of big government and big business. No sector of the economy, no part of society is safe from intervention, all done in the name of the people (subject to overnight polling and focus groups). The civic deity of this secular society is democracy. It's devolution from servant to master began as the rail splitter's handiwork, where various historians assert that lawbreaking was "justified" to support a cause more important than the law itself.

### The Tenth Amendment—the Reserved Powers

The Tenth Amendment to the Constitution, the final amendment in the Bill of Rights, is often referred to in the same sentence with "states rights." But since states rights is the political equivalent of a dirty word, it is intended as an epithet rather than a description. Nevertheless, the amendment is brief and easily understood.

> The powers not delegated to the United States by the Constitution, nor prohibited by it to the states, are reserved to the states respectively, or to the people.

The plain words say what they mean; if a power is not granted to the federal government by the Constitution, then that power remains with the states or the people. All that is required for one to do is to read the Constitution and catalogue the finite list of powers the federal government is allowed to exercise. The states and the people retain anything that is not on that list.

It didn't take long for the Supreme Court to address the issue of sovereignty. Within eighteen months of the court's original term beginning in August 1791, it issued a landmark decision in *Chisholm v. Georgia* (1793). The issue before the court was whether one state can be sued by citizens of other states in the federal courts. Georgia had protested that it could not be sued by citizens of another state without its consent. The court disagreed, in part because Georgia at that moment had suits pending in the federal courts against two South Carolinians and had already given its consent to be sued by citizens of another state when it ratified the "national compact," i.e., the Constitution. The court found:

> To the Constitution of the United States the term sovereign, is totally unknown. There is but one place where it could have been used with propriety. But, even in that place it would not, perhaps, have comported with the delicacy of those, who ordained and established that Constitution. They might have

announced themselves "sovereign" people of the United States: But serenely conscious of the fact, they avoided the ostentatious declaration. . . . Let a State be considered as subordinate to the People: But let every thing else be subordinate to the State.[68]

The words "sovereign" or "sovereignty" are not found in the Constitution. There is no overt claim to sovereignty by the government erected under the auspices of the Constitution. Even McPherson acknowledges this, without explanation as to its significance and without comment on the relationship to the Tenth Amendment.

Although the Supreme Court found in this particular case that Georgia is not a sovereign state as far as the union of states is concerned, it did uphold the principle that *the people of Georgia are sovereign* and retain their sovereignty and political supremacy. After all, it had been only five years since the people of Georgia ratified the Constitution, thus:

> At the Revolution, the sovereignty devolved on the people; and they are truly the sovereigns of the country, but they are sovereigns without subjects (unless the African slaves among us may be so called) and have none to govern but themselves. . . .

and,

> The Supreme Power resides in the body of the people. As a Judge of this Court, I know, and can decide upon the knowledge, that the citizens of Georgia, when they acted upon the large scale of the Union, as part of the 'People of the United States,' did not surrender the Supreme or Sovereign Power to that State; but, as to the purposes of the Union, retained it to themselves.[69]

Indeed, the citizens of Georgia "retained . . . to themselves" that supreme and sovereign power, the sovereign power to secede that is protected by the Tenth Amendment. And they exercised it again in 1861 in the same manner they had exercised it in 1788. In *Stone v. Mississippi* (1879), one of the legislative entrenchment cases, Chief Justice Morrison R. Waite stated in the court's ruling that no legislature can "bargain away" the sovereign police powers of the state. Waite further stated, "The people themselves cannot do it, much less their servants."[70] When one applies this principle to the larger question of sovereignty (which admittedly was *not* the legal issue in this case), the Waite court clearly indicated that sovereignty rests with the people that neither the people nor their elected servants can bargain away sovereignty.

In *McCullough* v. *Maryland* (1819), the argument before the Supreme Court was the issue of whether Maryland could lawfully impose a tax on the operations of the Second Bank of the United States, which had been rechartered by Congress in 1816 after the charter for the first national bank had expired in 1811. Chief Justice Marshall wrote the opinion of the court and found that among the implied powers of Congress is the power to charter a bank. Clearly, this was a blow to those who argued then and now that chartering a bank is one of the powers reserved to the states by the Tenth Amendment, as there is no explicit authority to do so in the Article I powers of Congress. The court struck down Maryland's tax on the bank in part because it had the effect of taxation without representation.

### The Fourteenth Amendment—Equal Protection of the Laws

The Fourteenth Amendment to the Constitution was declared officially ratified and in force by Secretary of State William Seward, July 28, 1868, with his certification of the approval of three-fourths (28 of 37) of the states.

Many over the years have questioned the legitimacy of Seward's declaration. The legislatures of New Jersey and Ohio rescinded their prior ratifications, yet Seward counted them anyway. The New Jersey legislature based the repeal of its ratification on the fact that the two-thirds vote of Congress to submit the proposed amendment to the states was fraudulently obtained. Article V of the Constitution establishes the process by which amendments are proposed and adopted. It also states that "no state, without its consent, shall be deprived of its equal suffrage in the Senate," which the New Jersey legislature claims happened when one of its senators, John P. Stockton, refused to support the congressional resolution to send the Fourteenth Amendment to the states, and was expelled from the Senate by the Radical Republicans. In his veto message of the resolution to rescind, New Jersey governor Marcus L. Ward claimed that once a state acted in the affirmative on a constitutional amendment, "the power of the Legislature over the subject is spent."

Governor Ward's reasoning is highly dubious for two reasons. First, under the principle of legislative entrenchment, any act a legislative body is competent to pass they are equally competent to repeal. In fact, the New Jersey legislature overrode Governor Ward's veto. Second, likely under the topic of "political correctness" and perhaps for reasons of its own, the New Jersey legislature voted in 2003 to ratify the Fourteenth Amendment. And just how did they accomplish this? They did the same thing the Southern states did; they simply revoked their 1868 resolution to rescind their original ratification. This was the very action Governor Ward erroneously warned them 135 years earlier they had no authority to do.[73]

The final three of twenty-eight states to ratify, North Carolina, July 4, 1868 (after rejecting it on December 14, 1866); Louisiana, July 9, 1868 (after rejecting it on February 6, 1867); and South Carolina, July 9, 1868 (after rejecting it on December 20, 1866), did so under duress. They were all still occupied by the U.S. Army and their readmission to the Union was contingent on ratification. One of the states counted among the twenty-eight by Seward was Oregon, which rescinded its ratification October 15, 1868, after the amendment was said to be in force.

Whether *de facto* or *de jure*, Section 4 of the Fourteenth Amendment contains language in the renouncement of debt clause that leads to the undeniable conclusion that secession was lawful and legitimate. It reads:

> The validity of the public debt of the United States, authorized by law, including debts incurred for payment of persons and bounties for services in suppressing insurrection or rebellion, shall not be questioned. But neither the United States nor any state shall assume or pay any debt or obligation, incurred in aid of insurrection or rebellion against the United States, or any claim for the loss or emancipation of any slave; but all such debts, obligations and claims shall be held illegal and void.

On the face of it, this clause accomplishes three things. It validates U.S. war bonds and other debt incurred by the war. It renounces the debt incurred by the Southern states in their own defense during the war. It bars any claim of compensation by a former slave owner for the loss of his chattel property.

The second part of this clause is revealing and important because the act of renouncement of Southern states' war bonds speaks to the legitimacy of that debt. There would be no purpose in declaring these debts "illegal and void" if that was the legal status of them to begin with. If the war bonds were not lawfully incurred, they would not be enforceable, or payable, in any case. Renouncement confirms that these war bonds were legitimate contracts that states were otherwise obligated to pay, unless renounced.

Under the general rules of contracts, a contract is not an enforceable, legitimate obligation unless all aspects of the contract pertain to lawful activities. In other words, a contract to repay money that was borrowed to fund an illegal purpose is no contract at all. Any break in the legitimacy of the chain of events from the making of the loan to the use of the loan to the legitimacy of the parties to enter into the loan contract would void its repayment. So, if the Southern states' war bond debt was legal and legitimate (the opposite of illegal and void) until renounced, it means that the defensive actions of the states were legal and legitimate, and the seceded state governments were themselves legal and legitimate and had every right to enter into a loan contract or war bond to defend themselves. Otherwise, the renunciation of this debt would be superfluous.

However, the renouncement of war bonds is only one part of this clause. The clause also places the legitimacy of U.S. government debt beyond question and bars any claim for compensation by a former slave owner for the loss of his slaves who were freed by the Thirteenth Amendment (adopted December 6, 1865). All three elements in this clause are treated equally, the legitimacy of federal debt, the renunciation of Southern states' debt, and the bar of compensation to any former slave owner. The first element of this clause established what will be paid without question (the federal debt), and the final two elements establish what will not be paid under any circumstances. The Radical Republican Congress would not have submitted to the states a provision in the proposed amendment to pay the federal debt without question, unless there was some question about this debt. Likewise, they would not have declared Southern war bonds "illegal and void" if they already were. Quite to the contrary, those bonds were legally contracted for, by legal parties (the Southern states), for the perfectly legal and legitimate purpose of self-defense.

The renouncement clause represents another political and legal dilemma for the federal government. If they allowed the Southern states to pay off the war bonds they had floated during the war, those states would be repaying banks, planters, and other wealthy individuals all across the South. If compensation had been provided for the loss of slaves, the former masters of those slaves would be made financially whole. But these were the very groups the Radical Republicans wanted to wipeout, leaving their assets vulnerable for carpetbaggers to pick up at pennies on the dollar. The only way to eliminate the ownership class in the South was to enforce a renunciation of war bond debt and bar compensation for the loss of slaves by constitutional means. In doing so, it confirmed that the Southern states acted lawfully and had every legitimate right to secede.

### Other Case Law during Lincoln's Career as a Lawyer

Lincoln received his license to practice law in Illinois in 1836 and entered into practice with John T. Stuart in Springfield the following year. It so happens that the same year Lincoln began his law practice, 1837, the Supreme Court decided a landmark case on state sovereignty that set out the clear and unequivocal relationship between the states and the national government.

In *New York* v. *Miln,* the Supreme Court went out of its way to establish principles in case law that survive into the twenty-first century. (This case was argued before the court when John Marshall was chief justice. However, Marshall died before the court rendered its decision. The new chief justice, Roger B. Taney of Maryland, did not participate in the decision.)

The court found that state sovereignty is similar in many ways to that of "any foreign nation." States have "the same undeniable and unlimited jurisdiction" over everything in their territorial limits "where that jurisdiction is *not surrendered or restrained* by the constitution of the United States." Furthermore, states not only have the right to exercise the authority they have retained, but also "the bounden and solemn duty" to do so.[72]

Interesting! Did you get that?

The Lincoln scholars and statists need to go back and find the specific language in the Constitution where the states actually "surrendered" their sovereignty, or where they are "restrained" from withdrawing from the Union. Surely, it is in there somewhere. Surely, the states had no constitutional basis to secede. Surely, Lincoln was right that the federal government was the supreme authority in the nation in *all* things, period. Surely the court didn't, couldn't, wouldn't, and hasn't let a decision like that rendered in *Miln* stand very long. We shall see.

Consider what the court meant when it referred to state sovereignty that was not surrendered or restrained. It meant that at the end of the American Revolutionary War, each state was sovereign and each had the infinite attributes of sovereignty enjoyed by "any foreign nation." In entering first into the Articles of Confederation and later into the Constitution, the states surrendered certain specific attributes of sovereignty to the national government and were restrained from the exercise of others. They could not have surrendered any attributes of sovereignty unless they first possessed them.

The authority thus surrendered is the finite list of the enumerated powers of Congress found in the Constitution in Article I, Sections 8 and 9 and other restrictions on the States in Section 10. Table 1 below shows the entire list.

Several years before the *New York* v. *Miln* decision, Marshall's opinion in *Cohens* v. *Virginia* (1821) stated that supreme power "resides only in the whole body of the people; not in any sub-division of them." Thus, as Stampp concludes, Marshall believed no state could simply unmake the Constitution. But the issue that Marshall left unsettled was whether a state had the right to separate peacefully from the Union it had voluntarily joined. This was the crucial question of the secession winter of 1860-61.[73]

### Table 1. Authority Surrendered by the States to the Congress

Authority surrendered by the states to the legislative branch (Congress) in Article I of the Constitution.

**Article I, Section 8**
- Lay and collect taxes, duties, imposts, and excises
- Pay the debts of the United States
- Provide for the common defense and general welfare

- Borrow money on the credit of the United States
- Regulate commerce with foreign nations, among the states, and Indian tribes
- Establish a uniform rule of naturalization
- Establish uniform bankruptcies law
- Coin money
- Fix the standard of weights and measures
- Punish counterfeiting
- Establish post offices and post roads
- Establish patents and copyrights
- Establish lower courts
- Define and punish piracies and felonies on the high seas
- Declare war
- Grant letters of marque and reprisal, and make rules concerning captures on land and water
- Raise and support armies, but no appropriation shall be for a longer term than two years
- Provide and maintain a navy
- Make rules for the regulation of the land and naval forces
- Provide for calling the militia to execute laws of the Union, suppress insurrection, repel invasions
- Provide for organizing, arming, and disciplining the militia
- Exercise exclusive legislation in all cases whatsoever, over D.C.
- Authority over places purchased by the consent of the legislature of the state in which forts, arsenals, dock-yards are located
- Make all laws which shall be necessary and proper for carrying into execution these powers

## Article I, Section 9
- Tax the African slave trade; authority to end it after 1808

## Article I, Section 10
- No state shall enter into any treaty, alliance, or confederation; grant letters of marque and reprisal; coin money; emit bills of credit; make any thing but gold and silver coin a tender in payment of debts; pass any Bill of Attainder, ex post facto law, or law impairing the obligation of contracts, or grant any title of nobility.
- No state shall, without the consent of the Congress, lay any imposts or duties on imports or exports

- The net produce of all duties and imposts, laid by any state on imports or exports, shall be for the use of the Treasury of the U.S.; and all laws shall be subject to the control of the Congress
- No state shall, without consent of Congress, lay any duty of tonnage
- No state shall keep troops, or ships of war in time of peace
- No state shall enter into any agreement or compact with another state, or with a foreign power, or engage in war, unless actually invaded, or in such imminent danger as will not admit of delay

Well, if the Lincoln scholars look in Article I for authority to use force to coerce the states; or for the transfer of sovereignty from the states to the federal government; or that the perpetuity of the Union that supersedes all other political obligations and options; or that the federal government is indivisible; or that the people of the states have relinquished their right to "alter or abolish" forms of government over them; or even that the federal government is the sole and exclusive arbiter and interpreter of its authority; then they are going to be woefully disappointed.

Authority "surrendered" by the states to the office of president (See table 2 below) is an even shorter list, that being the president's status as commander in chief of the armed forces including the state militias in actual service.

#### Table 2. Authority Surrendered by the States to the President

Authority surrendered by the states to the executive branch (president) in Article II of the Constitution.

**Article II, Section 2**
- President is commander in chief of the army and navy, and the militia of the several states, when called into the actual service
- Presidential power to grant reprieves and pardons for federal offenses, except impeachment
- Presidential power to make treaties with two-thirds concurrence of the senate
- Presidential power to appoint ambassadors, judges, other officials with the consent of the Senate

Lincoln was the greatest presidential power abuser of all time as he relied almost entirely on the presidential power as commander in chief to use the army to carry out his political will. His selective interpretation of constitutional authority never included the guarantee to the states in Article IV, Section 4 that the federal government "shall protect each [state] against invasion."

The word "shall" is mandatory. It connotes an obligation, a duty. It was and is a constitutional requirement for the federal government to protect the states against invasion, not to conduct an invasion.

Likewise, authority "surrendered" by the states to the federal judiciary (Article III) is the nationwide jurisdiction for all cases arising under federal law. See table 3, below. There was no judicial branch at all under the Articles of Confederation. Just as in the other attributes of sovereignty surrendered by the states, there is absolutely nothing in Article III of the Constitution that supports Lincoln's use of force, or that undercuts the states' right of withdrawing from the constitutional compact.

States are restrained from the exercise of certain authorities in Article I, Section 10 (entering separate treaties, granting titles of nobility, etc.); states must give "full faith and credit" to the public acts of every other state and recognize that the Constitution and the laws enacted there under are the supreme law of the land (Article IV). See table 4. Again, the Lincoln scholars strike out.

**Table 3. Authority Surrendered by the States to the Federal Courts**

Authority surrendered by the states to the judicial branch (federal courts) in Article III of the Constitution.

**Article III, Section 2**
- Judicial branch has jurisdiction over all cases arising under the Constitution, federal law
- Judicial branch has jurisdiction over all cases affecting ambassadors, admiralty, and maritime
- Judicial branch has jurisdiction over all cases to which the United States is a party
- Judicial branch has jurisdiction over controversies between two or more states; between a state and citizens of another state; between citizens of different states; between citizens of the same state claiming lands under grants of different states; between a state, or citizens thereof, and foreign states, citizens or subjects

### Table 4. Miscellaneous Authority the States are Restrained from Exercising

Authority the states are restrained from exercising by Articles IV and VI of the Constitution.

**Article IV, Section 1**
- States must give full faith and credit to the public acts, records, and judicial proceedings of every other state

**Article IV, Section 2**
- The citizens of each state shall be entitled to all privileges and immunities of citizens in the several states
- Extradition among the states
- States must return fugitive slaves

**Article IV, Section 3**
- No new states shall be formed within the jurisdiction of any other state; nor any state be formed by the junction of two or more states, or parts of states, without the consent of the legislatures of the states concerned as well as of the Congress

**Article IV, Section 4**
- Each state guaranteed republican form of government and protected against invasion

**Article VI**
- All debts before the adoption of the Constitution are valid
- Constitution and federal law is the supreme law of the land
- Judges in every state are bound by the Constitution and federal law
- Members of Congress and state officials must swear an oath supporting the Constitution
- No religious test is allowed for federal or state officials

Finally, there are the well-known, specific authorities surrendered by the states in various amendments to the Constitution. However, the first ten amendments, the Bill of Rights ratified almost immediately in 1791, consist of limits on the prerogatives of the federal government.

Therefore, the list of the attributes of sovereignty that the states surrendered, or are otherwise restrained from exercising under the Constitution, is a specific, limited, and finite list that is easily identified and catalogued.

That gets us back to the *New York* v. *Miln* decision.

In that case, the court held that except for those finite, easily identifiable authorities "surrendered or restrained" under the Constitution that the authority of a state is "complete, unqualified and exclusive."

There is no way any competent lawyer in the late 1830s, much less a prominent one, would not be familiar with this decision. So much for Lincoln the lawyer and officer of the Court, who was sworn to uphold the Constitution and the law.

A scant ten years later, at the height of Lincoln's law practice, the Supreme Court upheld the decision and powerfully elaborated on the meaning of "complete, unqualified and exclusive" jurisdiction of states.

In a grouping of cases from several states known as the License Cases (because they pertained to the regulation and taxation of alcoholic beverages), the Supreme Court under Chief Justice Roger B. Taney found that "the powers not conceded or prohibited by the constitution remain in the States *unchanged, unaltered, and unimpaired,* and as fully in force as if no constitution had been made."[74]

It gets better.

Defining the "great question of boundary between the sovereignties" of states and the federal government, the court explained with great clarity what was meant in *Miln* by the phrase "complete, unqualified and exclusive" authority by the states.

> If they are complete, the State has the whole and sole enjoyment.
>
> If they are unqualified, they remain as they were, unaltered and unchanged.
>
> If they are exclusive, there can be no participation in them by another.

Then the bombshell:

> The inference is irresistible, that such powers are independent of and paramount to the constitution of the United States, and therefore not subject to any supreme power of the federal government in cases of conflict.[75]

The Taney court held that the attributes of sovereignty not "surrendered or restrained"—in other words retained by the states—are independent of and supreme to the Constitution and the federal government.

It is an embarrassment to the nation for the Lincoln scholars to pass myths of what they wish had happened as if they were facts.

It is interesting to note that state sovereignty and the powers reserved to the states was not just a brief aberration of the law during the nineteenth century when only white men could vote. Three-quarters of a century after the Civil War, under the leadership of Chief Justice Charles Evan Hughes, the Supreme Court continued the fact and law of state sovereignty when it found that "all is retained [by the states] which has not been surrendered."[76]

In his December 4, 1860, message to Congress just days before the convening of the South Carolina sovereignty convention, President Buchanan expressed the mainstream views of every president before Lincoln on the constitutional powers of the executive and legislative branches of the government of the United States. He wrote:

> Apart from the execution of the laws, so far as this may be practicable, the Executive (Presidency) has no authority to decide what shall be the relations between the federal government and South Carolina. He has been invested with no such discretion . . . .
>
> Has the Constitution delegated to Congress the power to coerce a State into submission which is attempting to withdraw or has actually withdrawn from the Confederacy (Federal government)? If answered in the affirmative, it must be on the principle that the power has been conferred upon Congress to declare and to make war against a State. After much serious reflection, I have arrived at the conclusion that no such power has been delegated to Congress or to any other department of the federal government.[77]

Buchanan knew secession was a lawful and constitutional power that any state had the right to exercise. Next, we will explore the historic context of secession.

CHAPTER SIX

# Sovereignty and the Historical
# Context of Secession

*"Let a State be considered as subordinate to the People: But let every thing else be subordinate to the State."*

—Associate Justice James Wilson,
Signer of the Declaration of Independence and
Justice of the original Supreme Court

At the heart of Lincoln's political agenda was the accomplishment of drawing all power to the federal government. Lincoln wanted most what Jefferson, Washington, and the other Founding Fathers feared most: An all powerful, all ruling, all reaching, federal government; a totalitarian democracy of sorts. Washington warned that government, like fire, is a "dangerous friend and a fearful master." It sounds rather ho-hum in the nation's third century, but the fear of an all-powerful federal government was real and malevolent, its appearance fundamentally counterrevolutionary in the mid-nineteenth century.

In arguing against the First National Bank in 1791, Jefferson wrote that the Article I powers of Congress (the chains of the Constitution) are enumerated and limited. "To take a single step beyond the boundaries thus specially drawn around the powers of Congress is to take possession of a boundless field of power, no longer susceptible of any definition." Lincoln's real aim was this "boundless field of power" taken by counterrevolution, i.e., illegally exercising powers not given to the government thereby voiding the limits written into the Constitution.

The prevailing contemporary thought through the first seventy-five years of the Constitution was that the so-called "delegated" or "enumerated" powers of Congress (found in Article I, Section 8 of the Constitution) were the sum total powers of the federal government. The constitutional powers of the executive and judicial branches of government were deliberately limited by the Founding Fathers whose suspicion of those branches of government was galvanized during the struggle for independence. Only the legislatures in the Colonies supported the rights of the Colonists against the encroachments of the Royal-appointed executive and judiciary.

Jefferson argued that the Constitution restrains Congress from the exercise of even the enumerated powers except for necessity. In other words, not even the enumerated powers could be exercised except when it was necessary to do so. For Jefferson, the exercise of power based on convenience, such as chartering a national bank, was an abuse of power. He stated that to allow the exercise of any enumerated power simply for convenience is to give the federal government all power.

> For there is not [an enumerated power] which ingenuity may not torture into a convenience in some instance or other, to some one of so long a list of enumerated powers. It would swallow up all the delegated powers. . . . Therefore, it was that the Constitution restrained them to the necessary means, that is to say, to those means without which the grant of power would be nugatory.

Nor did Jefferson believe the Constitution gives any power to Congress to "do good." He wrote that while Congress had power to lay taxes to provide for the general welfare, "the laying of taxes is the power and the general welfare [is] the purpose for which the power to be exercised." Congress has no power to tax "*ad libitum* for any purpose they please; but only to pay the debts or provide for the welfare of the Union. In like manner, they are not to do anything they please to provide for the general welfare, but only to lay taxes for that purpose," according to Jefferson.

He further warned that "instituting a Congress with power to do whatever would be for the good of the United States . . . would be also a power to do whatever evil they please."

### Sovereignty, the Declaration, and the Treaty of Paris 1793

Where did the philosophy behind all these Supreme Court cases come from? The underlying philosophy arose prior to the adoption of the U.S. Constitution, during the War for Independence. The Colonies stated clearly in the Declaration of Independence that they (plural) "are, and of Right ought to be Free and Independent States." The plural, "states," was used because they were literally declaring their separate independence from British rule. "And that as Free and Independent States, they have full Power to levy War, conclude Peace, contract Alliances, establish Commerce, and to do all other Acts and Things which Independent States may of right do."

If there is any doubt as to the meaning of "free and independent states" that have "full power to levy war," historian Claude H. Van Tyne wrote one hundred years ago that "doubt would be dispelled by reading the resolves of the state conventions or assemblies in approving the Declaration."[1]

> The Pennsylvania convention passed a resolve approving, in behalf of themselves and their constituents, of Congress's resolution, declaring "this as well as the other United States of America, free and Independent," and declared "before God and the world that we will support and maintain the freedom and independence of this and the other United States of America." The Connecticut assembly approved of the Declaration and resolved "that this Colony is and of right ought to be a free and independent State."[2]

Van Tyne also notes that during the war and the years of the Articles of Confederation, the states took on and exercised powers common to independent nations. "South Carolina specifically endowed its government with the power to make war, conclude a peace, enter into treaties, lay embargoes, and provide an army and navy. Other states [Pennsylvania, North Carolina, Maryland, Delaware, and Massachusetts] specified some of these powers and implied the rest," including Virginia which actually ratified a treaty with France.[3]

The war brought a hard-earned independence that was acknowledged in detail in the Paris Peace Treaty of 1793, which officially ended hostilities. The explicit status of sovereign independence cannot be any more unmistakable than this:

> His Britannic Majesty acknowledges the said United States, viz., New Hampshire, Massachusetts Bay, Rhode Island and Providence Plantations, Connecticut, New York, New Jersey, Pennsylvania, Maryland, Virginia, North Carolina, South Carolina, and Georgia,

to be free sovereign and independent states, that he treats with
them as such, and for himself, his heirs, and successors, relinquishes
all claims to the government, property, and territorial rights of the
same and every part thereof.

Britain was the eighteenth-century equivalent of a superpower.
There simply was no more authoritative political source than a treaty
agreed to by the British Crown that acknowledged a state's sovereign
independence. And that's precisely the condition of each of the
former Thirteen Colonies upon signing the peace treaty.

In addition, the states themselves jealously guarded their sovereignty as well as one might expect. Although the words "sovereign"
and "sovereignty" do not appear in the U.S. Constitution, these
words were used in state constitutions then and remain in many state
constitutions after more than two centuries.

The people of Virginia adopted a constitution in 1776 just a
few weeks before the Declaration of Independence was signed.
The language in that document leaves no doubt that the people
are sovereign. The people have an "indubitable, inalienable, and
indefeasible right to reform, alter, or abolish [government] in such
manner as shall be judged most conducive to the public weal [sic]"
(Virginia Bill of Rights, Section 3).

In the resolution of the adoption of the constitution of New
York in 1777 much of the Declaration of Independence was copied
verbatim. "Governments are instituted among men, deriving their just
powers from the consent of the governed; that whenever any form of
government becomes destructive of these ends, it is the right of the
people to alter or abolish it." Clearly, the revolutionary principles of
sovereignty of the people flourished in the Empire State.

Vermont's constitution of 1777 declared "that it should be,
henceforth, a free and independent State," and that its "proper
form of government" should be "derived from, and founded on, the
authority of the people only." The same language was used again
when Vermont adopted another constitution in 1786.

Sovereignty was claimed in the Massachusetts constitution of 1780,
which was written during the War for Independence and predates
even the Articles of Confederation. The language used doesn't
sound as if they ever intended to give it up:

The people of this commonwealth have the sole and exclusive right of governing themselves as a free, sovereign, and independent State, and do, and forever hereafter shall, exercise and enjoy every power, jurisdiction, and right which is not, or may not hereafter be, by them expressly delegated to the United States of America in Congress assembled.

Notice that in the language of the time, the people of Massachusetts were only "delegating" certain authority to any other governmental entity. There was nothing permanent or irreversible about it.

When Illinois was admitted to the Union from the Northwest Territory, the preamble to its constitution of 1818 laid claim to the title of "a free and independent state, by name of the State of Illinois." Alabama used virtually identical language when it was admitted the following year, 1819. Moreover, as late at 1857, the preamble to Iowa's second constitution stated it is "a free and independent government."

The acknowledgment that all political power is inherent in the people, an essential and inescapable condition of sovereignty, was expressed in slightly different words but with the same meaning in numerous nineteenth-century state constitutions, including California, Connecticut, Michigan, Minnesota, and, Ohio.

## Congressional Action during the Secession Winter

During the secession winter of 1860-61, many proposals were submitted to Congress to address the question of secession. H. Newcomb Morse identifies four of the most telling of these, which reveal important principles in law. Each of the four was aimed in one way or another at limiting a state's right to secede unless authorized by a vote of Congress or by all the other states.

The first resolution Morse finds significant occurred on December 17, 1860, just three days before South Carolina seceded. New York congressman Daniel E. Sickles introduced a constitutional amendment that addressed the question of federal property in a state that secedes, and arguably establishes prior congressional approval for secession. It reads in part:

Whenever a convention of delegates, chosen in any State by the people thereof, under the recommendation of its Legislature,

shall rescind and annul its ratification of th[e] Constitution, the
President shall nominate, and by and with the advice and consent
of the Senate shall appoint, commissioners, not exceeding three,
to confer with the duly appointed agents of such State, and
agree upon the disposition of the public property and territory
belonging to the United States lying within such State, and upon
the proportion of the public debt to be assumed and paid by such
State; and if the President shall approve the settlement agreed
upon by the commissioners, he shall thereupon transmit the same
to the Senate, and upon the ratification thereof by two thirds of
the Senators present, he shall forthwith issue his proclamation
declaring the assent of the United States to the withdrawal of such
State from the Union.[4]

The second resolution came about on January 28, 1861, after
the secession of six states had already occurred, Pennsylvania
congressman Thomas B. Florence submitted a lengthy constitutional
amendment dealing with territories, statehood, fugitive slaves, and
secession, which read in part:

No State, or the people thereof, shall retire from this Union without
the consent of three-fourths of all the States.[5]

On February 11, Connecticut congressman Orris S. Ferry
introduced what Morse considers the third significant resolution:

Resolved, That the Committee on the Judiciary be instructed to
inquire into the expediency of so amending the Constitution of
the United States as expressly to forbid the withdrawal of any State
from the Union without the consent of two thirds of both Houses
of Congress, the approval of the President, and the consent of all
the states; to report by joint resolution proposing such amendment
or otherwise.[6]

The fourth resolution Morse found significant was introduced
March 2, 1861, by Wisconsin senator James R. Doolittle as a revision
to a previously proposed amendment to the Constitution:

No State or any part thereof, heretofore admitted or hereafter to
be admitted into the Union, shall have power to withdraw from the

jurisdiction of the United State; and this Constitution, and all laws passed in pursuance of its delegated powers, shall be the supreme law of the land therein, anything contained in any constitution, act, or ordinance of any State Legislature or convention to the contrary not withstanding.[7]

All four of these proposals, if enacted, would have restricted the right of a state to secede. The amendment offered by Doolittle was the most extreme because it would have established the perpetuity and inadvisability of the union through constitutional means. However, this proposal had an element of *ex post facto,* constitutionally prohibited in Article I, Sections 9 and 10, which might have voided it on those grounds.

In a 1986 *Stetson Law Review* article, Morse squarely hits the mark with a pair of rhetorical questions about these four proposals. "What would have been the point of the foregoing proposed amendments to the Constitution of the United States prohibiting or limiting the right of secession if under the constitution, the unfettered right of secession did not already exist?" Moreover, "Why would Congress have even considered proposed amendments to the Constitution forbidding or restricting the right of secession if any such right was already prohibited, limited or nonexistent under the Constitution?"[8]

The fact is none of these proposals would have completely withdrawn the right of a state to secede if enacted. To the contrary, these proposals would have merely restricted or regulated the right of secession. Why would restriction and regulation be proposed if the right of secession did not exist? Why indeed? Morse points out that Chief Justice John Marshall stated thirty-six years earlier in *Gibbons* v. *Ogden* that "limitations of a power furnish a strong argument in favor of the existence of that power."[9]

### Vermont and Texas Were Created by Secession
The Colonial governments in New York and New Hampshire disputed the jurisdiction over the territory composing Vermont from 1764 to its secession from New York and declaration of independence from both New York and Great Britain in 1777. Much of the dispute centered on which government would exercise taxing authority. The

first Vermont constitution adopted in convention that same year recites the history of New York's claim to jurisdiction, which that document notes, "Ever was, and is, disagreeable to the inhabitants" of Vermont. It was so disagreeable that Ethan Allen's Green Mountain Boys were organized in 1775 originally to resist New York. It was only in subsequent years that the Green Mountain Boys gained fame fighting the British in the American Revolution.

Vermont's 1777 constitution lists numerous causes for separation from both New York and Great Britain much like the Declaration of Independence the previous year. The preamble states, "It is absolutely necessary, for the welfare and safety of the inhabitants of this State, that it should be, henceforth, a free and independent State" based on the "common consent" of the governed. Vermont declared itself an independent republic, minted its own coin, and provided a separate postal service until 1791 when it was admitted to the union as the fourteenth state. Vermont exists today because it successfully seceded from New York.

Texas seceded from Mexico and won its independence at the battle of San Jacinto in 1836. The Texas declaration of independence, adopted in convention, reads, "Our political connection with the Mexican nation has forever ended, and that the people of Texas do now constitute a free, Sovereign, and independent republic, and are fully invested with all the rights and attributes which properly belong to independent nations."

Texas remained an independent republic for nine years and elected three separate presidents. The first president of the Republic of Texas was former Tennessee governor Sam Houston. The second and third presidents were Georgia native and former newspaper publisher Mirabeau Bonaparte Lamar and Dr. Anson Jones, a native of Massachusetts. (Massachusetts has never elected a Texan as their chief executive). In 1845, Texas gave up its status as a republic and was admitted as the twenty-eighth state.

The very existence of Vermont and Texas results from successful secessions. Both states adopted their first constitutions in convention, the same procedural mechanism the original states used to ratify the U.S. Constitution, and the same procedure followed by the Southern states to secede from the United States.

## The Conditional Ratification of the Constitution

Article VII of the Constitution established the mechanism by which its ratification by the states would be considered. It states, "The Ratification of the Conventions of nine States, shall be sufficient for the Establishment of this Constitution between the States so ratifying the Same." From the beginning, the switch from the Articles of Confederation to the Constitution was voluntary, and each state had the sole and exclusive authority to decide for itself. Though a two-thirds "super-majority" (nine of thirteen states) was required for ratification, the new government would operate only in the states "so ratifying," leaving in tact the domestic institutions of the other states that might not ratify. Five states placed conditions on their ratification, leaving only seven states that ratified unconditionally. Those seven had to assent to the conditional ratification of at least two other states in order to obtain the nine needed to erect the new government. Eventually, all the other states consented to all the states that placed conditions on their ratification of the Constitution.

The first state to ratify was Delaware, which ratified without conditions. The ratification resolution by the Delaware convention was simple, direct, and unanimous. It said that Delaware "fully, freely, and entirely approve of, assent to, ratify, and confirm" the Constitution. Unconditional ratification was passed by conventions in Pennsylvania, New Jersey, Georgia, Connecticut, Massachusetts, and Maryland.

The Massachusetts approval resolution says it agrees to enter into "an explicit & solemn compact" with the people of the other states, and it recommends nine amendments to the Constitution in order to "guard against an undue administration of the Federal government."

South Carolina, the eighth state to ratify, conditioned its approval with a concern about the control and conduct of elections. Its ratification resolution says, "The manner, time, and places of holding the elections to the Federal legislature, should be forever inseparably annexed to the sovereignty of the several states." Furthermore, the resolution states:

This Convention doth also declare that no section or paragraph of the said Constitution warrants a construction that the states do not retain every power not expressly relinquished by them and vested in the general government of the Union.

With the ratification of New Hampshire, the requisite nine states had agreed to erect a new government to operate in the nine. The decision among the remaining states, Virginia, New York, North Carolina, and Rhode Island, was whether to join this new government or remain free and independent states. In these final four states, only in the North Carolina convention was support for ratification overwhelming. Virginia ratified (conditionally) by a close 89-79 vote, with razor thin margins in New York (30-27) and Rhode Island (34-32).

As H. Newcomb Morse points out, it is legally and historically significant that these remaining four states each conditioned their ratification on the premise that ultimate authority belongs to the people of the states, and they can resume that power whenever they wish. The Virginia ratification resolution stated that "the powers granted under the Constitution being derived from the People of the United States may be resumed by them whensoever the same shall be perverted to their injury or oppression and that every power not granted thereby remains with them and at their will." Morse says this same language in the Virginia resolution "was later quoted in her ordinance of secession." He argues, "Because the nine states which were already members of the Union accepted Virginia's conditional ratification, they ostensibly assented to the principle that Virginia permissibly retained the right to secede."[10] But there is even more to the argument about assent than Morse developed.

New York, North Carolina, and Rhode Island also placed similar conditions on their ratification. The New York ratification resolution explicitly includes the right to secede: "That the Powers of Government may be reassumed by the People, whensoever it shall become necessary to their Happiness." New York would have to withdraw from the Union in order for its citizens to "reassume" the political power it surrendered when it voluntarily joined the union of states. The North Carolina ratification resolution says that "all power is naturally vested in, and consequently derived from the people," and that "the doctrine of non-resistance against arbitrary power and oppression is absurd, slavish, and destructive." Thus, the people of

North Carolina, in whom "all power is naturally vested," claimed to retain the power to make any decision they pleased regarding union with the other states. The Rhode Island ratification resolution asserted "the powers of the government may be reassumed by the people, whensoever it shall become necessary to their happiness," retaining conceptually the same power as New York.

The actions by the ratification conventions in North Carolina and Rhode Island include additional evidence that weighs powerfully in favor of Morse's argument about accession. Not only did the other states accede to the reservation of certain powers that these two states retained, so did the federal government that was already established and operating by the time these states acted. George Washington was sworn in as president on April 30, 1789. It was almost another seven months before North Carolina passed its ratification resolution on November 21, 1789. By the time North Carolina decided to join the United States, the first Congress had met and recessed from its first secession. It was the following spring before Rhode Island decided to ratify (May 29, 1790). By then, Washington had been in office for a full year. Even the U.S. Supreme Court met in its first secession, February 2, 1790, before Rhode Island joined the United States.

Not only did the other states accede to the conditional ratification of five of the states, but the president, Congress, and the Supreme Court of the United States acceded to North Carolina and Rhode Island's conditional ratification. Why would they not? After all, at the time, the thirteen sovereign states created the federal government under the Constitution, it had only been fourteen years since they, as Colonies, seceded from England.

Another point to consider in the topic of ratification of the Constitution is that the process was strictly *voluntary*. In fact, no state legislature was obligated in any way to call a ratification convention. There was no timetable, no schedule, and no requirement for any legislature to do anything. Rhode Island waited nearly two-and-a-half years longer than Delaware to call its convention. There were no threats. Neither the other states nor the federal government felt any threat from Rhode Island's delayed action. The process ratified a "solemn compact" as the resolutions of New Hampshire and Massachusetts said. A voluntary compact, or contract, that several states said they retained the right to withdraw from as their own decision.

## The Perpetual Articles of Confederation

The very first "perpetual" union in North America goes back to 1643. Four New England Colonies formed a "firm and perpetual" union that lasted for more than forty years. They entered this union as "free and independent sovereignties," according to Southern historians James and Walter Kennedy.[11] But of course, it wasn't perpetual.

The orthodoxy of the Lincoln scholars is that the federal government is a perpetual government based on the argument that the term "perpetual Union" is included in the Articles of Confederation. If a thing is perpetual, then no one can end it by any means. This argument had a great deal of attraction for Lincoln who made this dubious point in his first inaugural address on March 4, 1861.

Lincoln claimed we were made a perpetual nation by the Articles of Association in 1774. That is a preposterous argument. For among other reasons, the Colonies vow allegiance and affection for King George III in that document. It most definitely was not a governing document for any Colony or any group of the Colonies.

If Confederate leaders and, more importantly, leaders of the border and hold-out states that had not yet seceded, feared Lincoln didn't have a grip on the true meaning of the federal compact among the states—the compact that President Pierce referred to as the "congress of sovereignties"—Lincoln's inaugural address proved beyond a reasonable doubt that he did not.

Lincoln stated his theory that the union of the states is "perpetual" and that "no government proper ever had a provision in its organic law for its own termination." This was based in part on the sentence clause in the Preamble to the Constitution, "In order to form a more perfect Union."

It was a clever distortion by Lincoln to frame his argument about the perpetuity of the union in words that imply that the withdrawal of any state from the union terminates the union among all states. Such a notion existed in Lincoln's dialectic and nowhere else.

Lincoln claimed that the union was "much older than the Constitution," formed while the Colonies were still under the jurisdiction of and acknowledged loyalty to King George III. Lincoln continues:

> It [the Union] was further matured and the faith of all the then 13
> States expressly plighted and engaged that it should be perpetual,

by the Articles of Confederation in 1778. And finally, in 1787, one of the declared objects for ordaining and establishing the Constitution, was 'to form a more perfect Union.' But if destruction of the Union, by one, or by a part only, of the States, be lawfully possible, the Union is less perfect than before the Constitution, having lost the vital element of perpetuity.

Even the words to the Preamble "in order to form a more perfect Union" imply a degree of imperfection; otherwise, the Founding Fathers would have declared that the Constitution forms a "perfect" union. And what sort of perfection would it be if Lincoln needed the army to enforce it? Precisely because they knew the resulting union would not be perfect, the Founding Fathers made no such claim to ultimate perfection, only a stated goal of achieving a political arrangement among the states that was better than the one they had had under the Articles of Confederation. Nor did they limit the prerogatives of future generations that might want to "alter or abolish" this less-than-perfect union. They left that door open, deliberately.

Nevertheless, Lincoln concluded that "no State, upon its own mere motion, can lawfully get out of the Union"; he as president has no authority to "fix the terms for the separation of States"; and the "central idea of secession is the essence of anarchy."

It is ironic that Lincoln pointed out that the silence of the Constitution leaves him no authority to "fix the terms for separation of the States." He was entirely correct on this constitutional point. It is equally true that the Constitution is silent on authority to resist the separation of states, leaving him with precisely the constitutional authority to address secession as the Southern states contended: None.

Why would Lincoln stake his argument about a perpetual government on the Articles of Association? Why would he not be satisfied to stand on the term "perpetual Union" in the Articles of Confederation? One reason surely must be that the Articles of Confederation plainly and clearly recite a fact that Lincoln did not want to acknowledge under any circumstances.

Each state retains its sovereignty, freedom, and independence, and every power, jurisdiction, and right, which is not by this Confederation expressly delegated to the United States, in Congress assembled.

What were some of the powers not expressly delegated "to the United States, in Congress assembled?" The powers retained by the states under this "perpetual Union" include control of the military. The states elected the president of Congress for a one-year term. Congress could not declare war, make treaties, pass a budget, levy taxes, borrow money, or even appoint a commander of the army or navy without a two-thirds approval of the states. Furthermore, the perpetual Articles left the door open for Canadian provinces to join at any time, a door that was closed by the Constitution.

The obvious fatal flaw with the argument about the perpetuity of the Articles of Confederation is that the states voluntarily ended this confederation. The government under the Articles was not, in fact, perpetual. Stated differently, the Articles were perpetual only as long as the parties wanted them to be. As Kenneth Stampp notes, it was an embarrassment to declare that a new and perpetual union would be built upon the wreckage of the old.[12] But the alleged perpetuity of the Articles did not bind the Founding Fathers when they decided to move forward with a different foundational document.

This issue of perpetuity and whether it means something that is everlasting and irrevocable has been litigated before the Supreme Court. In 1932, the Supreme Court ruled that when Congress wanted to build a fire hall on land previously condemned and "perpetually dedicated and set apart as a public park" in the District of Columbia, it had every right to change its mind. In keeping with the doctrine of legislative entrenchment, the Hughes court ruled that the will of one Congress, even when it is a perpetual will, "does not impose itself upon those to follow in succeeding years" (*Reichelderfer* v. *Quinn*). In *Spratley*, the court ruled that the legislative branch is not "perpetually confined" by decisions it has previously made. The logic supporting the reasoning is just as obvious when applied to the issue of perpetuity of government.

Lincoln argued that the Articles of Association created a perpetual nation. Stampp disagrees. Lincoln argued half-heartedly that the Articles of Confederation created a perpetual nation. Stampp disagrees that a valid case of perpetuity can stand on the Articles of Confederation.[13]

What about the Constitution itself, does it create a "perpetual" government? Stampp concludes that it is ambiguous at best and neither side of the argument is so decisive that everyone is bound to accept it. He says Lincoln's argument that perpetuity is *implied* in the Constitution is the most persuasive argument anyone has ever devised. Stampp says Lincoln wisely placed the burden of proving the legality of secession on the secessionists, claiming they could not destroy the Union except by some theory or action not explicitly stated in the Constitution itself.[14] It is equally true, then, that Lincoln had no authority to preserve the Union except by means not specified in the Constitution itself.

Tragically, John Quincy Adams predicted in 1831 that the question of secession could only be settled at the barrel of a gun. Stampp notes that it was military force, not law, reason, or logic, that settled the secession controversy. That was accomplished at Appomattox, not a court of law.[15]

It is worthwhile noting that both Lincoln and a contemporary socioeconomic theorist, Karl Marx, held similar views on the primacy and indivisibility of central government. Marx's *The Communist Manifesto* was published in 1848 in several languages including English. It is purely speculative, but entirely possible, that Marx influenced Lincoln's beliefs about central government.

## Perpetual Treaties with Indian Tribes

Although the Constitution does not contain any form of the word "perpetual," other government documents use this word. It is important to examine such documents to understand the meaning of the word.

One place where the word is used by the federal government is in its treaties with Indian tribes. The 1798 Treaty of Tellico was an agreement between the United States and the Cherokee Indians. The preamble of the treaty states its purpose as "remedying inconveniences arising to citizens of the United States from the adjustment of the boundary line between the lands of the Cherokees and those of the United States, or citizens thereof." The boundary covered a large portion of east Tennessee.

Article I of the Tellico Treaty states, "The peace and friendship subsisting between the United States and the Cherokee people, are hereby renewed, continued, and declared perpetual."

In 1818, the federal government negotiated a treaty with the Chickasaw Nation known as the Jackson Purchase. It was so named because Andrew Jackson negotiated the purchase of this large section of western Kentucky, West Tennessee, and northern Mississippi. In return for the cession and sale of these lands, the Chickasaw Nation was grated a reservation in a large part of Mississippi.

Article I of this treaty states, "Peace and friendship are hereby firmly established and made perpetual, between the United States of America and the Chickasaw nation of Indians."

So, what did the federal government mean when it used the word "perpetual" with the Indian tribes? It clearly did not mean what Lincoln said the Constitution merely implied, because both of these "perpetual" treaties were broken. They lasted only until the 1830s, when the federal government forcibly removed the Indians from the very areas it had promised would be under their "perpetual" control.

### The Sovereignty Conventions in Arkansas, Virginia, and Missouri

On March 4, 1861, the day Lincoln took the oath of office, the Arkansas sovereignty convention assembled in Little Rock. At that time, Arkansas was still a state in the United States and subject to the laws and courts thereof.

Lincoln, in his inauguration speech, said, "No State, upon its own mere motion, can lawfully get out of the Union." If Lincoln believed what he said when he said secession is not lawful, then he must have believed that the states had no power to call a convention to consider exercising a power that they could not lawfully exercise.

Why then, did Lincoln fail to challenge the legal right of Arkansas to hold its convention? Why didn't Lincoln instruct his attorney general to petition the Supreme Court for an injunction? Why didn't Lincoln do something at the federal or state level to challenge a convention that he claimed was illegal? If he believed the Arkansas convention was illegal, did he not have a duty to challenge it?

The Arkansas convention debated the secession issue for two weeks before voting against secession in a close vote. The convention then recessed, subject to recall. There is more to this story.

The Virginia legislature enabled a sovereignty convention that convened in Richmond on February 13, the final month of the Buchanan administration. Missouri convened a sovereignty convention on February 28. Like the Arkansas and Missouri conventions, there was strong opposition at the Virginia convention to pass an ordinance of secession, at least in the early going. However, unlike Little Rock and Jefferson City, both of which are west of the Mississippi River, Richmond is only one hundred miles from Washington, D.C., practically under the federal government's nose.

Why didn't Buchanan do something about it? Why didn't he take legal action in the courts against Virginia? When Lincoln took office and inherited the problem, why didn't he take legal action against Arkansas, Missouri, and Virginia as all three were still subject to the federal court system?

Buchanan honestly believed that sovereignty remained with the states. He did not want to see any state leave the Union, but he clearly stated that the Constitution gives the government no power to coerce the states into remaining in the Union.

Lincoln's inaction shows an ulterior motive. Lincoln wanted war as DiLorenzo has ably established. He had no interest in peaceful resolution to the issue of secession. His aim was counterrevolution, to use force of arms to put an end to the principle of consent of the governed. Lincoln knew there could be no federal Leviathan as long as any state or group of states had the option of withdrawing.

Yet, Lincoln's inaction vis-à-vis the Arkansas, Missouri, and Virginia conventions demonstrate that these states had a legal right to do what they were doing. He had already acknowledged in his inaugural speech that the Constitution is silent on the issue of secession. Lincoln intended to settle the matter by sword and saber, outside the legal system, outside the Constitution.

### Five Living Former Presidents

Lincoln came to office on one of those rare moments when there were five former presidents still living: Martin Van Buren, John Tyler, Millard Fillmore, Franklin Pierce, and James Buchanan. John Tyler was the lone Southerner in the group. The only other time a president served when there were five living former presidents was Bill Clinton when Richard Nixon, Gerald Ford, Jimmy Carter, Ronald Reagan, and George H. W. Bush were all alive.

Top, left to right: *Martin Van Buren, John Tyler, Millard Fillmore.* Bottom, left to right: *Franklin Pierce, James Buchanan. These five former presidents of the United States were alive when Abraham Lincoln took the oath of office on March 4, 1861. Tyler was the only Southerner in the group; he initially opposed secession and later represented Virginia in the Confederate Congress. All five opposed Lincoln's war in one way or another. Fillmore, a New Yorker and former Whig, opposed the war throughout and never joined the Republican Party. Pierce was a vociferous critic of the war and Lincoln's police-state tactics in suppressing opposition in the North. Buchanan saw no constitutional authority to invade the states or stop secession. It took Lincoln only six weeks to precipitate what would become the bloodiest war in history up to that point, forcing the prompt secession of Virginia, North Carolina, Tennessee, and Arkansas.* (Courtesy Library of Congress)

To gauge how out of sync Lincoln's legal and philosophical theories were about the Union and whether it should be held together at any cost, no matter how expensive in treasure and loss of life, one needs only to consider his living predecessors.

**Martin Van Buren, New York**

By the start of the war, New Yorker Martin Van Buren (the eighth president) was elderly, and there is little evidence of political activity in the fading years of his life. He died early in the war, July 1862, at the age of seventy-nine.

However, Van Buren apparently opposed the war. Historian H. A. Scot Trask writes:

> After the firing on Ft. Sumter, Pierce wrote former President Martin Van Buren urging him to call all the ex-presidents to Philadelphia where they might issue an appeal for peace, calm, and political negotiations. Van Buren responded by suggesting that Pierce issue the call.[16]

Trask says Pierce was reluctant to issue the call because his reputation as a pro-Southern politician "would weaken the force of his appeal." Thus, both the elderly Van Buren and the younger Pierce missed the final opportunity for peace.[17]

Although Van Buren was the third-party presidential candidate of the antislavery Free Soil ticket in 1848, at least one biographer believes that effort was part of a strategy to control the Democratic Party in New York rather than an indication of anti-Southern bias. Joseph G. Rayback claims Van Buren's career in public office "never revealed any opposition to slavery" to say nothing of the myth that the war was, indeed about slavery, which it was not.[18]

Indeed other biographers, including Jeffrey Rogers Hummel claim that Van Buren was a decentralizer, and as president, he "reduced the power and reach of central authority," a distinctly un-Lincolnian idea, and one that was generally well received in the South.[19]

In fact, Van Buren's biographers agree that his public policies and political alliances were distinctly pro-Southern, a fact that is confirmed by his close political ties to Andrew Jackson of Tennessee and the Jacksonian wing of the Democratic Party. Van Buren served as Jackson's secretary of state in Old Hickory's first term and was placed on the ballot, becoming vice president in Jackson's second term. Jackson supported Van Buren's successful candidacy to succeed him as president in the election of 1836.

If Lincoln scholars are looking for a political or philosophical ally to the proposition of using war to preserve the Union, they will find no help from this former president.

### John Tyler, Virginia

Former president John Tyler, a Virginian, was a plantation owner and slave owner. Tyler, the tenth president, was the first vice president to become president upon the death of his predecessor, William Henry Harrison. Harrison was the first president elected on the Whig Party ticket and Tyler, who was not a Whig, was added to balance the ticket.

Following the secession winter of 1860-61, Tyler lent his prestige as a former president to a compromise movement in an attempt to avert war, a movement that Lincoln refused to discuss. When Lincoln came to office and war broke out, Virginia seceded, and Tyler soon took a seat in the Confederate Congress. Although Tyler was initially opposed to secession, he sided with his native state after Lincoln called for troops to invade the South.

The fact that John Tyler died in 1862 while serving in the Confederate House of Representatives is a part of history that often fails to receive even the proverbial footnote. All former presidents have a great deal of prestige. Prestige translates to political credibility. However, the historians who write the history books for the New York publishers who print and market those history books (studied in the classrooms across America) are not comfortable informing their students that a former president lent his credibility to the Southern cause much less served in the Confederate government. The fact that one did precisely this merits serious intellectual inquiry, a task the Lincoln scholars and the publishing houses are clearly uninterested in doing. Their agenda is easily attained by dismissing the Confederate government and the people it served as a pack of political extremists and racists, thus reserving unto them the monopoly of reasonable and rational explanation as to the cause of the war. Yet, if their explanation were as reasonable and rational as they insist, there would be no need to marginalize and denigrate alternative views.

In the person of John Tyler, we find another previous president who was an active enemy of Lincoln and Lincoln's strange legal theories to the extent of serving in elective office in the Confederate government.

**Millard Fillmore, New York**

Like Tyler, Vice Pres. Millard Fillmore became president when his predecessor died in office. Fillmore was a moderate Whig who preferred the states to address the question of slavery. He was a Buffalo, New York, lawyer who served ably but somewhat obscurely in the Congress for eight years and was serving as New York State comptroller when he was elected vice president.

Zachary Taylor died in July 1850, and Fillmore became the thirteenth president at a crucial moment during the debate over the Compromise of 1850. This compromise, which Fillmore was instrumental in passing, admitted California as a free state, compensated Texas for ceding New Mexico to the federal government, and defeated the Wilmot Proviso that would have closed the territories gained in the war with Mexico to slavery. Although the Wilmot Proviso is cited by Lincoln scholars as a purely antislavery proposal, it was equally a proposal that ensured the new territories in the West would be "white only."

Unlike Tyler, who succeeded a Whig president but was not himself a Whig, the Whig Party did not make that mistake when they put Fillmore on the ticket. Nevertheless, the Whig Party rapidly disintegrated over the issue of slavery and the passage of the Compromise of 1850. Most Northern Whigs joined the Republican Party, but Fillmore refused.

The official White House Web site says that Fillmore opposed Lincoln "throughout the Civil War," and he supported Pres. Andrew Johnson's more moderate form of Reconstruction over the Radical Republicans.[20] There can be no doubt that Fillmore paid a significant political price by refusing to join the Republican Party as most Northern Whigs after the war. It virtually shunted him away from the mainstream of Northern politics, which is to say national politics, for the remainder of his life. He died in 1874.

**Franklin Pierce, New Hampshire**

Franklin Pierce was a New Hampshire Yankee with strong political alliances and affections for the South. He was elected the fourteenth president as a Democrat in 1852. Pierce was the son of a

Revolutionary War hero and was keenly aware of the limits of central government. He was an army officer in the Mexican War and served in both houses of Congress prior to being elected president.

As president, Pierce coined the term "congress of sovereignties" to describe the relationship between the federal government and the states. Of the five living ex-presidents in 1861, Pierce was unquestionably the most constant and vocal critic of Lincoln and the war.

Pierce agonized as he watched the nation split apart during the secession winter of 1860-61. His private correspondence, a portion of which was published in 1905 in the *American Historical Review,* reveals a great deal of his assessment of Lincoln and the war. In exchanges of correspondence with his dear friend Jefferson Davis (who served along side Pierce in the Mexican War and later as Pierce's secretary of war), Pierce revealed his heartache over disunion and the prospects of war. Davis wrote to Pierce that war "has only horror for me." He explained to him that Mississippi's secession was "not a matter of choice but of necessity." Harking to the principles of the Declaration of Independence, Davis wrote to Pierce in the waning days of the Buchanan administration:

> Those who have driven her [Mississippi] to this alternative threaten to deprive her of the right to require that her government shall rest on the consent of the governed. . . .
>
> When Lincoln comes in he will have but to continue in the path of his predecessor to inaugurate a civil war and leave a soi-disant democratic administration responsible for the fact.[21]

When Lincoln called for 75,000 troops to invade the South, Trask writes: "Pierce believed that Lincoln's purpose in calling for troops was not to restore the union, for that could only be done through peaceful statesmanship, but to conquer the South." Pierce refused to support the war in any way.

> To this war . . . which seems to me to contemplate subjugation I give no countenance—no support to any possible extent in any possible way—except thro' inevitable taxation, which seems likely to bankrupt us all. Come what may the foul schemes of Northern Abolitionism, which we have resisted for so many years, are not

to be consummated by arms on bloody fields, through any aid of mine.[22]

Not surprisingly, such opposition placed Pierce in danger of being arrested by Lincoln, a fact of life that Pierce was well aware. In an 1863 stirring Fourth of July speech in Concord, New Hampshire, ironically, the day Lee evacuated Gettysburg, Pierce made it plain where he stood on the issue of state sovereignty and that he feared arrest by Lincoln:

> The Declaration of Independence laid the foundation of our political greatness in the two fundamental ideas of the absolute independence of the American people and of the sovereignty of their respective states.

In that speech, Pierce attacked Lincoln's suspension of the writ of habeas corpus and arrest of political opponents across the North. Pierce claimed, "Arrests are made, not so much for what has been done, as for what probably would be done" to laughter and applause. He also told the crowd, "True it is that any of you, that I myself, may be the next victim of unconstitutional, arbitrary, irresponsible power."

Shortly after hostilities broke out, Pierce received a letter from Chief Justice Roger B. Taney, who endorsed secession over Lincoln's tyrannical government. Taney wrote that the nation seemed almost to be in a state of "delirium." In describing the carnage of war, and his opposition to Lincoln's dictatorial rule, Taney stated the following:

> I hope [the war] is too violent to last long, and that calmer and more sober thoughts will soon take its place: and that the North, as well as the South, will see that a peaceful separation, with free institutions in each section, is far better than the union of all the present states under a military government.[23]

### James Buchanan, Pennsylvania
The Lincoln scholars reserve their most brazen polemics for former president James Buchanan of Pennsylvania.

They call the fifteenth president a traitor and smear him with the allegation of homosexuality. "In his betrayal of the national trust, Buchanan came closer to committing treason than any other president in American history," says history professor Jean H. Baker in her 2004 biography *James Buchanan,* coauthored with Arthur M. Schlesinger, Jr.[24]

And what, you may ask, constituted his alleged crime of treason? He left office without starting the war! He retired to the warm fireside in his Wheatland, Pennsylvania, home without getting any seventeen- and eighteen-year-old farm boys shot up.

Baker plays with fire on this issue of treason. Mind you, the U.S. Constitution, the document to which Lincoln scholars pay much empty, iconic reverence, defines treason in Article III, Section 3: "Treason against the United States, shall consist only in levying War against them, or in adhering to their Enemies, giving them Aid and Comfort."

"Them" is third person plural. "Their" is the third person plural possessive. The word "states" is plural. "Them" is the states, individually or collectively. "Levying war against them," the states, is treason. "Adhering to their Enemies," the states' enemies, the enemies who are levying war against the states, is treason.

Baker plays the semantic game of accusing Buchanan of treason for failing to start a war against individual states, when the levying of war against the states is the only thing that the Constitution actually defines as treason.

It was Lincoln who was the actual traitor, not Buchanan. It was Lincoln who actually levied war against the states. It was Lincoln who did not merely adhere to the enemies of the states. It was Lincoln who did not merely provide "aid and comfort" to the enemies of the states. Lincoln was the actual enemy of the states because it was he who levied war against them. As political economist Thomas DiLorenzo ably demonstrated in *The Real Lincoln,* war was part of Lincoln's agenda all along.

Other historians disagree with the imperialistic, militaristic lens through which Baker views Buchanan. Historian Frank Wysor Klingberg wrote in the mid-twentieth century, "Buchanan, as well as many other leaders, expected to avoid open conflict [war]." The Buchanan contemporaries that Klingberg lists are luminaries: former president John Tyler, who, as we saw earlier in this chapter, was initially opposed to secession of Virginia and worked feverishly for peace;

John Bell, the former speaker of the house and 1860 presidential candidate from Tennessee who was also initially against secession; the incumbent vice president of the United States at the time, John C. Breckenridge of Kentucky; Illinois senator Stephen A. Douglas; New York senator William H. Seward; New York publisher Thurlow Weed; and Kentucky senator John J. Crittenden, who offered the Crittenden compromises in 1861 as a way of avoiding war.[25] These men, plus Pierce, Fillmore, and Buchanan, worked in their own way to avoid war. After all, levying war against any state constituted the crime of treason.

Evidence that Buchanan's efforts to avoid war was in the mainstream of American politics can be found in the Missouri state convention. Numerous speakers at that convention "urged that Missouri and the border states stand firm for the old Constitution and the old Union and keep the two sections apart until their people awake and repudiate the fanatics and designing politicians." The Missouri convention endorsed compromise in the form of a national convention, a border state convention, and the Crittenden compromises. It admonished both sides to avoid precipitating war and then recessed prior to Fort Sumter. The convention reconvened after Fort Sumter, but by then, Lincoln had used the military to topple the lawful and legitimate state government in Jefferson City.[26]

One of the early biographers of Buchanan, George Ticknor Curtis, whose biography was published in 1883, pointed out Buchanan as a man trained in political compromise and diplomacy, which reflected the approach he took in the attempt to avoid war. Another contemporary apparently agrees. Maine native Horatio King, who served as postmaster general in Buchanan's administration, wrote in 1895 that Buchanan's preferred means to avoid war was to conciliate Southern secessionists "by all reasonable means."[27] That he successfully implemented his policy of avoid war through the close of his administration is precisely what the Lincoln scholars despise.

Historians at the turn of the twentieth century also saw civil war as something avoidable and unnecessary. *A History of the American People* is a five-volume work by Woodrow Wilson and published the same year he became president of Princeton University, 1902. Wilson wrote that Buchanan "believed and declared that secession was illegal; but he agreed with his Attorney General that there was no constitutional means or warrant for coercing a State. . . . Such, indeed, for the time seemed to be the general opinion of the country."[28]

Baker, under the tutelage of Schlesinger, gets so many things factually wrong about Buchanan and his times that it makes it virtually impossible for any informed reader to reconcile her book to the historic record. In a chapter that deals with the "final months of the Buchanan presidency," she seems almost as obsessed with Richard Nixon as she is with Buchanan's refusal to start a war. Nixon, incredibly, is mentioned four times in the chapter that covers Buchanan's final winter in the White House, 1860-61.

Another example of error is Baker's assertion that "the hot, dry, aggravating summer [of 1860] set tempers on edge."[29] The claim that climate influences human behavior and attitudes comes from a long-discredited theory of environmental determinism, which among other things, incorporates racial stereotypes to explain cultural differences between whites and blacks. That theory was supported by Ellsworth Huntington of Yale in *Mainsprings of Civilization* and Ellen Churchill Semple of the University of Chicago and Clark University.

Why Baker asks was Buchanan such a failure at warmongering against the South? In spite of the fact that the Pennsylvanian's only residence south of the Mason-Dixon line was Washington, D.C., Baker claims Buchanan was a closet Southerner.

> [Buchanan's] social and cultural identification [was] with what he perceived as the southern values of leisure, the gentleman's code of honor, and . . . "a soft dreamy deliciously quiet life . . . with all its sharp corners removed." Throughout his life James Buchanan enjoyed the company of southerners. Their grace and courtesy, even their conversational talents, attracted him.[30]

Imagine that, he "enjoyed the company of Southerners," so much so that he didn't really want to make war against them.

An irrelevant and unnecessary smear of Buchanan by Schlesinger's stable of obeisant scholars is the allegation that Buchanan was homosexual. This charge is made in lurid manner in Schlesinger's 2004 presidential-series biography *James K. Polk*, by John Seigenthaler.

In a section dealing with Buchanan's appointment as Polk's

secretary of state, Seigenthaler abruptly shifts to Buchanan's sex life. What follows is the discussion of a number of stories published about Buchanan's alleged relationship with Sen. William Rufus King of Alabama, who Seigenthaler claims was Buchanan's wife.[31] King had been Buchanan's roommate years earlier, a practice that was not unusual in Washington at the time.

Seigenthaler relates the story of when King was sent to France in 1844 as the U.S. ambassador. "His farewell letter to Buchanan expresses the hope that his roommate will find no one to replace him in affection," which Seigenthaler says he did not.[32]

The only significance of repeating these rumors and innuendos about Buchanan, other than the obvious smear of a president who the Lincoln scholars love to hate, is Seigenthaler's statement that the rumors made life difficult for Buchanan, not that the gossip had anything to do with his conduct in office. So, after smearing Buchanan with an admittedly irrelevant charge of homosexuality, Siegenthaler absolves himself by blaming everyone else for being interested in the story. "Whatever Buchanan's sexual preference, times were no more sympathetic to homosexuality in the mid-nineteenth century that in today's world of homophobia."[33]

Where did Buchanan stand among the five former presidents? He chose the more difficult of two paths, according to Klingberg, compromise and arbitration. War was "the easy alternative." And as long as Buchanan held power, the nation avoided war. Buchanan was fundamentally different from Lincoln. He was convinced "that the Union could not be cemented by the blood of its citizens."[34] Muscle, blood, and bone made all the cement that Lincoln needed.

Among Lincoln's living predecessors at the time he took office, Martin Van Buren was willing to participate in a peace conference with the five living ex-presidents if someone else would call it. Virginian John Tyler took up arms in open rebellion to the federal government's invasion of the South. New Yorker Millard Fillmore was opposed to the war "throughout" the conflict and refused to join the Republican Party even though almost all other Northern Whigs did so. New Hampshire Yankee Franklin Pierce was an outspoken opponent of the war as well as a harsh critic of Lincoln's use of the U.S. Army to suppress political opponents and close newspapers. And Buchanan refused to start the war because he believed the

Union could be held together only by consent of the governed, not by blood sacrifice.

### The Readmission of the Southern States

After the war, the federal government required the eleven states of the Southern Confederacy be readmitted to the Union as if they had never been part of it. This is evidence of those states exercising a valid right.

As Morse notes, the U.S. Army occupation troops were withdrawn from Arkansas, North Carolina, Florida, South Carolina, Mississippi, and Virginia only after these states had drawn up new constitutions agreeable to Congress that surrendered the right to secede. "How could they surrender a right, unless they had it in the first place," Morse asks?[35]

The Arkansas Constitution of 1868, adopted so as to end occupation, had as its first clause:

> The paramount allegiance of every citizen is due to the Federal Government in the exercise of all its constitutional powers as the same may have been or may be defined by the Supreme Court of the United States, and no power exists in the people of this or any other State of the Federal Union to dissolve their connection therewith, or perform any act tending to impair, subvert or resist the supreme authority of the United States.[36]

Not even conniving politicians come up with such poorly worded ideas; it must be the work of military bureaucrats. This provision not only surrenders the right of the people of Arkansas to secede, it purports in its own state constitution (undoubtedly dictated to the Arkansas legislature at bayonet point) to bind every other state to the same standard. When Arkansas was readmitted to the Union, the U.S. Army ended its occupation eight days later.

The people of North Carolina were made to adopt a constitution stating, "There is no right on the part of this State to secede." A similar story played out in South Carolina, Mississippi, and Virginia, "each adopting a new state constitution specifically relinquishing the right to secede."[37]

Morse squarely addresses the meaning of these actions the federal government forced the Southern states to take:

> Obviously, these promises not to secede were the price the former Confederate States had to pay for the withdrawal of the northern armies of occupation. But, by insisting that the former Confederate States surrender their right to secede, the United States government had implicitly admitted that those states originally had the right.[38]

There would have been no basis in constitutional law to incorporate a pledge not to secede in these states' constitutions if there was no *ab initio* right to do so.

## Summary

We have seen the evidence of the nature of the American experiment in government from Anglo-American legal and constitutional traditions to precedent-setting Supreme Court cases, from the Bill of Rights, the Treaty of Paris, and the Articles of Confederation to history as it pertains to Lincoln's predecessors in office and in the Constitution itself. This evidence leads to several inescapable conclusions:

- The Constitution is silent on sovereignty, perpetuity, irreversibility, dissolution, and secession, leaving those as powers reserved to the states and the people. Even when the federal government used the word "perpetual" in treaties, those treaties only lasted a few years.
- The legislatures of the states had every right to reconvene constitutional conventions in 1860-61 with the same authority as the original conventions in 1787-90.
- There is nothing in the Constitution that "unmistakably" transferred sovereignty from the people of the states to the federal government.
- The people have the same natural right to "alter, reform, or abolish" government today as they did in 1776.
- The Constitution guaranteed a republican (not military) form of government and protects the states from invasion (Article IV, Section 4).

- When Lincoln invaded the states for the purpose of toppling republican self-rule, he violated both clauses of Article IV, Section 4 of the Constitution and committed treason.

The war the federal government perpetrated on the South was an illegal counterrevolution conducted for the purpose of eliminating the principle consent of the governed that was established by the Declaration of Independence and the war of secession from the British crown. The republic of the Founding Fathers was replaced by a government limited only by the will of the political majority in power in Washington at any given moment. True limited government, the rule of law, has been displaced by "majority rule," which contemporary American society has utterly failed to recognize is nothing more than the rule of men.

The blood of 620,000 Americans is on one man's hands: Abraham Lincoln, the traitor. No one in history killed more Americans than Lincoln. Not Adolf Hitler. Not Hideki Tojo. Not Kaiser Wilhelm II. Not Ho Chi Minh. Not even all of them combined.

# CHAPTER SEVEN

# War Crimes: Lincoln Prosecutes the War on the South

*"I repeat my orders that you arrest all the people, male and female, connected with those factories, no matter what the clamor, and let them foot it, under guard to Marietta, whence I will send them by cars to the North."*
—Gen. William T. Sherman's order to
kidnap civilian women and children,
Roswell, Georgia, July 7, 1864

The central character of this chapter is Gen. William Tecumseh Sherman, a man who was lionized in the North for burning everything in the South within reach of his torch and later for his slaughter of the Plains Indians, which had begun in the West before the close of the Civil War. His name in many Southern towns is synonymous with ruthless, mindless destruction, cruelty, and privation.

Sherman was the United States Army's most prominent general officer to emerge from Civil War history as an unindicted war criminal. However, he was not the only one during the Civil War. There was Pope, Halleck, Grant, Sheridan, and Lincoln, who along with Sherman were the policy makers in the field and Washington. Certainly, lesser individuals were guilty of overt crimes or turning a blind eye. These men should have been tried for treason but not by Southerners. The United States government should have prosecuted them for war crimes because they broke the law. The federal government won the war, so they got away with it. In this war, as in all subsequent wars, winning was the only thing that mattered. If the Feds had lost, Northern history would have likely vilified, rather than idolized these men.

We have rediscovered from the historic record in previous chapters the philosophical and political connection between Germany and the United States. This connection eerily carries forward in the origins of war on civilians, i.e., total war. It reverberates on the pages of history in the nineteenth, twentieth, and twenty-first centuries in America, Europe, and Asia.

Before we consider the substantive material in this chapter, there are important moral questions to address. You should ask yourself: Under what circumstances do you condone taking another person's life, stealing their most valuable possessions, destroying their ability to make a living and feed their family, depriving them of shelter, or some combination of the above?

What about self-defense? Most people in Western culture would agree that one has the right to defend one's self and one's family. This is a natural right and is absolute. In self-defense, one is justified in the use of deadly force, especially if the aggressor escalates the conflict to the point that less violent alternatives would mean subjugation or death.

What about saving the Union? Is it morally right to kill in order to save the Union? Another way of analyzing this question is to consider whether the form of government established by the people who joined to create it is more valuable than the lives of the people themselves.

How about divorce? Is it morally acceptable for one partner to use force, even to the extremity of lethal force, in an effort to "save the marriage union"? Likely not. Most people would not endorse the idea that the marriage union itself is more valuable than the lives of the people who voluntarily entered into it, even if they vowed, "Until death do we part."

Would we consider it morally acceptable to kill for "progress," for the "greater good," or to "end all wars," as Wilson assured was the case in 1917-18? Do we consider it morally acceptable to kill in order to bring down an unjust regime, or to spread democracy?

We would likely answer in the negative if asked whether it is moral to kill people of another race or another culture in order to steal their land, but isn't that precisely what the federal government did with the Plains Indians? The Indians were viewed as racially and culturally inferior. They were dehumanized, and their resistance to being pushed off their land was a convenient excuse for the government to kill them off to make way for the railroads. The railroad companies were the nation's first corporate giants and perpetrators of an unprecedented raid of the nation's vast Western land domain. They were the first federally subsidized industry. This would set the stage for the robber barons toward the close of the nineteenth century; the military-industrial complex that would follow in the twentieth century; and the blurring of the line between big government and big business that seems to have taken hold in the twenty-first century.

## Origins of Total War

Although the term "total war" itself originated in the twentieth century, the concept of total war originated during the American Civil War. According to historian Lance Janda, the "library shelves groan with works pointing to the Civil War as a harbinger of 'total war'. . . a kind of macabre prelude to the world wars of the Twentieth century."[1]

The weaponry of the Civil War remained relatively crude and the ability to give meaningful medical assistance to the wounded and dying was even more primitive. Louis Pasteur's discovery that microorganisms are responsible for infection and disease came just before the war (1860), but it was of little help during the war, because it continued to meet significant skepticism at medical schools into the 1870s. There were few repeating rifles, few self-contained ammunition cartridges, and no high explosives. These innovations came later. Thus, it was neither the weaponry nor medical innovation during the Civil War that constituted an important shift toward total war.

"The real significance of the Civil War lies in its tactics, not its technology," according to Janda. If total war means the use of military force against noncombatant civilians, "then the Civil War stands as a watershed in the American evolution of total war theory." Although the use of force on civilians "had been around since the dawn of civilization," it was U.S. Army commanders who were "first in American history to use these tactics on a widespread scale, and they played a crucial role not only in the subjugation of the South, but in the conquest of native Americans as well."[2]

These commanders did not learn total war theory at the United States Military Academy at West Point. Quite the contrary, war on civilians was considered anathema and revolutionary during the period when Grant, Sherman, and Sheridan received their training there. In fact, Halleck, who became the army chief of staff during the war, was initially reluctant to sanction total war. He preferred defensive fortifications to invasion.[3]

The code of conduct for the U.S. military at the time was embodied in the Articles of War of 1806, which was in force until the Lieber Code (General Order No. 100) was approved by Lincoln in April 1863. The 1806 code stated, "Any officer or solider who shall quit his post or colors to plunder and pillage shall suffer death or other such punishment as shall be ordered by sentence of a general court martial." Such conduct stemmed from the Enlightenment, "which stressed that violence against noncombatants was barbaric and unworthy of modern military forces."[4]

**The Barbaric Reality**
How did this barbaric practice get into the United States military establishment? What was its origin?

From the outset of the hostilities, Lincoln misunderstood the nature of the conflict because he misunderstood the nature of Southerners. Though born in Kentucky, perhaps Lincoln failed even to understand that the "Southern experience" is something quite set apart from the American experience. He saw the war as a conflict of two distinct, separate economies and two separate political systems (centralized power versus distributed power). Clearly, this was true, but there was much more to it than financial interests or forms of political power.

As late as the summer of 1862, Lincoln labored under the delusion that a quick, knock-out punch of Lee's Army of Northern Virginia was possible and all that would be needed to force the South back into the Union. In July 1862, Lincoln wrote to the Northern governors pleading for them to send immediately 50,000 more troops. With these added troops, the army could "substantially close the war in two weeks."[5]

However, Lincoln failed to grasp that Southerners wanted to govern themselves, period. This fundamental truth drove both sides to the political crisis that ended in armed conflict. Southerners saw government as a tool to achieve and protect freedom, not an end unto itself. This view was the philosophy of natural law embedded in the Declaration of Independence and ingrained into the Southern mind and experience. To the Southerner, self-determination under a form of limited government was part of the very definition of being Southern. To the Southerner, there were things that no government should ever have the power to enforce upon a free man. Therefore, when the national government no longer served the interests of Southerners, they felt no obligation to serve it. In fact, they believed they had every right to "alter or abolish it, and to institute new government" as they saw fit, i.e., the right of revolution. That is what their grandfathers did in 1776, and as far as Southerners were concerned, they would no more serve Lincoln than their grandfathers would serve King George III.

Consequently, it was not simply the states as political entities that were in conflict with the government in Washington city, or even the economies of the North and South. It was the entire free population of the South that was intent on exercising its right of revolution.

To defeat and subjugate the South; to put an end to the Confederacy; to establish the perpetuity, indivisibility, and supremacy of the national government over the states; to centralize power into the national government; to break the "chains" of the Constitution; and to erect in its place a government of virtually unlimited authority, military victory alone would not be enough. The Southern people themselves would have to be "annihilated" as Adam Badeau wrote.

Badeau served on Grant's staff during the war and was brevetted as a brigadier general. He was with Grant at Appomattox when Lee surrendered. After the war, Badeau was rewarded with diplomatic posts to England and Cuba. He wrote several books about Grant and his diplomatic experiences. In the 1880s, Badeau wrote, "It was not victory that either side was playing for, but for existence. If the rebels won, they destroyed a nation; if the government succeeded, it annihilated a rebellion."[6] Of course, the South had no interest in "destroying" the U.S. government or altering anything in the North. Hence, this part of Badeau's statement is consistent with the false reasoning of Lincoln that the Lincoln scholars defend today. Nevertheless, Badeau's larger point is correct; the South was fighting for its very existence and the defeat of its armies in the field would be only part of the equation. The Southern people themselves would have to be annihilated, and this would require offensive warfare, and the deliberate application of military force on noncombatant civilians.

The first step on the slippery road toward total war came from Gen. John Pope and President Lincoln. Pope was one of the early commanders of the Army of the Potomac and suffered from Southern attack to his supply lines. Based on "military necessity," he obtained authority from Lincoln to "live off the land" when on Southern territory. This freed him from long, often disrupted supply lines, and it brought a degree of "retribution" to the Southern people by the requisition of their livestock and foodstuffs.

Military necessity was defined then much as it is today with the nebulous words, "those measures which are indispensable for securing the ends of the war," as attributed to Gen. David Hunter in 1862.[7]

Its implementation received a temporary setback when Lincoln appointed Gen. George B. McClellan commander of the Army of the Potomac. In an apology to one Virginia landowner for damage caused by his troops, McClellan wrote, "I have not come here to wage war upon the defenseless, upon non-combatants, upon private property, nor upon the domestic institutions of the land."[8]

It was Grant, the U.S. commander in the western theater, who would first employ the ruthless practice of total war. Sherman, his understudy, would raise it to a grizzly science. Early in the war in the West, Grant recognized that simply defeating Southern armies was not enough. "Grant's views on total war began to change after he gauged the depth of Southern resolve and found it so stalwart that new means would be necessary to ensure victory." As a result, after the battle of Shiloh in April 1862, Grant decided "to consume everything [of civilian property] that could be used to support or supply armies."[9]

By July 1862, an Illinois congressman advised Lincoln that he must "maul" the rebels. Lincoln responded, "Tell the people of Illinois that I'll do it." Further, Lincoln ordered Secretary of War Edwin Stanton to prepare an executive order so commanders in the field could "seize and use any property."[10] The harshest actions against Southerners were reserved for individual civilians.

Pope's Orders No. 11, issued July 23, 1862, ordered U.S. Army commanders to "proceed immediately to arrest all disloyal male citizens within their lines or within their reach in rear of their respective stations." Such civilian males were to take an oath of allegiance to the U.S. government or to suffer expulsion from their homes. If they returned to their homes during army occupation, they were to be shot as spies. If a man took the oath and was found to have violated it, the order said, "He shall be shot, and his property seized and applied to the public use."

The result was a "reign of terror" in Tennessee and parts of Virginia:

> Pope's soldiers went on a rampage, and they justified their theft and indiscriminate destruction of property by citing his orders. . . . A Union general in Stafford County [Virginia] observed, "our men know every house in the whole country, and . . . they now believe they have a perfect right to rob, tyrannize, threaten and maltreat any one they please, under the Orders of Gen. Pope."[11]

A British observer commented that Pope's new war policy had "cast mankind two centuries back towards barbarism." Indeed, there were numerous reports of rape and violence against free white women and slaves:

> If white women were not safe, then woe betide the region's unprotected black women, against whom acts of the "most beastly and infamous character" were perpetrated. No home was spared intrusion. The poorest families were deprived of food. White or black, rich or poor, no one was immune from Pope's concept of total war.[12]

So shocking was Pope's orders that some federal commanders protested. McClellan "bitterly opposed it;" he complained to Halleck that the war should be conducted in a civilized manner and "not against the people." Gen. Irwin McDowell said the orders had set "Satan loose," and he had no confidence in serving under Pope.[13]

By the spring of 1863, the doctrine of military necessity had been codified upon Lincoln's approval of the Lieber Code. Article 14 of the Lieber Code states:

> Military necessity, as understood by modern civilized nations,

consists in the necessity of those measures which are indispensable
for securing the ends of the war, and which are lawful according to
the modern law and usages of war.

Article 15 states:

> Military necessity admits of all direct destruction of life or limb
> of armed enemies, and of other persons whose destruction is
> incidentally unavoidable in the armed contest of the war . . . of the
> appropriation of whatever an enemy's country affords necessary
> for the subsistence and safety of the army.[14]

What did Lincoln have in mind when he approved the Lieber
Code? Historian John Frank describes Lincoln's Machiavellian
attitude. Lincoln's mind "worked in terms of basic ideas presented as
fundamentals." He had "the mental process of a pile driver landing
directly on point."[15]

To Lincoln, "the doctrine of military necessity had a powerful
attraction as organizing principle and foundation for political and
military action in defense of the Union." In short, Lincoln believed he
had the power to do whatever he deemed necessary to win the war.[16]
And since the reestablishment of federal authority over the states was
the objective, any means to that end could be viewed as necessary.

Grant was busy in the summer of 1863 demonstrating to Southerners what military necessity was all about. During the Vicksburg
campaign, which led up to the forty-six-day siege and capitulation
of the last Confederate strong point on the Mississippi River, Grant
decided to "cut loose from his base of supplies and live off the land,
practicing total war against the civilians of the South."[17]

Grant and his subordinate commanders, Sherman and Sheridan,
subscribed to the notion that Southerners were only getting what they
deserved. They believed "every man, woman and child contributed
to prolonging the war." Sherman put it this way in a letter to General
Halleck, "We are not only fighting hostile armies, but a hostile
people, and we must make old and young, rich and poor, feel the
hard hand of war."[18]

As the war dragged on, Lincoln's view of total war on everything
Southern—physical, cultural, institutional—widened. As Burrus
Carnahan notes:

By the end of the Civil War, then, the scope of destruction authorized by military necessity extended not only to property of direct military use, but, as Lincoln had written to [Illinois politician James C.] Conkling, to any property that "helps us, or hurts the enemy," including the economic infrastructure supporting the enemy war effort. The destructive implications of this doctrine were not fully realized until the development of strategic bombing in the Twentieth century.[19]

### Who Was Sherman—What Kind of Man Would Do This?

Gen. William T. Sherman was a failure at peace. His place in history, at least as the Lincoln scholars write history, was secured only by the opportunity to prove how destructive he truly was down deep in his soul.

Sherman's biographers and other historians describe him as:

- "A disappointed and unhappy man";[20]
- "A brilliant but tormented soul";[21]
- "A near emotional cripple" unable to loose himself from a "failed past";[22]
- A "dangerous man";[23]
- "Traumatized . . . marginalized . . . [and] self-loathing";[24]
- "Caged lion . . . angry";[25]
- "Frustrated, anxious, fearful of the future" as the war began;[26]
- In 1861, his wife noticed "obsessiveness, insomnia, loss of appetite, loss of realistic contact with others and delusional misjudgement";[27]
- Repeatedly suffered from "suicidal impulses" during the war and confessed to his wife a death-wish for himself and his most sickly child;[28]
- A man "trapped" by his own psychology "and harassed by pestering goblins that roamed freely in his mind";[29]
- By 1865, a man of "primal rage";[30]

The assistant secretary of war thought Sherman was insane and said so. Asstistant Secretary Thomas Scott said, "Sherman's gone in the head, he's luny [*sic*]." A U.S. Army surgeon, Col. Thomas M. Key, reported to his superiors that Sherman was unfit for command. General Halleck told General McClellan, "It would be dangerous to give him a command." The *New York Times* reported he had "disorders." The *Cincinnati Commercial* announced in a headline, **"GENERAL WM. T. SHERMAN INSANE."**[31]

Indeed, insanity ran in Sherman's family. His own life exhibited a strange mixture of dysfunctional relationships, failure in civilian life, cruelty, financial and emotional dependency, envy, guilt, shame, anti-Semitism, and vehemently racist attitudes toward blacks, Indians, and Hispanics. Historian Stanley P. Hirshson, who describes himself as a sympathetic biographer, notes that "Sherman's maternal grandmother, his maternal uncle, and his son Tom all died in, or spent years in, insane asylums." His brother Jim, died a drunk, and his brother John, who served as a member of both Houses of Congress, died mentally unstable.[32]

Sherman was born into an Episcopal family and raised by a Catholic family who had him rebaptized. His eight children were raised Catholic, and it was his wife, not he, who practiced the orthodoxy of the Roman church. One of Sherman's sons became a Jesuit priest, an event that displeased Sherman enormously.

Sherman's father died when he was a boy, leaving Sherman and his ten brothers and sisters scattered across various homes when their mother fell hopelessly into debt. The young Sherman landed in the home of a neighbor, Thomas Ewing, a physically large man and influential and prosperous attorney who served a term in the U.S. Senate.

Given only the name Tecumseh at birth, Sherman was baptized at the request of Ewing's wife, Maria, as a Catholic. She added what she considered a proper Christian name, William. (Thomas Ewing converted to Catholicism on his deathbed decades later, never having practiced the faith). The Ewings never formally adopted Sherman, perhaps out of respect for his mother who they knew. Sherman eventually married Ewing's daughter, Ellen, making his larger-than-life guardian also his father-in-law.[33]

The theme of Sherman's "self-loathing and shame" is discussed in sixteen different places in Michael Fellman's 1995 biography *Citizen Sherman*. It covers virtually every aspect of his life, professionally and personally. In the mid-1830s, as a West Point student, Sherman believed the Ewings never cared for him and was ashamed of this. In the 1840s, "he slipped into the first of what would prove a lifelong series of depressions" over his failure to see combat during the war with Mexico.[34] Early in the Civil War, he was given command of one Wisconsin regiment and three New York City regiments, all volunteers who he referred to as a "rabble" in his correspondence. As written by Fellman, "They hooted and jeered his attempts to discipline them," and after they broke and ran at the Battle of First Manassas, he wrote that he was "absolutely disgraced now" and wanted to "sneak into some quiet corner."[35] Near the end of his infamous March to the Sea, Sherman "found moral affirmation through organized violence, learning that war could provide a legitimate, even constructive outlet for his primal rage."[36]

Sherman's feelings of disgrace are so pervasive that they were a constant worry for his wife, his siblings, and even his army commanders. In 1862, he wrote his brother, John, by then a U.S. senator from Ohio, "I should have committed suicide were it not for my children."[37] On another occasion, he wrote, "I look upon myself as a dead cock in a pit, not worthy of further notice."[38]

Sherman's inability in the prewar years to earn enough money in the military to support his children and wife in a manner to which his wife had been accustomed led to his resignation from the army in 1853. He borrowed money from his father-in-law in order to make his way west to a promised banking job in San Francisco. His wife joined him two years later but did not stay long before returning to her father's home in Ohio. The bank failed in 1857, and Sherman confessed to one of his brothers-in-law that the experience left him "as poor as a church mouse, without profession, without confidence, without physical strength." As Fellman points out, Sherman was once again dependent on his father-in-law.[39]

During this time of economic turmoil, Sherman's dysfunctional family life was further irritated by his wife's insistence that he adhere to the Catholic faith, which he never followed as an adult. In ways, the couple was the most perfect imperfect match. "In the domestic arena these two warriors circled about each other and delivered about an equal number of brutal verbal blows."[40]

Sherman's prewar failures seemed to come to an end in 1859 when he finally won a job on his own as superintendent of Louisiana State Seminary of Learning & Military Academy (presently Louisiana State University). This job would take him and his young family away from Ohio and his dominant father-in-law, allowing Sherman to be his own man. The position seemed stable, would pay reasonably well, and would provide him the position and prestige he so desperately craved. However, even this was an illusion.

Sherman accepted the job and reported for work. In a matter of months, Louisiana seceded from the Union. Once again, Sherman's plans were dashed, but the looming war would open the door for him to return to the U.S. Army.[41]

Sherman's vehement racism toward nonwhites is well documented in the historic record, often in his own words. Since Sherman was a central figure in the Civil War, his words are important. They represent the general attitudes that explode the myth that the Civil War was a war of racial justice. Racial justice was the farthest thing from Sherman's mind. He believed that the free or enslaved Negro "is in a transition state, and is not the equal of the white man." He also felt that such attitudes "[were] shared by a large portion of our fighting men," i.e., Union soldiers. One of his most notable pronouncements on race was a letter to his wife:

> Niggers won't work now, and half my army are driving wagons, loading and unloading cars, and doing work which the very Negros we have captured might do, whilst these same niggers are soldiers on paper, but I can't get any—The fact is modern Philanthropy will convert our oldest & best soldiers into laborers whilst the nigger parades & remains in some remote & safe place. It is an insult to our Race to count them as part of the quota.[42]

Some of Sherman's correspondence found its way into newspapers in the North, generating a great deal of controversy. In a letter to Col. John A. Spooner, who had been commissioned by Massachusetts to raise a regiment among former slaves in Georgia, Sherman blamed the abolitionists for stirring up attacks against him:

> I don't see why we can't have some sense about Negros, as well as about horses, mules, iron, copper & c[   ] but say nigger in the U.S. and . . . the whole country goes crazy. I never thought my Negro letter would get into the papers, but since it has I lay low—
> I like niggers well enough as niggers, but when fools & idiots try & make niggers better than ourselves I have an opinion.[43]

As harsh as his views were against the black man, Sherman advocated nothing less than racial genocide of the Plains Indians. Biographer Michael Fellman describes Sherman's view:

> They were a less-than-human and savage race, uncivilized to white standards, and probably uncivilizable. They were obstacles to the upward sweep of history, progress, wealth, and white destiny.[44]

John Marszalek says Sherman viewed Indians much as he did recalcitrant Southerners during the war and newly freed slaves after the war. They were "resisters to the legitimate forces of an orderly society." The Indians needed a strong, stern father figure because Sherman believed they were "stubborn children who needed disciplining." The Indians' mobility and closeness to nature "represented the kind of anarchy he feared all of his life."[45]

In the mind of the American public in the late 1860s—which is to say the Northern public since the readmission of many Southern states into the Union that Lincoln said he fought to preserve had not yet occurred—Sherman and subordinate Philip Sheridan were the two most fierce Indian fighters. Of them, Marszalek says:

> Their names were forever tied to that philosophy through their joint linkage to the famous statement: "The only good Indian is a dead Indian." Sherman insisted that the phrase actually went back to colonial days and that "Miles Standish was the author of it." But by his own admission, "Sherman firmly believed in the doctrine."[46]

By 1868, Sherman ordered Sheridan to "attack without restraint." He gave him "prior authorization to slaughter as many women and children as well as men Sheridan or his subordinates felt was necessary when they attacked Indian villages."[47]

"During an assault," Sherman wrote, "the soldiers can not pause to distinguish between male and female, or even discriminate as to age. As long as resistance is made death must be meted out." Given Sherman's attitude, and his self-incrimination as a child killer, it is not surprising that the U.S. Army "purposely" campaigned against the Indians in winter when families were together, often wiping out entire villages.[48]

Fellman sums up quite well Sherman's merciless, malevolent, racist, and sometimes maniacal state of mind about the Plains Indians, writing:

> A great self-certainty that he was the agent of Progress, an overarching faith served by his equally deep and callous contempt for his enemy, one of those other, lesser races bound to lose in the harsh competition of History.[49]

Although Sherman had but brief contact with Hispanics during the Indian wars in what is now New Mexico, his attitude toward them is as predictable as it is unmistakable. Sherman informed his wife by letter:

> Santa Fe is the oldest town in the United States except for St. Augustine, but the People with a few exceptions are greasers of the commonest sort, and their houses gardens & c[   ] are about as they were when Moses was a baby—houses of adobe, no floors, no windows—the interior common to dogs, cats, bugs & fleas.

Sherman went on to complain to his wife that the inhabitants of Santa Fe are dependent on expenditures of the U.S. Army post to survive—akin to the same sort of economic dependency he experienced in his own life.[50]

### Just What Is Meant by Total War—What Did the Feds Say about It, Then and Now?

Before delving into the history of specific war crimes committed on civilians by the federal government through the U.S. Army, it is fitting to explore just what is meant by total war. What did the law of the land at that time say about it?

General Orders No. 100, otherwise known as the Lieber Code, was issued by the U.S. War Department in Washington on April 24, 1863. This order established the code of conduct for military operations of the United States government and set the limits of punishment for infractions thereof. The relationship between the U.S. Army and civilians in the South is summarized in paragraph 44 of the code:

> All wanton violence committed against persons in the invaded

country, all destruction of property not commanded by the authorized officer, all robbery, all pillage or sacking, even after taking a place by main force, all rape, wounding, maiming, or killing of such inhabitants, are prohibited under the penalty of death, or such other severe punishment as may seem adequate for the gravity of the offense.

The Lieber Code distinguished between "the private individual belonging to a hostile country and the hostile country itself, with its men in arms" (paragraph 22). "Private citizens are no longer murdered, enslaved, or carried off to distant parts" by the invading armies of civilized nations (paragraph 23). It established, ostensibly, that "protection of the inoffensive citizen of the hostile country is the rule; privation and disturbance of private property are the exceptions" (paragraph 25). The code eliminated retaliation on civilians for "mere revenge" but permitted retaliation in situations "only as a means of protective retribution" (paragraph 28). As an occupation force, it acknowledged a duty to protect individuals, private property, "and the sacredness of domestic relations" (paragraph 37). The code prohibited officers and soldiers from using their power or position "for private gain" in hostile territory (paragraph 46). Prisoners of war are not subject to punishment, revenge, "or any other barbarity" (paragraph 56).

The code offered freedom to escaping or liberated slaves who made it to U.S. Army lines. The only problem was that army commanders usually ignored or directly violated paragraph 43:

Therefore, in a war between the United States and a belligerent which admits of slavery, if a person held in bondage by that belligerent be captured by or come as a fugitive under the protection of the military forces of the United States, such person is immediately entitled to the rights and privileges of a freeman. To return such a person into slavery would amount to enslaving a free person, and neither the United States nor any officer under their authority can enslave any human being.

The Lieber Code also established and defined the principle of military necessity. This principle is discussed in only four of the 157 paragraphs of the code. Earlier in this chapter, it was established that the principle of military necessity was the undoing of virtually all the protections written into the code. Lincoln's objective in the war was the reestablishment of federal jurisdiction, which had been lost over the Southern states. As the war dragged on, Lincoln acted on the belief that virtually anything that helps achieve the reestablishment of lost jurisdiction is, in fact, a military necessity.

In keeping with much of what the Lincoln administration undertook, the Lieber Code contained fatal contradictions. All the apparent protections for opposing forces and noncombatants and all the apparent restrictions regarding conduct of U.S. Army personnel were subverted by the fact that the code pertained to armed conflict with a "hostile country." To Lincoln and Lieber, the Confederates were rebels and traitors and as such deserved no protection beyond that which commanders in the field found convenient. Paragraph 151 of the code was written to define the Southern states outside the protection of the law:

> The term rebellion is applied to an insurrection of large extent, and is usually a war between the legitimate government of a country and portions of provinces of the same who seek to throw off their allegiance to it and set up a government of their own.

The irony of this paragraph is that it precisely describes the attitudes and actions of the Colonial governments in 1776 when they adopted the Declaration of Independence. It is called self-determination, a natural right the Founding Fathers recognized, proclaimed, and fought for.

By defining the conflict as a rebellion, the Lieber Code becomes a self-gutting document at paragraph 155:

> The military commander of the legitimate government, in a war of rebellion, distinguishes between the loyal citizens in the revolted portion of the country and the disloyal citizens. The disloyal citizens may further be classified into those citizens know to sympathize with the rebellion without positively aiding it, and those who, without taking up arms, give positive aid and comfort to the rebellious enemy without being bodily forced thereto.

What is to be done with these disloyal citizens? Paragraph 156 states the commander in the field "will throw the burden of the war, as much as lies within his power, on the disloyal citizens." Here we see the smoking gun of a formally adopted government policy to wage war on civilians, to "throw the burden of war" on the very same civilians whose place in the union of states Lincoln purports to preserve. In the analogy of secession as political divorce, this policy is the equivalent of a divorce court sanctioning an abusive husband's increased battery of his plaintiff wife until she submits to the reinstatement of his authority—all done in the name of saving the (marriage or political) union.

Additionally, the Lieber Code considers any sort of resistance, "armed or unarmed," as war against the United States and therefore the crime of treason (paragraph 157). Since the code gave rise to subsequent developments of international law as it pertains to armed conflict (including the various Geneva Conventions), it is worthwhile to consider how rebellion or insurrection is treated by international law today. In fact, there are recognized criteria to determine when an internal conflict becomes an international one.

U.S. Army major John Embry Parkerson, Jr., writing in *Military Law Review*, published by the U.S. Army's Judge Advocate General's Legal Center & School, states when a civil war escalates to the intensity that rebel forces constitute a "belligerent" force, "the full body of international humanitarian law theoretically should apply to the conflict." Indeed, the U.S. Army's principal manual on humanitarian law (at least through the time of Operation Just Cause, the 1989 invasion of Panama) contains this statement: "The customary law of war becomes applicable to civil war upon recognition of the rebels as belligerents."[51]

Parkerson gives four elements as criteria for defining belligerency. The first criterion is "the existence of a civil war accompanied by a state of general hostilities." Clearly, the Civil War met this test as conflict raged from the Potomac to the Indian territories, Texas, and beyond. The Confederate flag even flew over Tucson after the U.S. Army withdrew and the locals passed an ordinance of secession.

The second criterion is "the occupation and a measure of orderly administration of a substantial part of national territory by the insurgents." Likewise, the Confederate states formed a government, adopted a Constitution, and administered government in many states. The Confederate government wanted to send a peace delegation to President-elect Lincoln who rejected the idea.

The third criterion is "the observation of the rules of warfare on the part of the insurgent forces a ting under a responsible authority."

Gen. Robert E. Lee was a former superintendent of the U.S. Military Academy at West Point. The curriculum there taught military law as it was before Lincoln twisted it. The principle of military necessity did not exist at that time, nor is there any record of Confederate abuse of Northern civilians or combatants. The Confederate forces had a clear chain of command and a civilian commander in chief.

Finally, there is "the practical necessity for third states to define their attitude in the civil war."[52] Note that Parkerson does not say it is necessary for the seceded, belligerent state to be recognized by third party nations, only that such nations take sufficient note of the conflict by defining an attitude about the conflict. Diplomatic officials in England, France, the Vatican, and perhaps other nations received Confederate emissaries. That England toyed with the proposition of recognizing the Confederacy is a well-established historical fact that sufficiently alarmed the Lincoln administration.

Thus, it would appear that the Civil War meets all the tests of modern belligerency and would have invoked the "full body of international humanitarian law" had such a law existed in the nineteenth century. This important conclusion dismisses as illegitimate the political cover for total war sanctioned in paragraphs 149-157 of the Lieber Code. In short, a true rendering of those paragraphs would enforce the rules of conduct imposed in the balance of the document, putting the U.S. Army high command as well as Lincoln and his cabinet in legal jeopardy. They levied war against the states, which the Constitution defines as treason.

This is not to say that Confederate forces were never guilty of abusive practices or crimes; history suggests that it is beyond human limitations for any government to put an armed force in the field that commits no crimes.

### Warfare on Civilians, War Crimes, and Atrocities

This section reviews a chronology of specific instances of military force on civilians; war crimes, or violations of the U.S. Constitution or law; or other notable atrocities committed in the field by Sherman, Grant, and others (often with the knowledge and consent of their military commanders as well as Lincoln). This list is intended merely to introduce a body of historical facts to the reader. It is a sample, not a complete compilation, of such events. The items on this list were chosen because they are outrageous and repugnant, because they are almost completely unknown to the average American, or both.

## Confederate POWs Forced to Clear Mine Fields, Williamsburg, Virginia, May 1862

The engagement of cavalry units at the Battle of Williamsburg, May 4-5, 1862, occurred during the Peninsular Campaign, Gen. George B. McClellan commanding the Army of the Potomac. This was the first attempt by the U.S. Army to take Richmond following the federal debacle at Manassas the previous summer.

After a sharp skirmish at Williamsburg, McClellan forced the Confederates under Gen. John Magruder to withdraw toward Yorktown but not before they covered their retreat with crude land mines, or torpedoes as they were called at the time. McClellan forced Confederate prisoners of war to clear these torpedoes.

He records in his memoirs, "The enemy had made a free distribution of torpedoes in the roads, within the works, and in places where our men would be apt to go—for instance, near wells and springs, telegraph-offices, and store-houses—so that some of our men were killed." He considered the use of torpedoes in an assault as "admissible under the current customs of war," but to use them in a retreat, he considered, was "barbarous in the extreme."[53]

McClellan's pursuit of retreating Confederates "was much delayed by the caution made necessary by the presence of these torpedoes." He wrote that he immediately "ordered that they should be discovered and removed by the Confederate prisoners. They objected strenuously, but were forced to do the work."[54]

Forcing Confederate prisoners of war (POWs) to clear land mines appears to have violated the Lieber Code, although it was not yet in force at the time. The Lieber Code, paragraph 75, spares POWs from "intentional suffering or indignity." Certainly, pressing POWs to clear land mines by hand would be extremely hazardous and likely lead to suffering. McClellan's actions would clearly violate today's U.S. Army regulations that proscribe the use of POWs in work that is "injurious to health or dangerous because of the inherent nature of the work."[55]

## Slaves Were Used to Build Fort Pickering in Memphis, Summer of 1862

This item in the chronology of war crimes incorporates all the complexities and contradictions of the Civil War. Up to one thousand slaves were used in 1862 to rush completion of Fort Pickering, an earthwork used to guard land approaches to the key commerce center of Memphis, Tennessee. It wasn't Confederate forces that compelled the slaves to labor, it was Sherman.

Within days of taking command in Memphis in the summer of 1862, Sherman had 750 slaves working on the fort.[56] And what was Sherman's contribution in Memphis to the war contemporary Lincoln scholars proclaim a war of racial justice? It was to "establish rules for slave labor" in order to hurry completion of Fort Pickering, which had been started by Grant. In fact, Sherman "required accurate book-keeping on the use of slaves for later payment to loyal slaveholders." Sherman "placed the slaves under his jurisdiction at work on Fort Pickering, and soon had a thousand working there, another two hundred working for the quartermaster on the levee, and three hundred to four hundred as teamsters and cooks in the regiments."[57]

Technically, Sherman's enforcement of the institution of slavery and his direct use of slave labor did not violate the Lieber Code because it was not issued until a few months after the Fort Pickering incident. This does not relieve Sherman from moral indictment by Francis Lieber who wrote in paragraph 42 of the code, "Fugitives escaping from a country in which they were slaves, villains, or serfs, into another country, have, for centuries past, been held free and acknowledged free by judicial decisions of European countries." In paragraph 43, Lieber states that in a war between the United States and a belligerent that allows slavery, if a slave is captured or otherwise comes under the "protection" of the U.S. government or its military forces, "such person is immediately entitled to the rights and privileges of a freeman."

The Confiscation Act was passed in the summer of 1862. Although the act emancipated any slave who had worked in the Confederate war effort, Sherman had little sympathy for its enforcement. He let it be known to members of the U.S. Supreme Court as well has his brother, John, who by then was a U.S. Senator, that it was "neither his duty nor pleasure to disturb the relation of master and slave." In correspondence to his brother, he offered, "Not one nigger in ten wants to run off."[58]

Sherman proved later in the war that he had no intention of abiding by these sections of the Lieber Code. In Sherman's defense, the code is riddled with inconsistencies. Even if applied *ex post facto,* one might successfully argue that Sherman's use of slave labor was a matter of military necessity as the slaves were used to construct a fort. In any case, a reasonable reading of the Lieber Code will yield much greater emphasis on the concept of military necessity than it will on freeing slaves.

Perhaps Sherman actually violated the law, but even if he did not, his actions were in clear opposition to any notion that the Civil War was a war of racial justice.

One final note on the Fort Pickering episode: There is not a single reference about Fort Pickering in Ketchum's huge pictorial history of the Civil War, in Randall and Donald's classic college text book, in Boatner's dictionary, or by McPherson in his many works. The U.S. Army's utilization of slave labor while allegedly waging war to eliminate it just doesn't fit the story line.

**Expulsion of Families from Memphis, September 1862**

While in command in Memphis, Sherman began to see the extent to which the Southern people would resist submitting to the federal government. He began to realize that normal tactics were not going to bring rapid progress in the war. Therefore, he developed a theory of collective responsibility, a sort of guilt by association, location, or happenstance. Historian John Bennett Walters explains, "Under this theory it was no longer necessary to establish individual or community guilt before inflicting punishment; he could retaliate upon any who happened to be within reach."

In late September, Sherman issued Special Order No. 254, which read in part:

> Whereas many families of known rebels and of Confederates in arms against us having been permitted to reside in peace and comfort in Memphis, and whereas the Confederate authorities either sanction or permit the firing on unarmed boats carry passengers and goods, for the use and benefit of the inhabitants of Memphis, it is ordered that for every boat so fired on ten families must be expelled from Memphis.
>
> The provost-marshal will extend the list already prepared so

as to have on it at least thirty names, and on every occasion when a boat is fired on will draw by lot ten names, who will be forthwith notified an allowed three days to remove to a distance of 25 miles from Memphis.[59]

Within a week of the issuance of this order at least two more steamboats were fired upon, leading to another atrocity.[60] At very minimum, these expulsions violated the constitutional guarantee against unreasonable searches and seizures (Fourth Amendment); the taking of private property without due process of law (Fifth Amendment); and the collective punishment of citizens deprived of the right of trial by jury and to be confronted with witnesses against them (Sixth Amendment).

### The Burning of Randolph, Tennessee, October 1862

Concurrent with the expulsion of civilians from their homes in Memphis, an obscure event was taking shape upstream. On October 4, 1862, Sherman had the town of Randolph, Tennessee, burned. One has to dig though history journals to find out about this incident because all the standard, mainstream histories of the Civil War (i.e., Randall and Donald, Ketchum, Boatner) make no mention.

The town of Randolph was located on the bluffs of the Mississippi River in Tipton County, Tennessee, a few miles north of Memphis. It was a small but growing river port platted with thirty to forty blocks in the 1820s. By 1834, Randolph was large enough to support its own newspaper, the *Randolph Recorder*.[61]

Sharpshooters in the vicinity of the town apparently inflicted serious small-arms fire on the government steamboats that supplied Sherman from upriver. Sherman ordered Lt. Col. Charles C. Walcutt to take his Forty-sixth Ohio Volunteers to Randolph and burn the town, which he did.[62] Sherman must have been pleased because he promoted Walcutt to full colonel in less than two weeks. Boatner records the date of Walcutt's promotion (October 16, 1862) without mention of the events that led up to it.[63]

In a written report to Grant, Sherman said the people of the South "cannot be made to love us, [they] can be made to fear us, and dread the passage of troops through their country." The firing on steamships stopped but only for a few days. Sherman seemed to think blind retaliation was the only thing that would force Southerners to

*Charles C. Walcutt took his Forty-sixth Ohio Volunteers to the town of Randolph, Tennessee. On October 4, 1862, the soldiers burned the city to the ground on the orders of Gen. William T. Sherman. Walcutt was promoted to full colonel two weeks later. After the war, he became warden of the Ohio State Penitentiary. Randolph was never rebuilt.* (Courtesy Library of Congress)

submit. "We must make the people feel that every attack on a road here will be resented by the destruction of some one of their towns or plantations elsewhere. All adherents of their cause must suffer for these cowardly acts."[64]

One of the many ironies of the war is that the original land grant for the town of Randolph was owned by a black man who obtained the title due to his service in the Revolutionary War. His successors in title settled the claim with the townspeople for $8,000 in 1835.[65]

By the end of October, Sherman sent Walcutt and his Ohio volunteers across the river to Arkansas "to destroy all the houses, farms and corn fields" for fifteen miles.[66] The Arkansas side of the Mississippi River is floodplain, low terrain that offers no vantage point from which to fire on boats. Thus, Sherman chose to demonstrate his policy of collective responsibility on the civilian population of Arkansas not because they had fired on his boats, but because they were Southerners. This constituted the same violation of the Bill of Rights as Sherman's expulsion of innocent citizens from Memphis.

### Expulsion of Jews from Paducah and Other Anti-Semitic Actions, December 1862

The story of the expulsion of the Paducah Jews from their homes is a dark, bizarre moment in American history, one that is almost completely unknown outside the Jewish community. The fact that the U.S. Army conducted its own form of *pogrom* right here on American soil, speaks volumes on the extent of ignorance about the atrocities that took place during the Civil War.

The United States government needed cotton during the war for uniforms, blankets, canvas, and other items. The Lincoln administration decided to permit trade with the South through trading licenses that were issued and regulated by the treasury and war departments. Much of this regulated trade occurred in and around Memphis and fell under the jurisdiction of the U.S. Army in June 1862. Naturally, some of the trade was conducted illegally, without license or official government sanction.

There are many references to cotton traders making a fortune during the war, some of whom were Jewish. One such cotton trader was Jesse Grant, father of the general. Jesse Grant signed a contract in December 1862 with three prominent Jewish brothers from Cincinnati, Harmon, Henry, and Simon Mack. The elder Grant promised to use

*Jesse Grant, father of Ulysses S. Grant, was a licensed cotton trader in West Tennessee. He was in a partnership with three Jewish brothers from Cincinnati when his son expelled all Jews from his area of command.* (Courtesy Library of Congress)

his influence with his son to obtain a permit that would allow the Macks to trade with the Southern states.[67] Even Lincoln knew something of the extent of the black market. He wrote to a friend, "The army itself is diverted from fighting the rebels to speculating in cotton."[68] Indeed, Gen. Stephen A. Hurlbut "participated in the smuggling himself" once he was appointed post commander in Memphis. He "then blamed Jewish merchants for the entire problem."[69]

Perhaps the actual presence of Jesse Grant and his Jewish partners in Holly Springs, Mississippi, prompted an indignant General Grant to issue the expulsion order.[70] Or, it might have been a message Grant received from Washington the day the order was issued.[71] There are numerous explanations, but since Grant made no reference to this matter in his *Personal Memoirs,* and his son, Frederick D. Grant, subsequently wrote in 1907 that the expulsion of Jews was a matter that was "long past and best not referred to," we will never know for certain.[72]

What we know is that Grant issued his infamous General Orders No. 11, December 17, 1862, from the field in Holly Springs back to his headquarters in Paducah. By the terms of this order, all Jews in his military district (northern Mississippi, West Tennessee, and western Kentucky) were to be expelled on twenty-four-hour notice. The order read:

> The Jews, as a class violating every regulation of trade established by the Treasury Department and also department orders, are hereby expelled from the department within twenty-four hours from the receipt of this order.
>
> Post commanders will see that all of this class of people be furnished passes and required to leave, and any one returning after such notification will be arrested and held in confinement until an opportunity occurs of sending them out as prisoners, unless furnished with permit from headquarters.
>
> No passes will be given these people to visit headquarters for the purpose of making personal application for trade permits.[73]

The order was issued under Grant's authority by his adjutant, John A. Rawlings, who was a lieutenant colonel at the time. It was preceded by two other orders on subsequent days in November 1862 aimed at the Jews. From LaGrange, Tennessee, on November 9, Grant sent this order to General Hurlbut in Jackson, Tennessee,

"Refuse all permits to come south of Jackson for the present. The Israelites especially should be kept out." The next day, Grant sent this order to General Webster also in Jackson, "Give orders to all the conductors on the road that no Jews are to be permitted to travel on the railroad southward from any point. They may go north and be encouraged in it; but they are such an intolerable nuisance that the department must be purged of them."[74]

Once issued, Order No. 11 was immediately executed in Paducah, Holly Springs, and Oxford, Mississippi, where Jewish soldiers under Grant's command were stationed. The order prompted the resignation in the field of a Jewish officer, Capt. Phillip Trounstine of Ohio. Trounstine's letter of resignation cited as cause of his resignation, among other things, "the taunts and malice, of those to whom my religious opinions are known, brought on by the effect that [General Order No. 11] has instilled into their minds."[75]

In Paducah, thirty Jewish men and their families were rounded up and hurriedly sent upriver to Cincinnati. Rabbi Bertram W. Korn says in his *American Jewry and the Civil War* that only two Jews were left behind. "Two dying women [were] permitted to remain behind in neighbors' care." Two of the Jewish men expelled with this group had already served enlistments in the U.S. Army.[76]

Historian John E. L. Robertson says the oral history of the contemporary Paducah Jewish community holds that the U.S. Army searched every house looking for Jews. Some were hidden by citizens during the searches. One story claims a soldier knocked on the door of a residence demanding to know, "'What are you?' The resident of the house answered truthfully, 'Tailor.' To which the soldier replied, 'Sorry to bother you Mr. Taylor, but I'm looking for Jews.'"[77]

Before the Jews were rounded up in Paducah, Cesar J. Kaskel dashed off a telegram to Lincoln protesting "this inhuman order, the carrying out of which would be the grossest violation of the Constitution and our rights as citizens under it, [and] which will place us . . . as outlaws before the whole world." According to Korn, this message was ignored because it was intercepted by the War Department, or Lincoln's secretaries set it aside, or Lincoln could "lend it no credence." It would be the protest messages from Jewish communities, publications across the North, and members of Congress that would eventually obtain Lincoln's reversal of the order.[78]

In Holly Springs, a party of Jewish businessmen from the North were forced to evacuate to Memphis on foot. One of the Jews, Lazarus Silberman from Chicago, had been imprisoned briefly in Holly Springs for violating the order by attempting to contact Grant.

In Oxford, a group of four Jews who had been traveling in the South at the outbreak of war and attempting to get back home in the North, were arrested the day after the order was issued. Their horse, buggy, and luggage were confiscated. One of the men repeatedly asked why this was happening to them. The answer given, "Because you are Jews, and neither a benefit to the Union or Confederacy."[79]

Historians are puzzled that at least two Tennessee Jewish communities were not affected by Grant's order, Jackson and Memphis. According to historian Stephen V. Ash, the order was reportedly not carried out in Jackson because the federal commander there, Brig. Gen. Jeremiah C. Sullivan, thought it was unjust and simply ignored it.[80] Sullivan's presence there was fortunate for the small Jewish community (the first Jackson synagogue was not organized until 1885); he commanded the Jackson post for only about five weeks, from November to December 1862.[81]

By far the largest Jewish community under Grant's control was in Memphis. The Jews in Memphis were not expelled, but no one seems to know why. Rabbi James A. Wax says Grant's order was first published in the Memphis *Daily Bulletin* on January 6, 1863, two days after Grant received orders from Washington to revoke the expulsion order. Grant rescinded the order the next day.[82]

Lincoln met with a delegation of Jewish leaders, including Cesar Kaskel on January 4, 1863. He sent them the same day to Gen. Henry Halleck, the supreme army commander, with a note to revoke Grant's order. Halleck's telegram that day to Grant was worded rather strangely, leading Korn to speculate that Halleck didn't want to send it.

> A paper purporting to be General Orders No. 11, issued by you December 17, has been presented here. By its terms, it expels all Jews from your department. If such an order has been issued, it will be immediately revoked.[83]

By the time the Kaskel delegation met with Lincoln, resolutions condemning Grant were in the works in the Senate and the House.

In the Senate, the Republicans were able to delay introduction of a resolution by Sen. Lazarus Powell of Kentucky until January 9, 1863, two days after the order was rescinded. Powell argued that even though the order was lifted, it was important to let the commanders in the field know "they are not to encroach upon the rights and privileges of the peaceable loyal citizens of this country." In debate on the Senate floor, Powell reminded his colleagues that "General Grant might just as well expel the Baptists, or the Methodists, or the Episcopalians, or the Catholics, as a class as to expel the Jews. All are alike protected in the enjoyment of their religion by the Constitution of our country." Sen. Henry Wilson of Massachusetts (a future vice president) spoke against debating the Powell resolution, saying it would be wrong "to strike a general in the field, and condemn him unheard," which, of course, was precisely what Grant had done to the Jews. The motion to table the resolution carried 30-7, thus ending Senate debate on the matter before it began. All seven votes against tabling the resolution came from border and western states, included both senators from Kentucky, both from Oregon, and one each from California, Missouri, and Delaware. Not a single senator north of the Mason-Dixon Line voted to debate Grant's outrage.[84]

Wilson's support of Grant's action against Jews seems to be consistent with his personal feelings. At the time, Judah P. Benjamin had resigned from the U.S. Senate following Louisiana's secession in 1861. Wilson pointed out tongue-in-cheek that Benjamin's "adopted country" protects the rights even of "that race that stoned prophets and crucified the Redeemer of the world." Another supporter of Order No. 11 was Tennessee unionist "Parson" William G. Brownlow. In a letter to the *Cincinnati Daily Times*, Brownlow wrote, "It is useless to disguise the fact that nineteen out of every twenty cases brought to light, of all this smuggling, turns out to be the work of certain circumcised Hebrews."[85]

Mysteries remain. History does not tell us why the Jews in Memphis were not affected by Grant's order. Ash offers no explanation why the order was not carried out there. Wax suggests it was because the order was not published in the Memphis paper until the eve of its revocation, but he does not explain why its publication was delayed. Korn suggests the order was not carried out in Memphis because it was not part of Grant's department, but this is erroneous.[86]

The fate of the Paducah Jews is another mystery. If they returned after the order was lifted, what did they find of their abandoned homes and businesses? Little is known, but given the record of widespread looting, stealing, and corruption during the war, it is doubtful that their property was still there.

Some of the Paducah Jews did return, but Cesar Kaskel apparently did not. Or if he did, he did not stay long. Kaskel soon settled in New York and opened a haberdashery store on Fifth Avenue that was in business for decades. Others moved to Louisville or back to Germany during or soon after the war's end.[87]

The expulsion of the Paducah Jews violated Article I, Section 9 of the U.S. Constitution. The expulsion had the same effect as a bill of attainder, which is specifically withheld from the powers of Congress. Enacting a bill of attainder makes it illegal for a person to be Jewish, or Christian, or Southern, or Cherokee, whatever the government decides. It is the power to declare the infamy of a person or a whole class of people. This event also raises the question of the federal government's power to deploy the military forces of the United States within its borders and rule by martial law or military decree even in a location where no emergency or act of insurrection exists.

### Attack on the Yazoo Valley (Mississippi), May 1863

In December 1862, Sherman left Memphis with 32,000 men on steamboats headed down river to wreak as much destruction as possible on the state of Mississippi. To add to the devastation, Sherman issued General Order No. 7, which allowed the boats shot at from the river bluffs to stop and burn the nearest houses and farms. The Confederates moved as much cordwood away from the river as possible in order to reduce the fuel supply for the steamships. When the steamboats needed fuel, troops with axes would disembark and chop up fences, houses, and barns.[88]

Occupying armies never fully subdued the countryside for long. The more brutal the tactics used, the more it galvanizes the locals to repel the invader. This lesson was learned by the Germans in France, Holland, and Norway; the French in Algeria; the French and Americans in Indo-China; the Americans in Iraq; and by the Israelis in Lebanon and the Gaza Strip.

By the spring of 1863, Sherman ordered Gen. Frank P. Blair, a Princeton University graduate, to "strip the Yazoo Valley." Blair burned a half-million bushels of corn and stole one thousand head of cattle and three hundred horses and mules. In retaliation against the civilians of Mississippi whose only "crime" was being civilians in Mississippi, Blair (under orders from Sherman) destroyed every grist mill in the valley.[89] Boatner does not even mention Confederate resistance during this "Yazoo Expedition," meaning there was no organized force opposing Sherman and Blair, and their military operations were carried out against civilians.[90]

The crimes of Blair and Sherman against the civilians of Mississippi violated paragraph 22 of the Lieber Code, which distinguishes between "the private individual belonging to a hostile country and the hostile country itself, with its men in arms." Blair and Sherman made no such distinction with a military operation conducted against civilians. Furthermore, they violated the Fourth Amendment by unreasonable seizures of private property; the Fifth Amendment by taking private property without due process of law; and the Sixth Amendment by imposing collective punishment of citizens through seizure and destruction of property without the right of a jury trial.

### Siege of Vicksburg, Mississippi, May 19-July 4, 1863

Grant was present for the campaign to besiege and reduce Vicksburg. Prior to the war, Vicksburg was a commercial center of 4,500 souls that occupied a high bluff overlooking a sharp meander in the Mississippi River. It was founded in 1820 and named for a conscientious objector to the war for Independence, Newitt Vick. Army gunboats attempted to take Vicksburg and open the river to federal operations in 1862 but were repelled.

The movement of military forces and the details of the fighting are unimportant. What is important is that the U.S. Army bombarded civilians, Americans on American soil. Americans whose place in the union of states the U.S. Army was ostensibly fighting to save. Americans whose town became the battlefield in the fighting between two armies. Americans who were indiscriminately starved into submission.

"Civilians were suffering from unceasing bombardment and the shortage of food."[91] During the siege, soldiers and civilians had been living largely underground due to bombardment. When rations ran out, they probably ate the horses first. When the horses ran out, they ate mules and rats.[92]

*Princeton University graduate Gen. Frank P. Blair followed General Sherman's orders to "strip the Yazoo Valley" in the spring of 1863. Blair devastated the area by burning corn and stealing livestock.* (Courtesy Library of Congress)

The Confederate commander at Vicksburg, Gen. John Clifford Pemberton, was a Pennsylvanian who sided with the South because his wife was from Virginia. Pemberton surrendered the Confederate garrison on July 4, 1863, because he thought he could get the better terms on that day of all days.

The bombardment and starvation of civilians violated paragraph 19 of the Lieber Code, which protects civilians, "especially women and children," from bombardment. Paragraph 25 of the code protects "the inoffensive citizen of the hostile country" from "privation." These actions also violated the Sixth Amendment in that criminal punishment was imposed on the civilians of Vicksburg without any procedural protections.

There is little wonder that the people of this small town did not again celebrate Independence Day until 1944.

### Destruction of Jackson, Mississippi, July 17-19, 1863

When Vicksburg surrendered on July 4, Grant ordered Sherman to move east and take the state capital of Jackson. The Confederate Army evacuated Jackson on July 16, leaving the U.S. Army to take the city without resistance. While U.S. soldiers destroyed the town, Sherman gave a banquet for his officers in the governor's mansion. After a three-day rampage, a Northern journalist reported:

> They left the entire business section in ruins, burned most of the better residences, dragged furniture into the streets to be demolished, and looted homes, churches, and the state library. A correspondent of the *Chicago Times* reported that the only fine residences left standing were those occupied by some of the general officers; and in summing up his impression of the sack of the town, he state that "such complete ruin and devastation never followed the footsteps of any army before."[93]

The destruction of private property in Jackson was a violation of paragraph 38 of the Lieber Code. "Private property, unless forfeited by crimes or by offenses of the owner, can be seized only by way of military necessity, for the support or other benefit of the Army or of the United States." It is hard to see that razing the business district, looting and burning private homes and churches, has anything to do with military necessity. Indeed, it is nothing but retribution and the venting of hatred.

One's imagination is taxed to the limit when attempting to understand the hollow viciousness that manifested itself in the destruction of the Mississippi state library and the states' irreplaceable records.

**Civilian Hostages Taken by the U.S. Army in McMinnville, Tennessee, Fall of 1863**

In an attempt to halt Confederate guerrilla activity in Middle Tennessee, the U.S. Army began taking civilian hostages in the town of McMinnville. Col. H. C. Gilbert ordered the arrest of two wealthy locals, Zenas Sanders and John Martin. Both men were known secessionists. When Gilbert arrested the men, he announced his intention "to hold them hostage for the lives and safety of the Unionist population" of the area. Sanders was released for the purpose of communicating with the Confederates in the hills east of the town, but Martin was held in the stockade.[94]

Other civilians were soon arrested. James M. Green was charged with harboring and encouraging bushwhackers. Green's son was alleged to be with the guerrillas. William Anderson was accused of being a secessionist and supporter of guerrillas. Isaac Deaton was arrested and released in order to get the word back to Confederate sympathizers that their lives and property would be in danger as long as Union sympathizers were attacked."[95]

According to historian Michael R. Bradley, who has researched and written extensively about the U.S. Army occupation of Middle Tennessee, "The 'get tough' policy did not work and guerrillas continued to be active throughout the area."[96] So much so, federals were forced to send expeditions to look for them.

On occasions, the guerrillas were found and some were killed. But when local residents declined to provide information about their whereabouts, the U.S. Army plundered or burned their homes and crops.[97]

The civilian hostage takings in McMinnville violated paragraph 23 of the Lieber Code, which states, "Private citizens are no longer murdered, enslaved, or carried off to distant parts, and the inoffensive individual is as little disturbed in his private relations as the commander of the hostile troops can afford to grant in the overruling demands of a vigorous war."

**Closing of Jewish Businesses in Memphis, December 1863**

Although the Jews of Memphis were spared Grant's expulsion

order of December 1862, they suffered other indignities the following year. In December 1863, Gen. Stephen Hurlbut issued his General Order No. 162 requiring all clothing stores in Memphis not having his permission "to keep and sell military clothing" to ship immediately such stocks of clothing North.[98] Apparently, there were only seventeen clothing stores in Memphis at this time, and fifteen were Jewish establishments. The order specified the following businesses as subject to these requirements:

- Sampter and Lepstadtch
- Scheadzki and Company
- Kohn and Company
- I. Schwab
- Loeb and Bro.
- M. Skaller and Company
- Fuld Bros. And Company
- Loeb and Company
- S. And L.S. Hellman
- H. Newmark
- G. F. Morris and Company
- Moss and Company
- Stow and Schapsky
- L. Mayer and Company
- Krouse and Company

"These 15 stores were all owned by Jews."[99] Rabbi Korn states, "Prejudice was the controlling factor" in the issuance of the order. How could all fifteen Jewish businesses be guilty of violating U.S. Army regulations and the only two non-Jewish businesses, innocent?[100]

Korn's analysis accurately reflects the deep anti-Semitism that Sherman had already evidenced in Memphis. Earlier in 1862, Sherman complained of having to deal with "swarms of Jews" in Memphis.[101] Yet, the anti-Semitism of the U.S. Army extended beyond Memphis. At almost the same time of the Memphis controversy, Gen. Benjamin Butler, federal commander in New Orleans, wrote Secretary of War Edwin M. Stanton and applied the word "treachery" to the Jews of New Orleans. He compared their profitable mercantile businesses to Judas's thirty pieces of silver.[102]

Perhaps it goes deeper than simple prejudice. According to

*Gen. Stephen Hurlbut accused every Jewish-owned clothing store in Memphis of illegally trading in military clothing and closed them in December 1863. He was charged with corruption in 1865 but was honorably discharged.* (Courtesy Library of Congress)

historian Selma Lewis, it wasn't the Jews who were guilty of smuggling, rather it was General Hurlbut. Instead of halting smuggling, Hurlbut participated in it "and then blamed Jewish merchants for the entire problem."[103] The contemporary Jewish press at the time charged that one of the two non-Jewish clothing stores, Tickner & Co., "not only knew in advance that such an order was to be issued, but were given permits to bring such military goods to Memphis and monopolize the trade."[104]

Perhaps greed was as much a motive as prejudice. If this is correct, and if Hurlbut participated in the scheme to monopolize the military clothing business to the detriment of the Jews and the benefit of his friends, then the Lieber Code paragraph 46 was violated. "Neither officers nor soldiers are allowed to make use of their position or power in the hostile country for private gain, not even for commercial transactions otherwise legitimate." In addition, it was an illegal taking to force the Jewish businesses to send their stocks North. This violated the Fifth Amendment by taking private property without due process of law. The order was tantamount to a verdict of guilty for the Jewish businesses without the opportunity to face their accusers or to a jury trail, a violation of the Sixth Amendment.

Later Hurlbut was charged with corruption, rightly so according to Boatner, but received an honorable discharge in June 1865. After the war, Hurlbut was elected to the Illinois legislature and again charged with corruption. He also served several terms in Congress.[105]

**Destruction of Meridian, Mississippi, February 1864**

At the beginning of 1864, Sherman moved his forces from the Chattanooga area, where they had imposed a brutal occupation on civilians, back to Vicksburg, Mississippi. He was disturbed by the Confederate forces operating in the state because they could threaten control of the Mississippi River. Once there, Sherman "resumed his campaign of terror on a more extensive scale" than before.[106]

Sherman moved eastward from Vicksburg toward Meridian, an important railroad center and supply base for the Confederates. In spite of that, Confederate forces withdrew from Meridian, and Sherman occupied the town without a fight on February 14. He spent five days "unofficially destroying the town." In his report to Grant, Sherman noted:

> For five days 10,000 men worked hard and with a will in that work
> of destruction, with axes, crowbars, sledges, clawbars, and with fire,
> and I have no hesitation in pronouncing the work as well done.
> Meridian with its depots, store-houses, arsenal, hospitals, offices,
> hotels, and cantonments no longer exists.[107]

Store-houses sound a lot like warehouses, which no doubt were
mostly civilian. After all, Meridian had been *a town* before Sherman
got through with it. This violated paragraph 38 of the Lieber Code,
which prohibits the destruction of private property except though
military necessity. But what could have been necessary about
destroying a town that was taken without resistance?

Hospitals, offices, hotels, what sort of military targets are these?
Sherman and his forces deliberately broke paragraph 34 of the code,
exempting hospitals and churches from military use, much less
destruction. Grant was also guilty because he failed to halt or punish
Sherman when he reported the destruction to him.

In his entry on the Meridian Campaign, Boatner whitewashes the
crimes committed against the people of Meridian. He mentions only
that Sherman destroyed railroads, resources, and facilities, which does
not adequately inform the reader of what actually took place.[108]

**Destruction between Meridian and Vicksburg, Mississippi,
February-March 1864**

The Confederates had skirmished with Sherman's forces here
and there, token resistance, as they moved east from Vicksburg
to Meridian. However, they left the state as Sherman approached
Meridian (except for Nathan Bedford Forrest); thus, the U.S. Army
faced no opposition in its destructive return to Vicksburg. Boatner
terminates his narrative of this campaign at Meridian, failing to
mention anything about the systematic pillage as Sherman retraced
his steps to Vicksburg.

Forrest continued to operate in the northeastern quadrant of the
state, and although he pulled off a stunning defeat of a superior force
at West Point, Mississippi, neither he nor any other Confederates
menaced Sherman during this period. This is important because
military necessity cannot credibly be invoked when there are no
opposition forces in the field. Furthermore, historian John Bennett
Walters notes that the lack of military opposition freed Sherman to
"[turn] his men loose on the towns, villages, and farms along the
return route to Vicksburg." Sherman's *Memoirs* fail to record the

havoc, but he notes that other sources including official reports and correspondence published in both Southern and Northern newspapers tell the story of "wanton waste, arson, looting, and other indignities visited upon the defenseless citizens by a ruthless soldiery." Even civilian food supplies were wasted. A refugee wrote that one could not hear a chicken crow within ten miles of the path of Sherman's troops.[109]

At one small town, Enterprise, no house was said to have escaped Sherman's thieves.

> Locks and bars availed nothing. Every room, trunk, wardrobe, and the beds and bedding were plundered and torn up. . . . Everything they could carry off was taken, and what they could not, was torn up and destroyed, even to servants' underclothes.[110]

Paragraph 43 of the Lieber Code states that "all robbery, all pillage or sacking . . . are prohibited under the penalty of death, or such other severe punishment as may seem adequate for the gravity of the offense.

In reality, this was the final tune-up in preparation of even more vicious attacks on the civilians of Georgia.

> As [Sherman] prepared to transfer his troops to a new theater of operations in Georgia in the spring of 1864, he could view his first full-dress performance in total war with satisfaction. He had accomplished his major objectives of destroying the resources of Mississippi and paralyzing its lines of communication, and he had demonstrated to the civilian population how terrible their lot could be made in a ware conducted without regard for orthodox rules.[111]

### Extortion, Torture, and Murder of Soldiers and Civilians in and around Jackson, Tennessee, February-March 1864

In the spring of 1864, in and around Jackson, Tennessee, the U.S. Army tortured and murdered prisoners of war; threatened, murdered, arrested, and stole and extorted money from civilians; and wantonly destroyed private property. These deeds were recorded in a report by Confederate lieutenant colonel W. M. Reed. He had been ordered to investigate the various allegations that came to the attention of Gen. Nathan Bedford Forrest. Reed's report became the basis for the demand by Forrest on the federal commander in Memphis to turn over the U.S. Army officers and enlisted men responsible for these crimes.[112]

Reed's report claims that U.S. colonel Fielding Hurst, a Tennessean from McNairy County commanding Tennessee Federal Volunteers, rode into Jackson on or about February 7, 1864, demanding money from the townspeople or else they would burn the town. Hurst extorted $5,139.25 from the Jackson civilians. The reason this odd amount of money was demanded is that the U.S. Army had assessed Hurst this amount for entering and robbing the house of a Mrs. Newman in Jackson in 1863. Hurst was going to have to pay restitution, so he went back to Jackson to steal the restitution money.

Reed's report also claims Confederate POWs were tortured and murdered. A Lt. Willis Dodds of Newsom's regiment in Forrest's command was said to have been arrested in his father's home in Henderson County, Tennessee, on March 9, 1864, and tortured to death under Hurst's orders. An eyewitness saw Dodds's body shortly after his murder.

> It was most horribly mutilated, the face having been skinned, the nose cut off, the under jaw disjointed, the privates cut off, and the body otherwise barbarously lacerated and most wantonly injured, and that his death was brought about by the most inhuman process of torture.[113]

Other murders documented in Reed's report include five officers and enlisted men who were shot by the U.S. Army, one of whom was forbidden burial for four days, and a helpless, crippled youth. "Mr. Lee Doroughty, a citizen of McNairy County, a youth about sixteen years of age, deformed and almost helpless, was arrested and wantonly murdered by [the] same command about 1st January, 1864."

Even the clergy was subject to arrest by the U.S. Army. On March 22, 1864, Forrest demanded the release of Rev. G. W. D. Harris of Dyer County, Tennessee, and several other citizens. Forrest threatened to execute five federal prisoners if Harris should die from ill treatment while in custody.[114] The lack of response to Forrest's demand for justice led him to proclaim Hurst's infamy.[115]

This is more of Sherman's implementation of collective responsibility on the civilian population of West Tennessee simply because they were Southerners, violating the Fourth, Fifth, and Sixth Amendments to the Constitution. Murder, torture, robbery, and extortion of civilians are crimes at all times and expressly forbidden as a capital offense in paragraph 44 of the Lieber Code.

## Battle of Yellow Tavern, Virginia, May 1864

The Battle of Yellow Tavern, Virginia, was an attempted cavalry raid on Richmond by Gen. Philip Sheridan. Gen. J. E. B. Stuart, Lee's famous cavalry leader, was mortally wounded in this battle. Although the federals won the battle, their attempt to raid Richmond was thwarted.

As the Confederates withdrew, they placed land mines, or torpedoes, along the likely route of the advancing federals. Sheridan wrote in his *Personal Memoirs* that many of the land mines exploded, killing horses and wounding soldiers.

> The torpedoes were loaded shells planted on each side of the road, and so connected by wires attached to friction-tubes in the shells, that when a horse's hoof struck a wire the shell was exploded by the jerk on the improvised lanyard. After the loss of several horses and the wounding of some of the men by these torpedoes, I gave directions to have them removed, if practicable, so about twenty-five of the prisoners were brought up and made to get down on their knees, feel for the wire in the darkness, following them up and unearth the shells.[116]

McClellan had done the same thing two years earlier at Williamsburg, except this time the Lieber Code was in effect. Forcing Confederate POWs to clear land mines was a violation of paragraph 75, which spares POWs from "intentional suffering or indignity." Pressing POWs to clear land mines by hand in the darkness would be extremely hazardous. U.S. Army regulations in effect today proscribe the use of POWs in work that is "injurious to health or dangerous because of the inherent nature of the work."[117]

## Civilians Executed by the U.S. Army in Fayetteville, Tennessee, June 1864

The U.S. Army's supply trains were under constant attack in Tennessee and elsewhere. Southerners, probably civilians as well as Confederate military, took potshots when the trains were at vulnerable locations. The army had been looking for one particular group of raiders and had received no help from the local people in tracking them down, according to historian Michael R. Bradley in his 2003 book *With Blood and Fire*.

Gen. Eleazer A. Paine of Ohio decided that retaliation would provide information on the raiders' whereabouts, or at least stop the harassment of trains. In June 1864, he and his command rode into Fayetteville, Tennessee, the county seat of Lincoln County (named for Revolutionary War hero Benjamin Lincoln). He seized hostages, dragged them to the court square, and announced that four would be executed unless someone came forward with information as to the location of the raiders.

One unarmed civilian hostage was released; three others were shot. ("They were executed at the spot where the Lincoln County Library now stands," according to Bradley.[118]) These murders were certainly not the first ordered by General Paine. Bradley claims Paine had routinely murdered Confederate prisoners (in uniform), a practice which earned him the nickname as the "Hanging General."[119]

Murder of unarmed civilians was expressly forbidden in the Lieber Code. Paragraph 44 of the code states, "All wanton violence committed against persons in the invaded country . . . all rape, wounding, maiming, or killing of such inhabitants, are prohibited under the penalty of death, or such other severe punishment as may seem adequate for the gravity of the offense." Paragraph 148 of the code forbids the proclamation of infamy on civilians and expresses abhorrence for such an outrage. Further, it states, "The sternest retaliation should follow the murder committed in consequence of such proclamation, made by whatever authority."

Clearly, General Paine was guilty of murder as were those who obeyed his illegal commands, and it is equally clear that they all went completely unpunished. Paine went on to become a businessman after the war.[120]

### Kidnapping and Murder in North Georgia, July-October 1864

Perhaps the most heinous mass-casualty crime of the war was the kidnapping of several hundred women and their children at Roswell, Georgia, in July 1864. Roswell was home to a large woolen mill and two cotton mills about twenty miles north of Atlanta. To the surprise of the U.S. Army, these mills were producing cloth right up to the time of their capture.

A U.S. Army unit commanded by Gen. Kenner Garrard took Roswell and burned the mills, one of which had a French flag flying over it (hoping for special treatment under a neutral flag). Garrard reported the destruction to Sherman on July 6 and advised him of the female workers at one of the cotton mills.[121]

Sherman ordered Garrard the following day to arrest the owners of the mills, charge them with treason, and hang them without trial should the "impulse of anger" overcome him. Garrard was also advised to kidnap the women and send them on a ten-mile forced march.

> To make the matter complete you will arrest the owners and employees and send them, under guard, charged with treason, to Marietta, and I will see as to any man in America hoisting the French flag and then devoting his labor and capital in supplying armies in open hostility to our Government and claiming the benefit of his neutral flag. Should you, under the impulse of anger, natural at contemplating such perfidy, hang the wretch, I approve the act before hand. . . .
>
> I repeat my orders that you arrest all the people, male and female, connected with those factories, no matter what the clamor, and let them foot it, under guard to Marietta , whence I will send them by cars to the North. . . The poor women will make a howl. Let them take along their children and clothing, providing they have the means of hauling or you can spare them.[122]

According to historian John Bennett Walters, the abducted women numbering approximately 500, were sent to Indiana perhaps to work in mills there, although this is not clear.[123]

In October 1864, Sherman ordered more indiscriminate murders of north Georgia civilians. Orders addressed to Gen. Louis Watkins, who was positioned near Calhoun, Georgia, state the following: "Cannot you send over about Fairmount and Adairsville, burn ten or twelve houses of known secessionists, kill a few a random, and let them know that it will be repeated every time a train is fired on from Resace to Kingston!"[124]

Murder and kidnapping are crimes at all times, irrespective of war or peace, irrespective of a soldier's uniform or a civilian's street clothes. As stated in the previous section, murder of unarmed civilians was expressly forbidden as a capital offense in paragraph 44 of the Lieber Code. Paragraph 47 of the code reads:

> Crimes punishable by all penal codes, such as arson, murder, maiming, assaults, highway robbery, theft, burglary, fraud, forgery, and rape, if committed by an American soldier in a hostile country

against its inhabitants, are not only punishable as at home, but in all cases in which death is not inflicted the severer punishment shall be preferred.

General Garrard was never punished for his deeds. After the war, he made a living in real estate and devoted his time to the study of history. General Watkins died on active duty in New Orleans after the war without any disciplinary action taken against him.[125] Sherman achieved celebrity status in the North and went west to slaughter Indians.

Overlooked reasons for Reconstruction are control of the conquered Southern states after the war and the installation of compliant governments, so as to avoid indictment and prosecution of the North's heroes after the war.

### Confederate Officers Used as Human Shields in Charleston, August 1864

Under the Lincoln administration, the United States government at its highest levels sanctioned the use of POWs as human shields in battle. In 1864, Secretary of War Stanton approved a plan to move six hundred Confederate POWs from Fort Delaware, where they were detained, to Charleston harbor. There they were to be placed in the line of fire between Confederate positions and U.S. Army lines. The plan was devised by Gen. John G. Foster whose job it was to construct fortifications. The orders came through from the army chief of staff, General Halleck, on August 8, 1864.

> Major General J.G. Foster, Department of the South:
> General: The Secretary of War has directed that 600 rebel officers, prisoners of war, be sent to you, to be confined, exposed to fire, and treated in the same manner as our officers, prisoners of war are treated in Charleston. No exchanges will be made without special instructions of the War Department. Any offer for exchange will be communicated here of the action of the Secretary of War.
> Very respectfully, your obedient servant,
> H.W. Halleck.[126]

This tactic violated paragraphs 56 and 75 of the Lieber Code, which spares POWs from "barbarity" and "intentional suffering or indignity," respectively. Halleck and Foster also violated paragraph

*Gen. John G. Foster used Confederate POWs as human shields in combat at Charleston, South Carolina, August 1864.* (Courtesy Library of Congress)

68, which states, "Modern wars are not internecine wars, in which the killing of the enemy is the object. . . . Unnecessary or revengeful destruction of life is not lawful." The order also clearly violates today's U.S. Army regulations that ban the use of POWs in activities "injurious to health or dangerous."[127]

Boatner's brief biographies of Foster, Halleck, (along with Grant, Sherman, Sheridan, McClellan, Hurlbut, Paine, Garrard, and Walcutt) record no charges against anyone at the command level for violating the Lieber Code. They got off scot-free. For them, there was no code.

### Sherman's Atlanta campaign and March to the Sea, 1864

In a period of only five weeks from mid-November to Christmas 1864, the so-called March to the Sea consisted of numerous war crimes and atrocities of which Sherman, his senior commanders, and many of his men were guilty. Neither Sherman nor any of his commanders were ever charged. The brand of total warfare he levied against the people of Georgia and South Carolina was so destructive, that one military historian (who is also an attorney) believes the Lieber Code was incapable of imposing sufficient restrictions to prevent abuse.

Writing in the *Emory International Law Review* in 1995, U.S. Army major Thomas G. Robisch states the Lieber Code "did not contemplate the type or scope of total warfare which Sherman conceived and practiced. As a result, the Code did not impose significant restrictions on the planning and execution of Sherman's campaigns in Georgia." Rather, Major Robisch's legal analysis focuses on whether Sherman met "the legal standards which are presently applicable to U.S. Forces." Robisch picked out numerous documented events during Sherman's march that show Sherman and his commanders violated U.S. law, international law, or both. We will look at five of those events.[128]

### Confiscation of Civilian Private Property

As a general principle of armies of occupation, Sherman "was required to treat civilians humanely and to desist from taking any action which caused physical suffering to the people under his control." It was Sherman's indiscriminate confiscation and destruction of civilian private property that violates current law, according to Robisch. Sherman took property without paying for it, accounting for it, or providing receipts. "Confiscation of private property under such circumstances is prohibited," Robisch states, citing requirements under the Hague Resolutions and Geneva Conventions.[129]

Sherman's annihilation of Georgia is legendary. Shortly before commencing his march, Sherman revealed his intention to one of his commanders. "I am going into the very bowels of the Confederacy, and propose to leave a trail that will be recognized fifty years hence."[130]

In Atlanta, Sherman made little or no effort to demolish or burn only military targets, leaving civilian houses and buildings alone. Some buildings "with no military value were ignited deliberately by soldiers under Sherman's command. The pillage or purposeless destruction of property constitutes a simple breach of the law of war."[131]

One of Sherman's self-styled sympathetic biographers wrote that he had "a reputation for winking at abuses." Stanley P. Hirschson relates a story of Sherman riding alone without his coat or rank insignia and coming upon a soldier "covered with plunder."

> When Sherman threatened him with arrest, the solder began cursing, using words like "damn" and "hell." Back and forth they argued, until Sherman indentified himself and demanded to know to whom he was speaking. Swinging chickens in his hands, the culprit answered: "Oh, hell, General, I am Abner F. Dean, Chaplain of the 112th Massachusetts." Without bothering to salute, the clergyman picked up whatever he had dropped and walked away.[132]

Following the U.S. Army's destruction at Milledgeville, Georgia, civilians picked over the federal campsites, "seeking anything they could find to eat." An account of the scene records that the roads were "lined with carcasses of horses, hogs, and cattle," and "fields were trampled down and hardly a fence was left standing."[133]

In a Christmas Eve 1864, report to General Halleck, Sherman anticipated the destruction he was about to unleash on the civilian population of South Carolina. "The truth is the whole army is burning with an insatiable desire to wreck vengeance upon South Carolina. I almost tremble at her fate, but feel that she deserves all that seems in store for her."[134]

## Killing Surrendering Confederate Soldiers in Atlanta

Robisch cites the disturbing instance of the murder of Confederate soldiers who were attempting to surrender in Atlanta. "Soldiers who attempt to surrender must be permitted to do so; through the act of surrendering, such personnel receive the status of prisoners of war."[135] The failure to allow surrender is the act of giving no quarter to the enemy, a clear violation of the Lieber Code, paragraphs 60 and 61, "It is against the usage of modern war to . . . give no quarter" (paragraph 60). The Lieber Code does not distinguish between wounded, dying soldiers, or those who have capitulated. "Troops that give no quarter have no right to kill enemies already disabled on the ground, or prisoners captured by other troops" (paragraph 61). Additionally, Robisch states that the killing of surrendering Confederates by U.S. Army infantry would be a violation of existing international law, Geneva Convention Relative to the Treatment of Prisoners of War, Articles 5, 12, and 13.

## Mistreatment of Runaway Slaves

Robisch describes Sherman's mistreatment of runaway slaves as "shockingly poor." As the U.S. Army moved deeper into Georgia, it accumulated a large number of runaway slaves seeking sustenance. Ever mindful of the question of supplies, Sherman repeatedly emphasized to his commanders that food, clothing, shelter, medicine, and transportation should be offered to runaway slaves only if it was available in sufficient supplies and had no affect on his army in the field.

Sherman did nothing to encourage the runaway slaves flocking to his army. Indeed, his actions were quite to the contrary. One of his commanders went so far as to deliberately burn bridges in order to isolate runaway slaves from his army. Robisch explains that under current regulations such persons "would be protected . . . under international law," and as such, "these former slaves would have been entitled to receive certain specific privileges, and as an occupying power, the Union army was responsible to protect these privileges." At very minimum, Robisch states that Sherman should have left behind ample food, medicine, and shelter for the runaway slaves, an action that should not have been difficult to do considering the bounty of foodstuffs his troops were gathering from the countryside.

Failure to do so places Sherman at odds with present requirements found under the Geneva Civilian Convention, Article 4.[136]

**Reprisals against Farmers**

Georgia farmers knew Sherman was coming. Many of them destroyed their own crops and livestock to deprive Sherman of their use, a strategy legal under present international law, as said by Robisch. By targeting for reprisal those Georgia farmers who had destroyed their own property, Sherman violated international law. "Reprisals against civilian and their property or other non-military targets are forbidden." Robisch cites the violation under an army publication from 1956, FM27-10 Change 1, "The Law of Land Warfare, Change 1." Additionally, Robisch notes that any reprisal on civilians is a political matter reserved to the president or the secretary of defense. "Under those modern circumstances, as a theater commander, Sherman would lack the discretion to resort unilaterally to such actions."[137]

**Forcing Confederate POWs and Civilians to Clear Land Mines**

Apparently, the U.S. Army's use of Confederate POWs to detect or clear minefields was a pervasive practice. As documented previously in this chapter, McClellan and Sheridan were guilty of this practice starting in the early days of combat. Sherman added his own twisted crime by using, or at least threatening to use, civilians as well as POWs to clear minefields.

In the field near Kennesaw, Georgia, Sherman ordered "wagon-loads of prisoners, or, if need be, citizens" to be drawn back and forth by long ropes over areas suspected of torpedoes. "Of course an enemy cannot complain of his own traps," Sherman wrote.[138]

> Sherman's use of Confederate prisoners in mine detecting and clearing activities also violated international law. . . . Prisoners must be protected from acts of violence or intimidation, and reprisals against them are prohibited specifically in the Geneva Prisoner of War Convention.[139]

Forcing civilians and POWs to do these sorts of dangerous tasks violate the Lieber Code. Paragraph 33 of the code says it is a "serious breach of the law of war to force the subjects of the enemy into the service of the victorious government." Paragraph 75 of the code was violated as well.

### Psychological Warfare by Sherman, the Terrorist

Was Sherman a psychological warrior? Was he the first terrorist of the modern era? Clearly, his biographers and even certain Lincoln scholars think so. More importantly, it is difficult to read many of Sherman's orders to his commanders without concluding that he thought himself so. The distinction of psychological warfare is important because it leads one to question if Sherman's nineteenth-century actions would be considered acts of terror under present-day standards.

Under the USA Patriot Act, passed in the aftermath of September 11 and reauthorized in 2005 and 2006, the crime of domestic terrorism is defined as any state or federal crime within the United States that appears to be intended to "intimidate or coerce" civilians; influence the policy of a government by intimidation or coercion; or "to affect the conduct of a government by mass destruction, assassination, or kidnapping."[140]

Sherman clearly intended to kill civilians, as evidenced by his use of the feminine pronoun "she" in a January 1864 letter to Maj. R. M. Sawyer. Such intention is indisputable because there were no women in uniform at that time. It is equally clear that as long as there was Southern military resistance in the field, Sherman believed it was open season on Southern civilians for political reasons.

> To those who submit to the rightful law and authority all gentleness and forbearance; but to the petulant and persistent secessionists, why, death is mercy, and the quicker he or she is disposed of the better. . . .
>
> Next year their lands will be taken, for in war we can take them, and rightfully, too, and in another year they may beg in vain for their lives.[141]

Later that year, November 1864, Sherman wrote Halleck that if Southerners wanted to rid themselves of his "barbarity and cruelty," they must stop the war. In other words, his mass destruction and violence was intended to change the policy of the Confederate

*Maj. R. M. Sawyer was ordered by General Sherman to kill civilian men and women in Georgia, January 1864. This act of psychological warfare was carried out on civilian Southern sympathizers.* (Courtesy Library of Congress)

government. It was at this moment, according to biographer Michael Fellman, that Sherman "attained his most fully conscious and self-acknowledged role as a psychological warrior." Though there were military arguments for much of what Sherman did, "his greater purpose was to strike terror into Southern hearts."[142]

Most Lincoln scholars acknowledge Sherman's overindulgence and the application of military power on civilians, but blame the cruelty of war rather than any individual. Randall and Donald explain:

> It cannot be denied that Sherman's march was marred by unjustifiable excess; yet his campaign, being directed against property and Southern resources, was conceived as a substitute for further human slaughter. . . . The fact that he was operating, not against substantial armies but against Southern morale and upon the people, made his presence particularly offensive."[143]

Sherman clearly stated his intentions to kill Southern civilians and inflict massive destruction, which shows premeditation on his part. The object of this violence was bringing about a policy change by the Confederate government. Therefore, his actions meet the elements of domestic terrorism under current law. What's more, Robisch establishes quite convincingly that Sherman violated present-day U.S. military and international laws as well as the code of law of the nineteenth-century United States Army.

### Sherman and Lincoln, War Criminals

World War II was only one life span removed from the bloody hands of Sherman's Southern campaigns, even less than that from the warfare he levied on the Plains Indians. At the close of World War II in 1945, the Allies commissioned and erected an international tribunal to bring top Nazis to justice.

The Charter of the International Military Tribunal, known as the Nuremberg Trial Proceedings, has an eerie and familiar reverberation to it. Title II, Articles 6-13 of this charter establish the jurisdiction of the tribunal. Article 6 enables the tribunal to try and punish individuals' crimes including:

*Gen. William T. Sherman, America's first domestic terrorist. Among his many atrocities, Sherman ordered the murder of civilians, the kidnapping of women and children, the use of POWs to clear minefields, and the deliberate destruction of civilian property and cattle.* (Courtesy Library of Congress)

(a) CRIMES AGAINST PEACE: namely, planning, preparation, initiation or waging of war of aggression . . .

(b) WAR CRIMES: namely . . . murder, ill-treatment or deportation to slave labor or for any other purpose of civilian population of the occupied territory . . . killing of hostages, plunder of public or private property, wanton destruction of cities, towns or villages, or devastation not justified by military necessity;

(c) CRIMES AGINAST HUMANITY: namely, murder . . . deportation, and other inhuman acts committed against any civilian population

Clearly, Sherman and Lincoln were guilty on numerous counts of the crimes listed above. As the political head of state, Lincoln's guilt of "crimes against peace" and initiating and waging a war of aggression cannot be controverted. DiLorenzo has well established that Lincoln had war at the top of his agenda. Sherman's crimes against humanity have been detailed in this chapter. They were war criminals.

**Conclusion**

Lincoln, his administration, and his generals introduced the modern world to the concept of total war. The principle of military necessity was developed and defined for the first time in the Lieber Code. Lincoln's generals first used military necessity in a very limited way, pertaining only to military targets, tactics, and supplies needed to defeat the Confederate forces in the field.

As the war dragged on, the Lincoln administration began to view military necessity in a different light. The objective of the war was to reestablish political authority over the Southern states. Gradually, any action that would likely hasten this was viewed as militarily necessary. Therefore, kidnapping, murder, torture, destruction of food stores and livestock, and massive destruction of the means of food production came to be an acceptable consequence of restoring lost federal authority. As Grant's aide said, the Southern people, not just Southern armies, had to be "annihilated." Civil War destruction and death was on a scale unprecedhiled in human history to that point.

This chapter explodes the myth that the Civil War was civil, or that its conduct was perhaps even righteous. Lincoln scholars and statists assure their readers that the war was conducted in a "relatively restrained" manner.[144] Yet, it is important to expose the savagery of the U.S. Army toward the civilians of the South because military commanders, political theorists, and despots worldwide watch and learn from that which was tolerated in the past in order to apply it to future wars.

The federal government's Civil War theory of military necessity and of total war, originated by Americans to justify the butchering of other Americans, opened Pandora's proverbial box. Next time, the whole world would be involved. It would take another fifty years and the invention of the internal combustion engine, the machine gun, and high explosives before a more costly conflict (World War I) could eclipse the scale of the Civil War in terms of battle deaths. In World War II, the justification for the haphazard destruction of London and massive fire bombings of German and Japanese population centers were the twin evils of military necessity and total war.

# CHAPTER EIGHT

# Secession: Legal in 1860, Legal Today

*"If centralism is ultimately to prevail; if our entire system of free institutions as established by our common ancestors is to be subverted, and an Empire is to be established in their stead; if that is to be the last scene of the great tragic drama now being enacted: then, be assured, that we of the South will be acquitted, not only in our own consciences, but in the judgment of mankind, of all responsibility for so terrible a catastrophe, and from all guilt of so great a crime against humanity."*[1]  —Alexander H. Stephens

The Declaration of Independence established the philosophical framework from which all government in the United States has devolved. Every office erected in the Constitution, every power of government, every limit to the government's reach established therein must be read in the context of the Declaration of Independence. One cannot fully understand the American experiment in government with the Constitution alone.

The fundamental thesis of this book is that the war commonly known as the American Civil War[2] was *not* a war between the Northern and Southern states. Secession was a lawful and legitimate power to be exercised by the states. Lincoln did virtually everything he could to reestablish control of the Southern states, which was outside the law and counterrevolutionary to the principles of the founding of the nation in 1776.

If the Civil War had merely been a power struggle between the Northern and Southern states, with the winning of the war leaving the Northern states with political power over the Southern states, the likely long-term effects would have inflicted much less damage to all the states. No, this war was a war between the Southern states and the federal government in Washington. It was a war to resist the centralization of economic, cultural, political, and military power. It was a war to uphold the most revolutionary principle ever asserted by man. That principle, the "consent of the governed," was the basis upon which the Thirteen Colonies seceded from England.[3]

The Declaration of Independence, the prerequisite to the understanding of the Constitution, articulates one, sole role for government and one, sole source of legitimate power. Read carefully:

> We hold these truths to be self-evident, that all men are created equal, that they are endowed by their Creator with certain unalienable Rights, that among these are Life, Liberty and the pursuit of Happiness.—That to secure these rights, Governments are instituted among Men, deriving their just powers from the consent of the governed.

As expressed by Jefferson and unanimously adopted by the Founding Fathers, the sole purpose of government is to secure the rights of its citizens—nothing more, nothing less, nothing else. Securing those rights is the only reason government among men is established. Moreover, the sole source of government's "just powers" is based on the "consent of the governed." The concept of consent of the governed is the ultimate revolution, which throws off the shackles of tyranny from whichever direction it comes on the political spectrum.

In intellectually conformist twenty-first-century America, few seem to consider why the principle of "consent" remains relevant. It remains relevant because consent is a vital attribute in the fullness of human experience. No sale occurs and no contract between parties is enforceable if either of the parties withholds their consent, or are under duress and cannot exercise consent.

Consider that the difference between a weekend of house arrest and merely staying at home is a matter of consent. The police impose the former while the latter is one's own preference. The difference between sexual assault and intimacy between a man and a woman is consent. Similarly, the difference between extortion and contribution, between a voluntary gift and robbery is consent.

Perhaps the most important cultural influence on Western civilization is Christianity, in which Christ's Crucifixion served as a redeeming sacrifice for all mankind. Just hours before Christ's death, he prayed, "Yet not My will, but Thine be done" (Luke 22:14).

Christ consented to his own death as an offering of sacrifice. If he had not expressed his consent, it would have been willful murder rather than redeeming sacrifice.

Consent is the very basis for civilization, for personal interaction between individuals, and for government itself.

Before we recap the legal basis for secession of the Southern states in the context of the United States Constitution, it is well worth considering what the Civil War accomplished and failed to accomplish.

## What the Civil War Did Not Accomplish

The Lincoln scholars attribute the freeing of the slaves and the preserving of the Union to the federal government's winning of the war, as if no other course of events could have possibly accomplished the same result. Their belief system about history is quite nearly one of predestination.

Their reasoning is that because slavery was ended following the war, war was the only way slavery could have ended. Their viewpoint ignores the demise of slavery in the rest of the world in the nineteenth century. They point instead to the *Texas* v. *White* decision as proof that the Southern states' secession was illegal and Lincoln was merely enforcing the law rather than breaking it. They embrace the concept known as hindsight bias, which has been intellectually developed by historians David Hackett Fischer, John Lewis Gaddis, and others.

The Lincoln scholars make several arguments. The first argues that because secession was illegal and only slave states seceded, then those states fought to preserve slavery. Secondly, the South fought to preserve slavery, and the federal government fought to end it. Thirdly, since the South used force in an attempt to preserve slavery, then the use of violence by the federal government to end it was inevitable. Finally, since the war was inevitable, the federal government is absolved from all violence, carnage, and crimes against the states, the Constitution, and civilians. This is the essence of the contemporary argument by Lincoln scholars.

Arthur Schlesinger, Jr., saw the same moral imperative in the defeat of Jefferson Davis in 1865 as he saw in Adolf Hitler's defeat in 1945. Speaking in 1949 about the Civil War, Schlesinger stated,

"The unhappy fact is that man occasionally works himself into a log-jam; and that log-jam must be burst by violence. . . . We know that well enough from the experience of the last decade." Schlesinger dismissed revisionist historians who examined the cause of the Civil War in its true complexity as "sentimentalists." As historian Edward L. Ayers has noted, Schlesinger believes such revisionists were "insensitive to the evil of slavery and excessively squeamish about using violence to end it."[5]

Schlesinger's hindsight bias constitutes a near simpleminded-ness. The war was not fought in order to free the slaves, generating a by-product of maintaining federal jurisdiction over the states while altering (on a protracted but temporary basis) the body poli-tic. Quite to the contrary, the purpose of the war was to reestablish federal jurisdiction over the states, period. The by-product of that war was the temporary alteration of the body politic that allowed the political demise of slavery. If Schlesinger is correct about the war be-ing caused by slavery, do you suppose the federal government would have called off the war and sent the Ohio and Illinois farm boys back home if the Confederacy had ended slavery in 1863? Of course not.

**The War Did Not Free the Slaves**
Neither Lincoln nor the war itself freed the slaves. That should not be too much of a surprise when one considers that Lincoln was a lifelong white supremacist who favored exclusion of all blacks from the western territories and supported the forced deportation of free blacks back to Africa. As black historian and publisher Leronne Bennett, Jr., has pointed out, the first time any black person was invited to the White House to meet with the president was a meeting of free black businessmen called by Lincoln for the purpose of soliciting their support for their own deportation.

The Thirteenth Amendment to the U.S. Constitution accom-plished instantaneous emancipation. Prior to the war, when the Northern states abolished slavery, it took decades to accomplish and no individual born a slave was ever actually freed, as explained in chapter two. The only place where slavery was instantaneously abol-ished was the South by constitutional amendment.

There is no denying that the individual Northern states moved toward emancipation sooner than the Southern states. Northerners ended slavery under terms favorable to the slave owners. Under the Northern model of manumission, slave owners never freed a single slave by force of law, and they received many years of compensatory work from the freeborn children of their slaves to make up for the expense in rearing them. Additionally, when Northern states enacted their various manumission laws, each of those states subsequently enacted the original Jim Crow laws in order to control or deport free blacks. The elective franchise for free blacks was fanatically opposed in almost every Northern state. It was briefly given to free blacks following the Revolutionary War but quickly taken away in Connecticut, Delaware, New Jersey, New York, Pennsylvania, and Rhode Island.

By the mid-nineteenth century, the tide of history was running against slavery worldwide. The fact that slavery had peacefully ended in dozens of countries around the world during the nineteenth century is evidence of powerful economic, rather than racial, factors in America. Indeed, slavery was an enormously profitable labor system that was not only competitive with the budding wage system of industrial production in the North, but also more efficient according to Robert Fogel and Stanley Engerman. Slavery was not simply "dying out" in America as is portrayed in government schools. Its legal demise was part of the social, economic, political, and military destruction of the South during Radical Reconstruction. In 1860, Mississippi was one of the wealthiest states. From Sherman's destructive rampage back and forth across the state in 1863 to its harsh occupation during Reconstruction, Mississippi became one of the poorest states and remains so today.

Nowhere in the world, save the United States, was there a nineteenth-century war associated with the ending of slavery. The "peculiar institution" was ended peacefully everywhere else.

### The War Did Not Preserve the Union

The idea that the Civil War was fought to "preserve" the Union is one of the most ridiculous ideas foisted on history. The only thing preserved was the federal government's authority over the Southern states. Lincoln certainly fought to keep the Southern states under Union control as conquered provinces, not states.

The last thing the Republicans wanted was the Southern states functionally back in the Union, represented in Congress, and casting electoral votes for president. This would have meant that eleven Southern states would have immediately sent twenty-two Democrats to the U.S. Senate in 1866. It would have pushed the Republicans out of power in the Congress. The Democratic nominee for president in 1868, New York governor Horatio Seymour, might have even beaten Grant with the South delivering the deciding votes and holding balance of power.

The Republican power structure in the North *had* to continue military occupation after the war in order to keep the Southern states out of the Union. If they had allowed the Southern states to come back in, the party that wanted the war, started the war, and won the war would have lost power to the very people they had defeated on the battlefield. Therefore, there was simply no way the Radical Republicans were going to let that happen. As a result, Congress came up with the radical Reconstruction of the South (a misnomer that should have been called the radical Destruction of the South), which established military government for Southern states. The Southern states were forced to ratify the Fourteenth Amendment of the Constitution and renounce secession in their constitutions. Reconstruction, i.e., military occupation, finally collapsed as part of a political deal to allow Republican candidate Rutherford B. Hayes to win the presidency in 1876 by the margin of a single electoral vote.

In 1866, we saw the U.S. Supreme Court rule that "national authority was overturned" by secession in Virginia "and the courts driven out" (*Ex Parte Milligan*, 1866). Likewise, national authority was "overturned" and "driven out" in Tennessee. Similarly, Georgia was governed after the war under the Reconstruction Acts, not under her own laws as she had done prior to military occupation by the U.S. Army. As Justice Swayne noted in *White* v. *Hart* (1871), Georgia was governed under the Reconstruction Acts "from the close of the rebellion until [she] was restored to her normal relations and functions in the Union." It's a verbose admission that secession took Georgia out of the United States until Congress restored her statehood. Furthermore, it is an admission that Georgia was under some form of governance other than the laws of the United States prior to the close of the rebellion. That authority of governance came from the Confederacy, which Georgia voluntarily founded and joined in 1861 just as it had voluntarily founded and joined the United States by its ratification of the Constitution in 1788.

The readmission of Tennessee in July 1866 is additional evidence that Congress did not believe the Union was preserved by the war; Congress wanted quite the opposite. A Senate amendment to the readmission resolution, which was approved by the House on July 23, 1866, plainly states that Tennessee "can only be restored to its former political relations in the Union by the consent of the law-making power of the United States."[6]

Just what was Tennessee's "former political relations in the Union?" Why, it was admission to statehood of course, achieved in 1796 and maintained until the secession plebiscite approved by its citizens in June 1861 had the effect of withdrawal from the Union. One is compelled to inquire how Congress restores a condition of statehood unless a state had it and lost it? Clearly, the historic record shows that Tennessee was admitted to statehood in the United States in 1796; it seceded in 1861 and was admitted to statehood in the Confederate States. It was readmitted to statehood in the United States in 1866 when Congress restored its "former political relations," a power which Congress declared only its approval can accomplish.

Lincoln's whole point of invading the Southern states was to reassert by force of arms the federal authority that had been legally and peacefully abolished by the Southern people. The analogy to the American Revolution, i.e., the First War of Secession, is a one-to-one fit. The only difference is the outcome. Where King George III failed and let the Thirteen Colonies have their independence, erecting whatever political apparatus they thought best, Lincoln succeeded in defeating both the self-determination of the Southern states and the principle of "consent of the governed." Lincoln was profoundly counterrevolutionary: The Federal government need not seek the consent of a defeated state on any political matter. In this regard, the Northerners who supported the federal government's power grab lost what the Southern states lost. Henceforth, states could only argue against federal abuse in the federal government's own courts.

### The War Did Not Change What the Founding Fathers Fought to Establish

Neither the war nor the subsequent rulings of the Chase court altered the basis upon which the Constitution was adopted. It didn't settle the legal and philosophical arguments about secession either. All it established was a *de facto* legal basis from which a centralization of power, and eventually finance and the economy, was to proceed.

The Constitution was a voluntary arrangement among the states whose sovereignty was already established. Article VII of the Constitution called for conventions in the states to be the means of ratification. There is no provision anywhere in the Constitution that required the legislatures of the states to call a ratification convention. Nor did the executive branch under the Articles of Confederation have any means by which to force a state to call a convention, short of one or more of the states themselves mobilizing their militia to invade a neighbor. The entire process of framing and adopting the Constitution was voluntary and consensual. There was not even a hint of the use of force by any state at any time.

In the years after the war, Chief Justice Salmon P. Chase would have been aware that there was no Supreme Court ruling on whether states had the legal right to secede. He set out to find a case where he could write his opinion into legal precedence, clearly calling secession illegal.

A centerpiece of the Lincoln scholars' argument for the illegality of secession is the Supreme Court's ruling in *Texas* v. *White* (1869). This case gave Chase an opportunity to incorporate his own political views into common law. The court ruled, "The Constitution, in all its provisions, looks to an indestructible Union, composed of indestructible States." Actually, it settled nothing because the controversy of the case was moot two years before it was argued and the decision handed down.

As previously discussed, the Constitution is silent on the question of perpetuity. This silence places the question in the jurisdiction of the Tenth Amendment, i.e., powers not given to the federal government by the Constitution, or prohibited to the states, "are reserved to the states respectively, or to the people." The Founding Fathers left it that way because they knew they could not get the Constitution ratified if it were, in fact, intended to be an irreversible commitment by and among the states. Furthermore, there is ample evidence that at least some of the Founding Fathers wanted a way out of the Constitution if it proved to be a mistake. Thus, the ruling that the Union is "indestructible" flies in the face of the spirit and letter of the Constitution.

History must ignore *Texas* v. *White* because Chief Justice Chase was guilty of unprecedented misconduct that was so sweeping as to strike at the very integrity of the United States Supreme Court. From a substantive standpoint, *Texas* blatantly violated the Tenth Amendment by completely ignoring it, accomplishing precisely what Chase intended, the creation of a *de facto* centralization of power in the hands of the federal government while eliminating the states' ability to withdraw there from.

Chase violated his oath of office to uphold the Constitution and to "impartially discharge" his duties under the Constitution in three ways. First, Chase was a virtual party to the case, who as Lincoln's secretary of treasury had formulated policies from which the case partially rose. He wrote the court's ruling and quoted in that ruling actions and policies he formulated from his days as treasury secretary. Second, biographer John Niven says Chase made "public comments" about the status of the wartime government in Texas, which was the whole point of the court's ruling. Third, Niven states Chase traveled in the South to make observations that would likely prejudice his thinking about cases that would come before the court. His prejudicial words and deeds strike at the essence of principle of an impartial tribunal.

Chase proved to be the most biased, opportunistic, politically ambitious, unprincipled, and unethical jurist ever to lay his hand on the Bible, swear an oath of office, and not be impeached. For these and other reasons discussed in previous chapters, historians must discard *Texas* v. *White* as a definitive answer to the question of the legality of secession. Rather than establish that secession is illegal, which *Texas* attempts but fails to do, it establishes that the Lincoln scholars will gleefully use any point, no matter how disreputable, to support the founding of the unitary, central state.

There are no questions from the Lincoln scholars as to why Lincoln never took any legal action to ascertain the legality, or illegality, of secession. His call for troops in April 1861 was a *de facto* declaration of war against the Southern states. Not only did he fail to seek the approval of Congress for his war, but Congress was not even in session. That was just as Lincoln wanted. His call for troops states, "The laws of the United States have been for some time past and now are opposed, and the execution thereof obstructed [in the seceded states] by combinations too powerful to be suppressed by the ordinary course of judicial proceedings, or by the powers vested in the marshals by law."

However, there were no "judicial proceedings," ordinary or extraordinary. Lincoln filed no suit challenging any state's right to secede, nor did he even ask his own attorney general for an opinion on the matter. He simply declared war without authority from Congress and got the shooting started in earnest before he called Congress into a special session. By then his counterrevolution to the Founding Fathers was in full swing.

## What Did the Civil War Actually Accomplish?

### The Death of "Consent of the Governed"

Lincoln envisioned a powerful central government that would decimate the political power of the states. DiLorenzo and others have established that Lincoln wanted a monster that would be powerful enough to subsidize the corporations and politically well connected and punish his enemies in political and economic terms.

It would be impossible to remake the federal government into today's Leviathan as long as a single state or group of states could exercise their consent and withdraw from the Union. It was imperative for Lincoln to force the issue of secession in order to overturn the principle of consent and eliminate the self-limiting reach of government that secession represented. The military winner on the battlefield does not need the consent of the defeated, disarmed, and destitute.

Secession stood in the way of Lincoln's dream of the almighty, dominant central state. One must think of Lincoln's dilemma with the same vicious opportunism of an abusive husband who refuses to give his wife a divorce. If the law that provides for divorce is repealed and the abused wife has no way out of the relationship, does one believe she will receive better or worse treatment from the husband?

During the fifteen presidencies prior to Lincoln's, the states were often consulted, and they voiced their objections to a variety of issues. The federal government generally paid close attention to these objections. Prior to 1860, no one except Lincoln and perhaps a few others believed the federal government would ever attempt to remove by force of arms the lawfully elected government of any state.

The day has long past in the United States of America when the federal government considers the political concerns of states. Consider the issue of the tax on incomes. Article I, Section 9 of the Constitution plainly states that Congress has no power to lay any direct tax on the people except in proportion to the population of each state. This disability was overcome in 1913 by the Sixteenth Amendment, though there have been and continue to be various tax protest groups who disagree. Some consider the personal income tax to be a form of nationalization of incomes in the same way various countries have nationalized mining and other extractive enterprises including petroleum production. Clearly, there is no proportionality among the states on the income tax. The states have been completely neutered in the process.

### The End of Self-determination

When state governments in the North aided Lincoln's federal campaign against the South, they did not know they were helping establish the precedent that self-government (self-determination) of any state is a thing of the past. Self-determination became a mere footnote to history, unless a state was willing to fight and die for it. The lesson of the Civil War is that the willingness to fight for self-determination is quite inadequate without the means to attain military victory. As H. L. Mencken noted about Lincoln's Gettysburg Address, the argument that the Union soldiers who died there "sacrificed their lives to the cause of self-determination" is untrue. Mencken suggests it was the U.S. Army that fought to put down the South's move toward self-determination. "It was the Confederates who fought for the right of their people to govern themselves."

## The "Chains" of the Constitution Were Broken

Thomas Jefferson inspired, and perhaps even personally wrote, the Kentucky and Virginia Resolutions of 1798-99, resolutions passed by those states' legislatures to protest the Alien and Sedition Acts. Jefferson believed the acts greatly overstepped constitutional authority by limiting political speech critical of government. He used the term "chains of the Constitution" in the Kentucky Resolution to describe a system of limited government.

> Free government is founded in jealousy, and not in confidence; it is jealousy and not confidence which prescribes limited constitutions, to bind down those whom we are obliged to trust with power: that our Constitution has accordingly fixed the limits to which, and no further, our confidence may go; and let the honest advocate of confidence read the alien and sedition acts, and say if the Constitution has not been wise in fixing limits to the government it created, and whether we should be wise in destroying those limits. Let him say what the government is, if it be not a tyranny, which the men of our choice have conferred on our President. . . . In questions of power, then, let no more be heard of confidence in man, but bind him [the president] down from mischief by the chains of the Constitution.

Jefferson feared tyranny from an elected president who abused his power just as much as he did from the king of England. He knew there was only one way this could be guarded against in the Constitution. Every state would have to reserve to itself the right to judge whether the federal government has violated its limited constitutional duties. Only if the people of the states retained the legal right and the necessary means to resist any abuses of the federal government, could limited government be maintained. The Kentucky Resolution stated that the federal government created under the Constitution "was not made the exclusive or final judge of the extent of the powers delegated to itself." That judgment must be left in the hands of the states, each of which "has an equal right to judge for itself."

When it comes to matters of federal power exercised under the Constitution, Jefferson and Lincoln agree on one point. They both believed tyranny could not truly be perpetrated on the people so long as the states' jealously maintained the constitutional "chains" that prohibit it. Lincoln knew he needed to break those chains, and the best way to do it was to use military force to end the debate about secession as well as to silence his critics in the North as necessary. Unfortunately, he accomplished both.

## The Beginning of the Imperial Presidency

Many people believe the first administration justly accused of creating an "imperial presidency" is that of Richard M. Nixon. However, this is far from the truth. In fact, other than petty violations that led to his political downfall and ignominious resignation from office, Nixon's abuse of office was trivial compared to Lincoln's.

Lincoln asserted that as commander in chief of the military forces of the United States under Article II, Section 2 of the Constitution, he was entitled to order these forces to do whatever he pleased. He stated in his first inaugural address that the Union is perpetual even though the Constitution is silent on the issue of perpetuity. Therefore, Lincoln took the position that he was entitled to do whatever was necessary to preserve his perpetual Union, even though there is neither authority nor mandate under the Constitution for the president or Congress to do so. In fact, embedded within his purpose of preserving the Union was the remaking of the Union into a strong centralized national government. The revolutionary ideal of government being limited only to those areas to which the citizens have given their "consent" was out the window.

Lincoln's belief in preserving the perpetual Union was so strong that he felt entitled to order the U.S. Army to take actions that were clearly in violation of expressed prohibitions in the Constitution. Lincoln suspended the writ of habeas corpus by executive order, a violation of Article I, Section 8, which reserves that power to Congress.

He sent the army to arrest members of the Maryland legislature on the way to a special session, depriving the state of a republican form of government, a violation of Article IV, Section 4. Lincoln violated that same clause when he sent the army to Jefferson City, Missouri, to topple the state's duly elected government.

Lincoln sent the U.S. Navy to blockade Southern ports, which was an act of war that violated another clause of Article IV, Section 4, protecting states from invasion. The blockade also violated a clause of Article I, Section 8, prohibiting Congress from requiring vessels bound to or from one state to enter or clear a port in another state.

If Congress did not have this authority, the president could not have it either.

He used the army to arrest newspaper editors and publishers (in violation of the First Amendment, freedom of press) and denied them a speedy trial (in violation of the Sixth Amendment). Lincoln banished a member of Congress, Rep. Clement Vallandigham, who was a fiery opponent and political thorn in the flesh. Expelling Vallandigham from Congress was in violation of Article I, Section 2, which leaves expulsion in the hands of the Congress itself and not the president or the judiciary.

Lincoln's call for troops to invade the South had the "practical effect" of a declaration of war as Lincoln scholars Randall and Donald admit. This, too, violated the Constitution, which reserves power to declare war to Congress (Article I, Section 8).

### The Doctrine of Military Necessity and the Era of Total War

Military necessity was first defined in paragraph 14 of the Lieber Code. Frances Lieber defined it as "those measures which are indispensable for securing the ends of the war, and which are lawful according to the modern law and usages of war." This formed the basis for international agreements on the rules of armed conflict that would come later at the Hague and Geneva Conventions.

Contemporary international law incorporates certain limitations on the use of military action as applied with the law of military necessity. The action must be intended to help in the military defeat of an enemy limited to a military objective, and collateral harm to civilians or private property must be proportional, not excessive. Article 52 of the Additional Protocols to the Geneva Convention (1977) defines "military objectives" as "those objects which by their nature, location, purpose or use make an effective contribution to military action and whose total or partial destruction, capture or neutralization, in the circumstances ruling at the time, offers a definite military advantage."

The distinction between political and military objectives was a dilemma that plagued Lincoln. After all, his objective in the Civil War was reassertion of federal control of the Southern states. Defeating the Confederate Army was only part of the consideration. Sherman was even more confused as he embraced the application of military force with spiritual and psychological concepts of destiny and divine will. With such a frightening and bizarre combination of muddled ideas, it is little wonder that Lincoln's war turned the South into a Machiavellian orgy of total warfare on civilians and military alike. To these men, all Southerners were enemies; all enemies were military targets.

Twentieth-century application of these concepts shows that very little has changed. Writing in the *American Journal of International Law,* military analyst Burrus M. Carnahan hears a "distant echo" from the Lincoln administration following the Christmas bombing of North Vietnam in 1972. President Nixon ordered the bombing of military installations or war-supporting industries in Hanoi and Haiphong, North Vietnam. Although the targets were clearly military in nature, the purpose of the attack "was not to respond to a new military threat from North Vietnam. Rather, it was to induce the North Vietnamese Government to return to the negotiating table."[7]

Similar arguments have been made for the firebombing of German cities, the atomic bombings of the almost exclusively civilian targets of Hiroshima and Nagasaki, and even the Doolittle raid on Tokyo (which did little damage). All such acts of total warfare had dual intent, harm the enemy's military and destroy the enemy's ability for its civilian populations to escape the horror of war.

There is no question the concept of "total war" originated in the U.S. Army during the Civil War. Even the Lincoln scholars admit this. Prof. James McPherson gleefully speaks of Lincoln's policy of "total war" against the South, apparently unconcerned that his words indict the object of his approbation as a war criminal.[8]

### Did Lincoln, Sherman, and Others Inspire the Nazi Policy of *Lebensraum?*

The conquest of the South was not the only aggressive policy executed during the Lincoln administration. The racial genocide of the Plains Indians begun by Lincoln was well underway during the Civil War.

Circumstances associated with the simultaneous defeat of the South and the Indians bear a chilling parallel to the twentieth-century policy of *lebensraum* by Nazi Germany. *Lebensraum,* the German word for "living space" was the Nazi policy of forcibly clearing Slavic,

Polish, and Jewish populations from Eastern Europe in order to make "living space" for the colonization of those areas by Germans.

The similarities begin with the way Sherman described the military tactics and policies he carried out against the Indians when he took command of the western United States after the war. His private correspondence mentions "the final solution of the Indian problem." It was not Joseph Goebbels or Adolf Hitler who came up with that terminology, it was William T. Sherman's, the hero of the Civil War. The Nazis borrowed Sherman's phrasing seventy-five years later, merely substituting the word "Jewish" for "Indians." But there was much more to it than just similar terminology.

Both *lebensraum* and the clearing of the Indians were perpetrated by governments that claimed strong central power. Ironically, these governments were headed by men who came to power by elections of the people rather than military coup.

Both governments viewed the racial majority (white, Northern Europeans) under their jurisdiction as superior to the cultures and peoples they sought to eliminate. The racial minorities were seen as inferior and deliberately dehumanized. They occupied vast territories that were agriculturally productive and home to extremely valuable natural and mineral resources, on which they developed their own traditions. In both cases, the governments of the racial majorities encouraged fictitious sagas of their fulfillment of destiny as justification for aggression against the racial minorities. "Go West, young man," was the cry of the day in America while German designs on Eastern Europe were motivated by the cult of the peasant.

Force was used not only to remove the undesired minorities, but also to exterminate the entire population to the extent possible. With *lebensraum*, the Nazis sought to eradicate the non-Germans of Eastern Europe. Those who remained after the slaughter were penned in ghettos. In the United States, the few surviving Indians were restricted to reservations, which deprived them of traditional hunting grounds and created a dependency on the federal government for food, fuel, and shelter.

Is it mere coincidence that the United States and Germany, two nations that so readily exchanged intellectual, cultural, and political office holders during the 1850s, '60s, and '70s, developed such a similar approach?

## Secession in 1860—Did the States Break the Law?

The United States of America was founded on secession, with the Colonies seceding from England. They took this action for the common purpose of virtually every secession in history—self-determination.

There are many successful secessions in history; most were peaceful, some were not. Vermont seceded peacefully from New York in 1777 during the American Revolution. Belgium seceded peacefully from the Netherlands in 1830. Texas seceded from Mexico in 1836 by revolution. West Virginia seceded from Virginia in 1863 to join Lincoln's illegal federal cause. Pres. Theodore Roosevelt precipitated the secession of Panama from Colombia in 1903. Norway peacefully seceded from Sweden in 1905. Pakistan seceded from India in 1947, precipitating war. Bangladesh subsequently seceded peacefully from Pakistan in 1971. And of course fifteen former Soviet republics seceded peacefully from the Soviet Union in 1991. What did these peoples and countries have in common? They all wanted to govern themselves.

The Thirteen Colonies wanted to govern themselves with institutions they erected of and among their own people. When the Constitution was adopted, there was no mandatory timetable for states to consider it. North Carolina and Rhode Island were so hesitant to enable a ratifying convention, they weren't even a part of the Union until after Washington was elected president and sworn into office. Yet there was no demand for them to take action, they were allowed to consider their affiliation with the other states on their own terms without outside interference. It is ironic as well as instructive that the very first state to be added to the Union after the adoption of the Constitution was Vermont, itself a product of secession.

Likewise, the Southern states wanted to govern themselves without interference from Northern intellectuals, radical Unitarian clergy representing the state-established church in New England, or the federal government.

The Southern States were well within their legal rights to leave the Union in 1860 by the authority of the common law of the land. Three doctrines stemming from the U.S. Supreme Court, unmistakability, legislative entrenchment, and equal footing, guided the court's judgment from the early days of the nineteenth century to today. If there is a compelling argument that secession was a legal and constitutional option in 1860, it remains a legal and constitutional option today. The fact that secession was defeated by force of arms in 1865 settled only the practicality of it for the Southern Confederacy. The legal issues remain unchanged, unaddressed, and subject to future political and legal consideration.

### Unmistakability

The unmistakability doctrine holds that the government cannot agree by contract to limit any of its sovereign powers except in "unmistakable" terms. If this doctrine is applied to the circumstances of the ratification of the Constitution, one would find that there was no "unmistakable" transfer of sovereignty from the states to this new government. In fact, the records of the ratification conventions are filled with assurances to the contrary. Even at the Pennsylvania convention, there was discussion regarding convening another convention to rescind the action of the first if ratification was a mistake.

The Philadelphia Convention attendees knew they would never get the Constitution ratified by the states if they had included an explicit transfer of sovereignty. Perhaps some at that convention favored a full or partial transfer of sovereignty, but many opposed it. Either way, the issue of sovereignty was deliberately left out of the Constitution. There was no "unmistakable" transfer of sovereign power from the states.

### Legislative Entrenchment

The fundamental question regarding the doctrine of legislative entrenchment is this: If the original states were competent to write and adopt the Constitution, forming a Union as a purely voluntary and consensual act, how could they not retain the right to reconsider?

The act of creating a political union is like the union of two people in marriage. It is in fact a political marriage, and secession is a political divorce. Every Western society recognizes divorce to some degree. Only a few authoritarian regimes fail to do so. Why?

Individuals make mistakes. Sometimes a person enters a relationship that seems good at first but later proves to be a mistake. What sort of hellish relationships would people be in if every marriage was perpetual, without divorce for any reason at any time? If individuals are capable of making mistakes about relationships, societies are too.

A basic feature of self-government and the essence of the doctrine of legislative entrenchment is that any past decision made by a legislative body can be repealed or amended in the future. Any act that a previous legislature had the authority to enact, a future legislature has the same authority of amendment or repeal. No generation has the right or the ability to bind for all time a future generation. Each generation, each legislature has all the rights and prerogatives of its predecessors. This is natural law, and it is just as natural as the growth of one's child to adulthood.

Of course, the Lincoln scholars and statists argue that the United States is perpetual, that the Constitution must always be. Such notions of permanency fail to square up with the simple fact that the Constitution can be amended and has been twenty-seven times. Fourteen of those amendments have come since Chase's shameful declaration that the Union is "indestructible."

Consider the Eighteenth Amendment (Prohibition) and the Twenty-first Amendment (repeal of Prohibition). Prohibition was a failure and provided the opportunity for crime to organize itself into a powerful enterprise. Prohibition was a mistake that was specifically repealed by a subsequent amendment. Thus, the Constitution, which is subject to amendment, cannot be perpetual and "indestructible" because any given amendment can change anything and everything in the document. The people of the states have a right, through their legislatures, to amend the Constitution. Article V gives Congress the authority to propose amendments but leaves the sole and exclusive authority to ratify amendments in the hands of the states.

As we have already seen, the right to amend is the same right to adopt or repeal, according to Supreme Court precedence. Each succeeding legislature holds the same authority and power as its predecessors. "The later have the same power of repeal and modification which the former had of enactment, neither more nor less."[9]

What's to stop the states from adopting an amendment that specifically gives every state the right to withdraw from the Union at any time? Although such an amendment is not necessary if the Tenth Amendment means anything, there is no reason why it couldn't be adopted. Furthermore, there is no reason why the states couldn't repeal the Constitution and go back to the Articles of Confederation.

The position by the Lincoln scholars and statists that the nation is "one nation," "indivisible," "perpetual," and "indestructible" is intellectually flawed. It is a bogus argument created to preempt legitimate debate about the nature of the American union. The central state establishment does not want a public discussion on this topic. They have way too much to lose.


**Equality of the States**

The power of the original thirteen states to withdraw from the Union extends to all states under the doctrine of equal footing. All states are legally on an equal footing with each other. They all have the same rights and prerogatives. The Supreme Court agreed with the argument that there "is, and must be, from a constitutional necessity, a perfect and unchangeable equality among the states"[10]

What Massachusetts may do, Arkansas, and Oregon, and Alaska may do. What Congress cannot force Massachusetts to do, it cannot force Tennessee, or Utah, or West Virginia to do.

The historical, philosophical, and legal basis for secession remains unchanged. The original thirteen states existed for more than one hundred years as colonies before seceding from Great Britain. In war, they gained their independence and international recognition as sovereign states.

The Constitution was written and submitted to the domestic government of each state for its consideration and voluntary ratification if agreeable. The power to ratify is the power to repeal. No state can give up this or any other attribute of sovereignty without an express intention to do so, which is absent from the Constitution. There was no transfer of sovereignty expressed in any state's ratification resolution.

Each state retains the legal right to withdraw from the Union. That was the law in the nineteenth century, and it remains the law in the twenty-first century. In 1860, the Southern states exercised their legal rights of secession. It was not until three years after the war that the flimsy arguments against the contemporary exercise of this right appeared in the rulings of the U.S. Supreme Court (*Texas* v. *White*). Secession was and is a natural right of the people to alter or abolish government. It was understood that the federal government's powers are limited to the express grants of authority in the Constitution, including the powers reserved to the states and the people in the Tenth Amendment.

Chief among the reserved powers is the power to secede. As Justice Swayne wrote in 1880, the question of secession was settled "by the arbitrament of arms" (*Daniels* v. *Tearney*). However, no question of political relationship can be permanently settled by force alone. Any attempt to do so will only delay the final debate. As secession is nothing more than a political divorce, and every divorce embodies a property and debt settlement, its day in court is yet in our future.

# CHAPTER NINE

# One Nation Under Surveillance: Will the Republic Terminate in an Empire?

*"Folks used to pray to God for rain, and now they call Washington."*
—Bro. Dave Gardner, comedian, c. 1960

This chapter takes a step back from history to look at where America stands today, a perspective on fifteen immediately preceding decades of unrelenting centralization.

I believe the American republic is in trouble. I believe this because America has acquired an empire through aggressive military action, and an empire is inherently inconsistent with a republic. Rome was a republic for four hundred years during which time it acquired an empire, and the empire eventually swallowed the republic. The same thing is likely to happen in America because the dynamic forces associated with the acquisition and maintenance of an empire are more powerful than those associated with a republic. History teaches that unless the republic terminates the empire, the empire will terminate the republic. These United States are very close to that tipping point.

There are many alarming trends in American government and society today, not the least of which is the diminishing ability to distinguish between the two. One of the most alarming is the direct surveillance and compilation of information about individual citizens by the central government Leviathan. Why does the federal government need so much information about its own citizens? Does it fear a threat to our security and is it protecting us from some outside malevolent power or force? If that is the case, the government needs more information about those who pose such a threat, not about its own citizens.

Perhaps the federal government fears a fifth-column movement in America. If so, why do congressional leaders and the president pander to every conceivable voting block, even those that might potentially threaten national security? We have already seen presidents and presidential candidates take large campaign contributions from groups with questionable or conflicting ties to foreign governments. Some former presidents and presidential candidates have murky ties to foreign trading and consulting organizations, governments, and sovereign monarchs that bring them millions of dollars of personal income.

Alternately, does the Leviathan fear that the average American will become a threat to its own security? Government does not know the answer to this question, so it keeps its options open by gathering or purchasing from private vendors information about its citizens. Yet by this process, it almost seems as if the federal government is stalking its citizens, gathering information, learning our habits and weaknesses, cultivating its allies among us, marshaling and staging its forces and supplies waiting for the opportunity to strike.

There are other alarming trends, including the militarization of civilian police forces, the explosion in the number and deployments of SWAT teams, the perpetual war on drugs and terrorism with the exercise of perpetual war powers, and the domestic incarceration rate. Government secrecy; lack of fiscal accountability and outright fraud; the evisceration of First Amendment rights of speech and to petition the government for redress of grievances; the frightening preparations the executive branch of government has made for emergency, dictatorial rule (only a few in either party in Congress has opposed); and the plan to surrender American sovereignty to a North American Union are trends representing the ultimate, supranational centralization of economic, political, and legal power.

There is only one political principle on Earth that can counteract these powerful trends—secession. Only the power of the states to secede can rein-in runaway centralization of authority and save the American republic.

The relationship between the public and the federal Leviathan has all the characteristics of an abusive relationship. Leviathan makes all decisions without consideration of the wants and needs of individuals; its spending habits are uncontrollable, piling up debt at an alarming rate, constantly demanding more money; it chronically lies to the American public and expects them to believe the lies; it demands undivided loyalty yet remains distant and inattentive; and it spies on the people just like an irrationally jealous husband.

The present political party structure will not, because it cannot, stop centralization. In fact, the Republicans and Democrats are much the cause of it as they have willingly prostituted themselves for their share in the centralization of power and wealth. These two political parties have been likened to the Genovese and Gambino crime families, separate entities that are branches of the same criminal enterprise. They are little more than factions of a one-party empire that masquerades as a free enterprise, capitalistic democracy based on the traditions of Judeo-Christian pluralism.

Only the power to secede can bring about the decentralization necessary for the peaceful demise of the empire and the survival of the American republic. The power to secede is the power to instill discipline and reimpose limits on the federal government. Discipline is needed to govern by consensus, which is to say the restoration of the consent of the governed; the very thing Lincoln worked the hardest to end.

Let's look at just a few things that threaten the republic.

**The FBI v. the States**
From 2005 to 2008, the Federal Bureau of Investigation conducted corruption investigations of the legislatures in seven states: Tennessee, 2005; New York and Alaska, 2006; Massachusetts and Rhode Island, 2007; and Oregon 2008. In 2008, the Feds tapped the phone of Illinois governor Rod Blagojevich. These are only the ones we know about from the public record. There may be others that remain unknown. Perhaps all state legislatures are under investigation at this moment. Perhaps these investigations are on going on a permanent basis. We don't know how many state legislatures are being investigated at any given moment, but we do know such investigations constitute a very high priority of the FBI.

In 2006, the FBI launched a Web site to ferret out corrupt state and local government officials. The site says, "Public corruption is one of the FBI's top investigative priorities—behind only terrorism, espionage, and cyber crimes." The FBI places public corruption at such a high priority "because of its impact on our democracy and national security."[1] The FBI learned long ago, under J. Edgar Hoover, that when you can't rationally explain why the FBI is doing what it is doing, you can always invoke "democracy" or "national security."

However, the tactics the FBI used in its investigation of the Tennessee legislature in 2005 leaves thoughtful observers wondering whether the Feds were conducting a supervision of or an investigation of the Tennessee legislature.

Two days before the Tennessee General Assembly was set to adjourn, FBI agents swooped in and arrested three state senators, one former state senator, and one member of the Tennessee House of Representatives on bribery and extortion charges. Other individuals who were not office holders were also arrested. The FBI had conducted a sting operation in an attempt to entrap legislators who took cash pay-offs in return for support of a bill.

The FBI chartered a phony recycling company in Georgia, E-Cycle Management, Inc., using assumed, fictitious names of its agents to apply for incorporation. This violated the Georgia code, which makes it a misdemeanor to make a statement on incorporation documents that is "false in any material respect." In the case of the FBI's dummy corporation, it was false in all respects.

> A person who signs a document he knows is false in any material respect with intent that the document be delivered to the Secretary of State for filing shall be guilty of a misdemeanor and, upon conviction thereof, shall be punished by a fine not to exceed $500.00. (Georgia Code, § 14-2-129)[2]

January 29, 2004, Georgia secretary of state Cathy Cox issued a Certificate of Incorporation (control number 0406877) to E-Cycle Management, Inc. and sent it to the company's ostensible CFO, John Morrow, except John Morrow doesn't exist. He is a persona who exists only because a real FBI agent falsely and illegally assumed it.

Then the FBI agents, identities obscured, crossed into Tennessee to conduct a sting on the general assembly. While in Tennessee, the agents violated other laws, but in true Lincolnian form, it was for a higher cause, the ferreting out of public corruption. They hosted breakfast receptions to lure members of the legislature, and in doing so violated Tennessee ethics laws by falsely representing themselves. In fact, they repeatedly misrepresented themselves.

# Secretary of State
## Corporations Division
### 315 West Tower
### #2 Martin Luther King, Jr. Dr.
### Atlanta, Georgia 30334-1530

CONTROL NUMBER : 0406877
EFFECTIVE DATE : 01/29/2004
JURISDICTION : GEORGIA
REFERENCE : 0044
PRINT DATE : 02/06/2004
FORM NUMBER : 311

JOHN MORROW
5579B CHAMBLEE DUNWOODY ROAD
#137
DUNWOODY, GA 30338

## CERTIFICATE OF INCORPORATION

I, Cathy Cox, the Secretary of State and the Corporations Commissioner of the State of Georgia, do hereby certify under the seal of my office that

**E-CYCLE MANAGEMENT, INCORPORATED**
**A DOMESTIC PROFIT CORPORATION**

has been duly incorporated under the laws of the State of Georgia on the effective date stated above by the filing of articles of incorporation in the Office of the Secretary of State and by the paying of fees as provided by Title 14 of the Official Code of Georgia Annotated.

WITNESS my hand and official seal in the City of Atlanta and the State of Georgia on the date set forth above.

Cathy Cox
Secretary of State

ARTICLE OF INCORPORATION
OF
E-CYCLE MANAGEMENT, INCORPORATED

I.

The name of the corporation is "E-CYCLE MANAGEMENT, INCORPORATED".

II.

The corporation is organized pursuant to the provisions of the Georgia Business Corporation Code.

III.

The corporation shall have perpetual duration.

IV.

The corporation is a corporation for profit and is organized for the following purpose: to engage in any lawful act or activity for which corporations may be organized under the Georgia Corporation Code.

V.

The corporation shall have authority, acting by it's board of directors, to issue not more than 10,000 shares of a common class having a par value of $1.00 per share.

VI.

The corporation shall not commence business until it shall have received consideration of not less than $1,000.00 in value for the issuance of it's shares.

VII.

The shareholders of the corporation shall not have any preemptive rights to acquire any unissued shares of the corporation.

VIII.

The initial registered agent of the corporation is John Morrow, and the offices of the initial registered agent of the corporation is 5579B Chamblee Dunwoody Road, Suite 137, Dunwoody, Georgia, 30338, Fulton County, Georgia.

IX.

The initial board of directors shall consist of five members, the name and address of each is as follows:

Joseph Carson
Director
5579B Chamblee Dunwoody Road
Suite 137
Dunwoody, Georgia, 30338;

L. C. McNiel
Director
5579B Chamblee Dunwoody Road
Suite 137
Dunwoody, Georgia 30338

John Morrow
Director/Secretary
5579B Chamblee Dunwoody Road
Suite 137
Dunwoody, Georgia, 30338;

The initial name and address of the incorporator(s) is: John Morrow, 5579B Chamblee Dunwoody Road, Suite 137, Dunwoody, Georgia, 30338.

The mailing address of the corporation will be 5579B Chamblee Dunwoody Road, Suite 137, Dunwoody, Georgia, 30338.

IN WITNESS WHEREOF, the undersigned incorporator has executed these Articles of Incorporation.

This ___ day of January, 2004.

CORPORATIONS DIVISION

2004 JAN 29  A 11: 11

SECRETARY OF STATE

John Morrow, Incorporator

BUSINESS INFORMATION AND SERVICES
Suite 315, West Tower
2 Martin Luther King Jr., Drive
Atlanta, Georgia 30334-1530
(404) 656-2817

Secretary of State
State of Georgia

TRANSMITTAL INFORMATION FOR GEORGIA
PROFIT OR NONPROFIT CORPORATIONS

DO NOT WRITE IN SHADED AREA - SOS USE ONLY

| | | |
|---|---|---|
| DOCKET # | PENDING CONTROL # *P566209* | CONTROL # *0406899* |
| Docket Code | Corporation Type | |
| Date Filed *1/29/3004* | Amount Received $ | Check/Receipt # *1563* |
| Jurisdiction (County) Code | | |
| Examiner | | Date Completed |

NOTICE TO APPLICANT:  PRINT PLAINLY OR TYPE REMAINDER OF THIS FORM.
INSTRUCTIONS ARE ON THE BACK OF THIS FORM.

1. *0406376255*
   Corporate Name Reservation Number
   E-CYCLE MANAGEMENT, INCORPORATED
   Corporate Name (exactly as appears on name reservation)

2. JOHN MORROW
   Applicant/Attorney                                    Telephone Number
   5579B CHAMBLEE DUNWOODY ROAD, #137
   Address
   DUNWOODY                 GEORGIA                      30338
   City                     State                        Zip Code

3. NOTICE:  THIS FORM DOES NOT REPLACE THE ARTICLES OF INCORPORATION.  MAIL OR DELIVER
   DOCUMENTS AND THE SECRETARY OF STATE FILING FEE TO THE ABOVE ADDRESS.  DOCUMENTS
   SHOULD BE SUBMITTED IN THE FOLLOWING ORDER.  (A COVER LETTER IS NOT REQUIRED.)

   1. FORM 227 - TRANSMITTAL FORM (ATTACH SECRETARY OF STATE FILING FEE OF $60.00 TO
      THIS FORM)

   2. ORIGINAL ARTICLES OF INCORPORATION

   3. ONE COPY OF ARTICLES OF INCORPORATION

   I understand that the information on this form will be entered in the Secretary of
   State business registration database.  I certify that a Notice of Incorporation or a
   Notice of Intent to Incorporate with a publishing fee of $40.00 has been or will be
   mailed or delivered to the authorized newspaper as required by law.


   _____          _____
   Authorized Signature                          Date

BSR Form 227 (06-95)

Eventually, the FBI agents got several legislators to sponsor legislation in both houses of the general assembly—false legislation. No crime had been committed by any of the defendants, at least that the government was aware of, until the FBI solicited it. Initially there were no specific targets of the investigation, the FBI simply waived the bait around (cash), focusing on those who they thought might take it.

Several Tennessee lawmakers took the bait, and they were arrested two days before the assembly adjourned at the state capitol. Three were booked in Nashville and released the same day they were arrested. State senator John N. Ford was driven to Memphis, two hundred miles away, and kept in federal custody until after the legislature adjourned. The other legislators were released and back at the legislative session by the afternoon.

State representative Frank S. Niceley (Republican, Strawberry Plains) witnessed the assembling of FBI agents the morning of the arrests, moments before they made the arrests. Niceley entered the capitol in a little-used basement door and surprised several FBI agents. "There were five or six of them with dark suits and shinny shoes. They looked startled. I went on about my business but I figured something was up," Niceley recalls.

Niceley and others legislators have expressed concern at the heavy handedness of the investigation and the arrest of legislators during session. As for the actual bill, a bogus bill, the FBI paid to have introduced, Niceley said in a personal interview that it was a "reasonable sounding bill" that could have passed. "They posed as a recycling company that would recycle obsolete computer hardware that the State is always generating." He said the irony of introducing a bogus bill is that "it could have actually passed, and probably would have been signed by the governor."

No one seems to know what the status of such a law would have been had the bill moved forward. Niceley plainly does not like FBI entanglement in the legislative process: "There's plenty of damn corruption at the Federal level for them to work on."

This episode represents the federal government's attitude toward the operation of the legislatures of the fifty states. Let's recap federal interference and law breaking in this case:

- The FBI lied in its application to incorporate in Georgia, which broke Georgia law.
- The FBI lied to members of the Tennessee General Assembly, violating state ethics rules when its agents used false identities to lobby for legislation.
- It solicited the introduction of bogus legislation, which was subsequently enrolled by the engrossing clerk in both chambers of the Tennessee legislature.
- It arrested members of the legislature while in session and restrained one state senator who was not allowed to return.

In fairness to the FBI, it should be noted that all four arrested Tennessee legislators have resigned, pled guilty, and been sentenced to prison. The FBI videotaped them taking cash; their guilt was unquestionable. Nevertheless, the FBI's methods are quite disturbing.

The bureau's intimidation and lawbreaking constitutes a dangerous interference with state government. The power in the hands of the FBI to entrap legislators and arrest and detain them during session is the power to control votes on the floor of the legislature. The audacity of the FBI to use bogus legislation as enticement is a mockery of state government, striking at the very nature of representative government. Article IV, Section 4 of the Constitution guarantees "to every state in this union a republican form of government." Yet, republican, or representative, government is impossible when the federal government usurps the power to arrest and detain legislators during session. Imagine what the U.S. Congress would look like if the FBI arrested all the crooks. Congress might not even have a quorum to conduct business if the District of Columbia had enough jail space to incarcerate all criminals.

No one defends crooked politicians. The investigation and prosecution of state legislators who sell their offices, or are otherwise on the take, should certainly be pursued with a great deal of vigor but not by federal law enforcement. The Feds are sending a clear message that federal law is better, cleaner, and superior to any of the states' laws. Furthermore, Federal agents are free to lie and commit crimes under state law at will and with complete impunity in order to entrap and bring down state officials.

The federal prosecution of former Alabama governor Don Siegelman is even more troubling. Paul Craig Roberts, a Republican and a deputy treasury secretary under President Reagan, has exposed the abuse of power by the George W. Bush administration in bringing down Governor Siegelman, a Democrat. These details are well known and have been published by various sources.[3]

Roberts tells the story of Siegelman's frame-up by Bush-appointed prosecutors and his unfair treatment by a Bush-appointed federal judge. It is difficult to recall any other story where the criminal prosecution of a prominent public official was alleged to have been tainted by a stolen election, suborned perjury by government witnesses, engaged in prosecutorial jury tampering, and paid off a federal judge. If Roberts's assertions are true, Gov. Don Siegelman is a political prisoner guilty only of being in the way of Bush's political allies in Alabama.

As Representative Niceley said, there's plenty of corruption in the federal government to keep the FBI busy. However, perhaps that's precisely why the FBI has made state and local corruption a priority. The headlines in Nashville, Boston, Albany, New York, and Salem, Oregon, are a nice public relations diversion from the major-league corruption in the federal government's multitrillion-dollar budget. The public gets to see the goodness of federal law enforcement and evidence for why we need to give up even more of our freedoms to Washington. Centralism never rests.

### Secrecy and Surveillance

Ordinary government secrecy exists solely to withhold from its own citizens the knowledge of what it is really doing. Why, one might ask, would a government do that? The answer is always the same on all continents, in all cultures, and in every language: The government has plans that the citizenry would resist if they were informed of them in advance. This is the ugly reality of centralization of power, and it is why a republic cannot long endure when the government is shrouded in secrecy and spying on its own citizens. The very nature of government secrecy repudiates a republican, or representative, form of government because it undermines apparent government with mendacious stealth.

Oddly, the government can never seem to determine who its enemies are. As a result, the government defaults to its "safety net" of assuming that nearly everyone either is or might become its enemy. Therefore, everyone is suspect and subject to surveillance, supervision, and intimidation.

Where does America stand today in the continuum between citizen and subject? How much is jeopardized by secrecy and surveillance?

Police departments in the multicounty metropolitan area of Atlanta acted quickly following the 2001 al-Qaeda attacks in New York and Washington. With a $12 million counterterrorism grant supplied by the federal government, suburban DeKalb County set up one of the first police intelligence units in the nation, according to the May 8, 2006, story in *U.S. News & World Report.* Of course, no one asked whether there had ever been a terrorist threat, much less an attack, in suburban Atlanta, at least not after Sherman marched off with the town smoldering behind him.

Within a year, the wheels had fallen off this counterterrorism program. The secret agents had turned their interests away from impending attacks by jihadists to vegan activists who handed out antimeat leaflets at a local Honey Baked Ham store. This story sounds completely foolish, and it is. The agents, their supervisors, and the entire law-enforcement establishment in DeKalb County should be held up to public ridicule for such an asinine stunt. An editorial in the *Atlanta Journal-Constitution* concluded that glazed ham is "safe" in DeKalb County.

Nevertheless, real damage was done by this antispy unit. They tracked the movements of a DeKalb County executive suspected of misspending public funds. Additionally, *U.S. News & World Report* reported that it found "nearly a dozen cases in which city and county police, in the name of homeland security, have surveilled or harassed animal-rights and antiwar protesters, union activists, and even library patrons surfing the web."[4]

Other federal government plans are even more chilling and directly threaten liberty. *The Wall Street Journal* reported that the Department of Homeland Security plans a $15 billion *domestic* spy satellite. Spying on Americans is justified by statists on the left and right, and their news media sycophants, on the basis that it protects the access to the Internet "and involves government protection of domestic computer networks," the *WSJ* news story said. The leadership of either party in Congress offered hardly a whimper of protest or even caution.

However, plans continue. *WSJ* reports Homeland Security is "in the middle of a public debate over domestic spy powers, kicked off by the revelation two years ago that the National Security Agency [NSA] had been eavesdropping on some conversations in the U.S. without a warrant." What's more, the new spy satellite will produce "imagery" that will be shared with other federal agencies and local authorities under the planned National Applications Office.[5] In one of the bright spots regarding privacy, the Obama administration might actually eliminate the spy satellite program.

Much of the eavesdropping conducted by the NSA, the CIA, and the FBI is illegal. The federal government has been systematically breaking the law, believing it is above the law. Such ideas didn't just appear out of thin air. They are the same justifications Lincoln used 145 years ago, and the same justifications the Lincoln scholars use today. Authorities are free to break the written statutory law as long as they are obeying a "higher" law, such as "preserving the Union" or "keeping us safe from terrorist attack."

This is not to say that Lincoln is to blame for the contemporary violation of laws and trampling of constitutional guarantees to citizens. Far from it, present leaders must stand in account for that. Lincoln's crimes were perpetrated on Americans. He levied (made) war on the states, the Constitution's definition of treason.

Chalmers Johnson revealed another grave threat to liberty in his 2004 book *The Sorrows of Empire*. Johnson explains that the international apparatus for domestic spying has been around since the early days of the Cold War. He says that since 1948, the governments of the English-speaking countries of the United States, United Kingdom, Canada, Australia, and New Zealand have allowed each other's spy agencies to operate in each other's countries to circumvent their own nation's laws that prevent domestic intelligence gathering.

Thus, if the CIA wanted to gather information on an American in the U.S. (which is illegal for it to do), it would simply ask the Canadians or the Brits to do it and deliver the information. Johnson cites a former Canadian operative who claims that Margaret Thatcher, while prime minister of the U.K., authorized the Canadians to spy on her domestic political foes in England.[6]

The gathering of information is also accomplished by private credit-reporting bureaus, which ultimately sell information about you to the government. One of the three credit bureaus, Experian, acknowledges on its Web site (www.experiangroup.com) that its clientele includes the government. It provides a great amount of detail about its services to private individuals and financial institutions but nothing about the information it sells to the government. Neither Equifax nor TransUnion reveal anything about having the government as a client.

Fringe news sources on the Internet claim that the credit bureaus have custom-detailed data packages available for sale to the government on everyone who has ever had a bank account or credit card. Supposedly, these data packages include the names and addresses of your current and former neighbors and where they work and bank. If these claims are true, God help us.

But don't look to the federal court system for any help. The U.S. Supreme Court recently turned down an appeal from the American Civil Liberties Union (ACLU) to pursue a lawsuit against Pres. George W. Bush's now defunct Terrorist Surveillance Program.

In 2007, the Bush administration announced it would put all intercepted communications on U.S. soil under the jurisdiction of the Foreign Intelligence Surveillance Court (FISC). The *New York Times* reported on February 17, 2008, that the FISC provided the FBI with every e-mail address on a particular computer network instead of the single e-mail address the FBI had authorization for. The news story explained that in the cyber world this incident "is equivalent of law enforcement officials getting a subpoena to search a single apartment, but instead having the landlord give them the keys to every apartment in the building."[7]

The *New York Times* reported that the government has routinely continued wiretaps for days or weeks beyond what was authorized by the court. These revelations were the result of a lawsuit by the Electronic Frontier Foundation, a nonprofit group that advocates greater privacy protections. Marcia Hoffmann, an attorney for the foundation, said there are troubling questions about the policy controls that the FBI has in place to guard civil liberties. "How do we know what the FBI does with all these documents when a problem like this comes up?"[8]

In early 2008, the U.S. Congress passed an amnesty bill that relieves telecommunications companies that cooperated with the government from all criminal and civil penalties and removes all court jurisdictions. Those abuses are effectively buried. We will never find out what really went on.

There is also growing secrecy in the federal court system, and it is not simply limited to sealed records. There is a separate, secret docket for the U.S. District Court in Washington, D.C. and other locations around the country, at least forty-six. A group known as the Reporters Committee for Freedom of the Press has established these facts. The steering committee for this group has included such media luminaries as Dan Rather, the late Tim Russert, Fred Graham, and Judy Woodruff.

According to the organization's Web site, federal as well as state courts have created secret dockets, which "never appear on the public docket or are hidden using pseudonyms, such as 'Sealed v. Sealed; or 'John Doe v. Jane Doe.'" What's more, the courts won't even directly acknowledge the existence of secret dockets.[9]

The Associated Press requested a tally of secret federal criminal cases from the Administrative Office of the U.S. Courts. The tally revealed there were 5,116 defendants whose cases were complete in 2003, 2004, and 2005, yet the records of those cases remained sealed. This is precisely the point, the public cannot criticize what it does not know is happening.[10]

Notice what the Sixth Amendment in the Bill of Rights has to say about the right to a "speedy and public trial."

> In all criminal prosecutions, the accused shall enjoy the right to a speedy and public trial, by an impartial jury of the state and district wherein the crime shall have been committed . . . and to have the assistance of counsel for his defense.

There is nothing optional about this; the government has no "flexibility." "Shall" is a word that takes all the options away. All people accused of a crime shall have the right to a public trial. This is another egregious violation of basic rights of citizens as well as a violation of the oath of office for the president, the attorney general and district attorneys, and federal law enforcement agents. It is not merely a wrong signal that the federal government is sending to its own citizens, it goes far beyond that.

Through the years, we have criticized governments in Argentina, Chile, El Salvador, Haiti, Cuba, China, and the former Soviet Union for secret government prosecution and secret imprisonment. Yet, our own elected officials who have sworn to uphold the Constitution are using the same repressive, medieval tactics right here at home. This is too much concentration of power in the hands of the few. It matters not whether a communist dictator or a duly elected president is trampling your rights. It is an ugly thought to entertain that the federal government can spy on you in secret, arrest you in secret, convict you in secret, and imprison you in secret.

One of the key differences between an open society ruled by law and a former Eastern bloc-type police state or a banana republic-type dictatorship is due process in courts that are open to the press and the public. The willingness for the federal government to prosecute Americans in secret, even for what is says is terrorism, puts the U.S. on a fast track to dictatorial rule. This tactic leads to the "disappearance" of individuals in regimes that the U.S. government criticizes as repressive.

### Police State, Incarceration, and SWAT Teams

Every fifteen minutes a police SWAT (Special Weapons and Tactics) team beats down a door to serve a warrant somewhere in the United States. The police spokesperson always refers to it as a "deployment." What's more, the civilian police forces in America, which have been exclusively locally controlled, are becoming more like the military in training, weapons and equipment, tactics, and rhetoric. How often have you heard the police refer to gang-controlled neighborhoods as a "war zone," or that the police are "combating" gangs? These are military words brought into the civilian lexicon.

A Google search for "police state USA" will return seventeen million entries. When you Google "police state in America," the number goes up to fifty-two million. That is not surprising when one considers that in 2008 the United States crossed an unenviable threshold in the rise of imprisoned adults. America has become a benevolent police state.

The idea for a paramilitary-type SWAT team originated in the Los Angeles Police Department in the 1960s. It became popular with mayors, police chiefs, and the public in 1966 when former Marine Charles Whitman barricaded himself atop the clock tower at the University of Texas and killed fifteen people with a deer rifle. The police could do little more than watch.

Creation of individual SWAT teams units were concentrated mostly to big cities, and the actual deployment of these units remained limited to hostage takings, hijackings, or prison escapes throughout the 1970s. According to criminology professor Peter Kraska, beginning in the early 1980s to 2001, SWAT team deployments have risen from 3,000 a year to 40,000 a year.

The Cato Institute's 2006 report "Overkill: The Rise of Paramilitary Police Raids in America" identifies several new federal laws and a new emphasis on the war on drugs that changed the situation dramatically in the 1980s. These changes "allowed nearly unlimited sharing of drug interdiction intelligence, training, tactics, technology, and weaponry between the Pentagon and federal, state, and local police department."[11]

> In 1997 alone, the Pentagon handed over more than 1.2 million pieces of military equipment to local police departments. . . . The Los Angeles Police Department was offered bayonets. The city of St. Petersburg, Florida, bought an armored personnel carrier from the Pentagon for just $1,000. The seven police officers of Jasper, Florida–which has all of 2,000 people and hasn't had a murder in 14 years–were given a military-grade—M-16 machine guns, leading one Florida paper to run the headline, "Three Stoplights, Seven M-16s." The sheriff's office in landlocked Boone County, Indiana, was given an amphibious armored personnel carrier.[12]

And what did police departments across America do with all this stuff? They formed thousands of SWAT teams. Kraska found that ninety percent of cities with populations of 50,000 or more had at least one paramilitary unit. Although these units are sold to the public as being necessary to thwart terrorism or intervene in school shootings, "in practice, the teams are used mainly to serve search warrants on suspected drug dealers."[13]

The frequent use of SWAT teams introduces tremendous firepower into situations where it is most often not needed, or in the wrong place, subjecting innocent citizens and children to highly charged situations entirely by mistake. A Google search for "SWAT team knocks on wrong door" generates 165,000 returns. There are repeated news stories of SWAT teams receiving the wrong address or arriving at the wrong house for a variety of reasons.

In the report "One in 100: Behind Bars in America 2008," the Pew Center on the States reports that after thirty years of growth in prison populations around the nation, "for the first time, more than one in every 100 adults is now confined in an American jail or prison." The total U.S. prison population of 2.3 million is greater "than any country in the world, including the far more populous nation of China."[14]

These statistics are even more staggering when the number of citizens who have previously served prison time are added to those who are there now. That number is more than 5.6 million Americans, according to the *Christian Science Monitor.*

The growth rate for incarceration is being led by the federal prison system, according to the Sentencing Project, a nonprofit advocacy group in Washington, D.C. This organization notes that mandatory minimum sentences are likely to drive prison populations higher, and in 2002, the federal system outgrew any of the state systems.

The "war on drugs" is the primary culprit responsible for the explosion in the prison population. But that doesn't mean that any real progress is being made in fighting drugs or the highly organized enterprises that deliver the product. Kentucky justice secretary J. Michael Brown said it is not the drug lords that his state is putting in jail. "We're just getting the people who went out and got caught. It's the low hanging fruit."[15]

### Toward a North American Union: The Waco Protocol and the USNORTHCOM Agreement

The one-world-government supporters in the prestigious Council on Foreign Relations (CFR) clearly have a friend in George W.

Bush. Bush, a member of CFR, is one of their own; however, this is not unique among American presidents. Every president since Eisenhower was first a member of CFR, including Barack Obama. The only exception is Pres. Jimmy Carter, who turned over the State Department to CFR insiders. In fact, no man or woman has served as U.S. secretary of state without first being a member of CFR in nearly two generations. In 2008, the only major candidate for president in either party who was not a CFR member was Congressman Ron Paul.

Perhaps no president of the United States has done as much as George W. Bush to lay the foundation for the surrender of United States sovereignty to a coming North American Union. For the true believers of centralization, the Bush administration has been an answer to a prayer.

In 2005, President Bush, Mexican president Vicente Fox, and Canadian prime minister Paul Martin signed an agreement to establish the Security and Prosperity Partnership of North America (SPP). The SPP was signed at their meeting in Waco, Texas, and is available on the official White House Web site. The agreement is also known as the Waco Protocol.

The agreement states that the security and prosperity of the three nations is "mutually dependent and complementary." It establishes a "North American framework" to address border security, economic development, and increasing harmonization of regulations, i.e., the remaking of the three nations into a single political unit.

The control of the porous U.S. southern border is a controversial issue the Washington establishment promises to fix. But the SPP agreement does not attempt to secure the U.S. border with Mexico. Why do that when the leaders of the three countries are talking about merging them into a single union? Indeed, the U.S. has agreed in this document to "minimize" its border with Mexico. It is Mexico's southern border with Guatemala and Belize, not the U.S. border, that President Bush has agreed to defend.

Other dangers lurk in the flowery words of mutual assistance. One of the concrete proposals in this agreement is the North American Free Trade Agreement superhighway, which will run from Mexico City to Toronto, splitting Texas, Oklahoma, Missouri, and every other state in its way. The SPP refers to it as a "multimodal corridor" that could include pipelines, rail, and electric power transmission lines in addition to a superhighway. This plan is being debated in Texas and options include ownership and operation of this monstrosity by a private company, perhaps even an internationally owned company. The intent is to wipe out any significance of the U.S. border with Mexico.

The SPP also pledges "a common approach to emergency response." Most Americans are likely to be surprised to read that Bush thinks so little of the Federal Emergency Management Agency's (FEMA) ability to respond to disasters that he got the Mexican government to promise in writing it would help. After all, in 2008, Bush put $8 billion of taxpayer money into FEMA.

In addition to FEMA, under the USNORTHCOM command, the U.S. Air Force signed a Civil Assistance Plan with the Canadian military that some critics say creates a North American army without a vote by the U.S. Congress or the Canadian Parliament. The Civil Assistance Plan was signed February 14, 2008, by U.S. Air Force general Gene Renuart, the commander of USNORTHCOM. According to USNORTHCOM's Web site, the plan "allows the military from one nation to support the armed forces of the other nation during a civil emergency."[16]

What sort of "civil emergency" does the president anticipate? What constitutional provision authorizes the president of the United States to use foreign military forces on his own people? These questions are rhetorical because the Constitution obligates the federal government to protect states from invasion, not to lead an invasion by foreign troops. That would be the moral and legal equivalent of King George III using Hessian mercenaries during the American Revolution. What could happen here that might necessitate an invasion of Canadian military forces to restore order? From whom would Canadian troops crossing the U.S. northern border (the longest unfortified border in the world) take orders?

In the early 1930s after Adolf Hitler was elected chancellor of Germany, the Nazi Party could not win enough seats in the Reichstag to authorize rule by decree (martial law). So, they burned the Reichstag and blamed it on the communists. The nation was so incensed by the phony crime that Hitler was immediately given power to rule by decree, and all political opposition was smashed. Is a "Reichstag fire" in America's future?

**Setting the Stage for Rule by Decree**

Over the years, the office of the president of the United States has accumulated the kind of power that would make Lincoln blush. Today, upon proclamation of a national emergency, the president can take your property without due process; he can seize your gold, your bank accounts, your cash money; he can take control of all telephone service as well as access to the Internet; he can regulate or stop all travel on the interstate highway system; he can declare martial law and send the National Guard to your door to demand your guns. These are awesome powers that most Americans know nothing about and do not believe even exist.

The Congressional Research Service (CRS) knows these powers exist. In a 2007 report to Congress, CRS listed the emergency powers that have been delegated to the president by statute:

> The President may seize property, organize and control the means of production, seize commodities, assign military forces abroad, institute martial law, seize and control all transportation and communications, regulate the operation of private enterprise, restrict travel, and, in a variety of ways, control the lives of United States citizens.[17]

Apparently, former president George W. Bush thought these powers were inadequate, so he created additional authority by an executive proclamation known as National Security Presidential Directive 51/Homeland Security Presidential Directive 20.[18] President Obama has done nothing to undo it. Under these directives, and in the name of "continuity of government," the president claims authority to coordinate activities of the Congress, the Supreme Court, and the entire federal judiciary. During a "catastrophic emergency," which the president can proclaim on his own, his powers extend to the "orderly succession, [and] appropriate transition of leadership" in all three branches of government. In other words, the president can "pack" the Congress and the Supreme Court with partisan cronies beholden only to him. It is a breathtaking step toward dictatorship and the end of the rule of law and civil rights of any sort. At the stroke of a pen, all those who died for freedom from Bunker Hill to Normandy and beyond will have died in vain. Their sacrifice will be instantly rendered meaningless.

This dangerous directive is filled with all sorts of ominous, military-sounding acronyms such as COG (continuity of government), COOP (continuity of operations), and COGCON (continuity of government readiness conditions). It is exactly the sort of language you would expect from a military-type dictatorship.

Under this directive, the president is authorized to declare a "catastrophic emergency" when there is "any incident, regardless of location, that results in extraordinary levels of mass casualties, damage, or disruption severely affecting the U.S. population, infrastructure, environment, economy, or government functions." In other words, it means almost anything the president says it means.

Another World Trade Center-scale attack that results in "extraordinary levels of mass casualties" could trigger this directive. A recession that results in a "disruption" of the "economy" could trigger it. A hurricane that affects the "infrastructure" or the "environment" could trigger it. Maybe even another Oklahoma City-type bombing of a federal building could disrupt "government functions" and trigger it. Almost any unusual event could be enough of an excuse for the president to declare martial law under NSPD-51.

Where, you might wonder, was the news media when this directive was issued? Why wasn't it covered? Those are good questions. The extremely limited coverage can be blamed at least in part on the corporatization of news networks and publications. The greater share of the blame lies with the fact that no one in the congressional leadership of either party offered a whimper of opposition.

The *Washington Post* covered the story the day after the directive was signed, placing it on page twelve. The news item was little more than a rewrite of a White House press release without any reference to political or civil libertarian objections.

The Bill of Rights to the Constitution is one stroke of the pen away from deletion. History shows that once a dictator, emperor, generalissimo, ayatollah, or führer emerges, his removal will be very costly in treasure and blood.

**Conclusion**

Future presidents will look back at the administration of George W. Bush and appreciate his clever ability to arrange a perpetual war on terrorism because it facilitates the federal government's perpetual exercise of war powers. War powers consist of bending the rules of the Constitution while the nation is at war. The federal courts have long allowed the executive branch to exercise temporary, special powers while the nation is at war and its sons are in harm's way. Naturally, these perpetual war powers were turned over to Pres. Barack Obama without any objection on his part. In coming years, he will likely turn over the same (or even greater) powers to his successor.

During World War II, FDR and Earl Warren (governor of California at the time), forcefully removed Japanese Americans from their homes and interred them in a series of camps for the balance of the war. FDR and Warren questioned their loyalty in spite of the fact that no American of Japanese ancestry was ever convicted of sabotage during the war. When the war ended, the government's special war powers ended. The Japanese Americans were released. Things went back to normal, just as they had done at the end of World War I, Korea, Vietnam, and even the Civil War.

But the Trotsky-influenced neo-conservatives have figured out a way to conduct war for years, perhaps decades, and thus perpetuate war powers. I fear they intend for matters never to return to normal, that a shift in government has occurred. I fear they never intend to relinquish the awesome and unprecedented power they have centralized in the federal government and concentrated in the office of president. I fear what appears to be two competing political parties in the U.S. are nothing more than factions of the same welfare/warfare/empire party, whose bickering is indispensable in fooling the American public into believing that elections matter.

I fear the centralization of power and money has reached a tipping point. If not, we are very close. The thing that saddens me the most is that the American public has demanded security; we have demanded more police, more SWAT teams, more prisons, harsher punishment, and more surveillance.

In a thousand ways, we have demanded the president to "do something" about whatever are the day's headlines, whether or not the Constitution gives him authority. Somehow, mistakenly, we believed the federal government can educate children better than parents and local communities. We believed FEMA should be able to respond to weather emergencies better than charities and churches.

We believed the Federal Reserve Bank could manage the national economy even as centrally planned economies collapsed around the world. And we even believed the federal government should police the world and bring democracy and justice for all.

Both political parties have dutifully complied with the demand for greater central control in every aspect of life in America. "We the People" have come full circle from subjects of the king in 1776. We escaped that trap to become citizens of thirteen free sovereignties in 1781. However, since 1861, we have been on the path of centralization. Lincoln started it; Theodore Roosevelt provided much of the philosophical support for it; Woodrow Wilson made great strides toward it; Franklin Roosevelt perfected it in wartime; and George W. Bush and his clever Skull and Bones myrmidons figured a way to perpetuate a state of war and war powers. Pres. Barack Obama also seems to be a true believer in the war on terror and the perpetuation of war powers. It seems every president leaves behind a little more surveillance and central control of the American public.

Just what is the objective of this centralism? It is to roll back the clock and turn Americans back into subjects of the government: Subjects, no longer citizens. It is to replace the phrase "We, the people" with "They, the masters."

And so, the government that was created by the states has, like a cancer, swallowed the states and all the citizens thereof, or is positioned to soon do so. That which was created as the servant of the people has become the master. The American people have no one to blame but themselves.

Time will tell if it is already too late.

# Notes

**CHAPTER ONE**

1.  Mario M. Cuomo, *Why Lincoln Matters: Today More than Ever* (New York: Harcourt, Inc., 2004), book jacket.

**CHAPTER TWO**

1.  Mike Toner, "Digs Unearth Slave Plantations in North," *Atlanta Journal-Constitution*, 2 March 2003, sec. A1.
2.  Robert William Fogel and Stanley L. Engerman, *Time on the Cross* (Boston: Little, Brown, 1974), 35.
3.  Leo H. Hirsch, Jr., "The Slave in New York," *The Journal of Negro History* 16, no. 4 (1931): 391.
4.  George DeWan, "Slavery Died a Slow Death in New York," Newsday.com, http://www.newsday.com/extras/lihistory/5/hs511a.htm.
5.  Herbert S. Klein, *The Atlantic Slave Trade* (New York: Cambridge University Press, 1999), 62-63.
6.  Ibid., 104.
7.  Herbert J. Foster, "Partners or Captives in Commerce? The Role of Africans in the Slave Trade," *Journal of Black Studies* 6, no. 4 (June 1976): 430.
8.  Robert Paul Thomas and Richard Nelson Bean, "The Fishers of Men: The Profits of the Slave Trade," *The Journal of Economic History* 34, no. 4 (December 1974): 908.
9.  Klein, 103.
10. Thomas and Bean, 900.
11. Klein, 63.
12. Thomas and Bean, 908.
13. James High, "The African Gentleman: A Chapter in the Slave Trade," *The Journal of Negro History* 44, no. 4 (October 1959): 287.
14. Klein, 105-6.
15. Ibid., 107
16. Donald W. Livingston, "Slavery as the Cause of the War Between the States," League of the South Institute, http://lsinstitute.org/Slavery.htm.
17. David Harper, "Slavery in the North," http://www.slavenorth.com.
18. Ruth J. Simmons, "Slavery and Justice: We Seek to Discover the Meaning of Our Past," Steering Committee on Slavery and Justice, *Report*, April 26, 2004.
19. Harper.

20.   Edgar J. McMannus, *A History of Negro Slavery in New York* (Syracuse, NY: Syracuse University Press, 1966), 26.

21.   Ibid., 31-32.

22.   James G., Lydon, "New York and the Slave Trade, 1700 to 1774," *The William and Mary Quarterly*, 3rd ser., 35, no. 2 (April 1978): 394.

23.   Harper.

23A. Anne Farrow, Joel Lang, and Jenifer Frank, *Complicity: How the North Promoted, Prolonged, and Profited from Slavery* (New York: Ballantine Books, 2005), 122.

24.   McMannus, *History of Negro Slavery,* 26.

25.   Ibid., 32.

26.   Fogel and Engerman, 4-5.

27.   Ibid., 4.

28.   Thomas Sowell, "Rattling the Chains," Townhall.com, http://www.townhall.com/columnists/thomassowell/ts20040324.shtml.

29.   Ibid.

30.   Thomas Sowell, "Twisted History," Townhall.com, http://townhall.com/columnists/thomassowell/printts20031217.shtml.

31.   Fogel and Engerman, 13.

32.   Ibid., 14.

33.   Ibid., 29.

34.   Leon F. Litwack, *North of Slavery* (Chicago: University of Chicago Press, 1961), 15-16.

35.   Jacque Voegeli, "The Northwest and the Race Issue, 1861-1862," *The Mississippi Valley Historical Review* 50, no. 2 (September 1963): 236.

36.   Ibid., 244.

37.   Ibid., 242.

38.   Litwack, *North of Slavery,* 64.

39.   Ibid., 65.

40.   Reginald Horsman, "Scientific Racism and the American Indian in the Mid-Nineteenth Century," *American Quarterly* 27, no. 2 (May 1975): 161.

41.   Ibid., 158, 160.

42.   Lerone Bennett, Jr., *Forced into Glory* (Chicago: Johnson Publishing Co., 2000), 115.

43.   Litwack, *North of Slavery,* 84.

44.   Ibid., 31.

45.   Sue Macy, "A Look Back at Slavery in Maine," *The Maine Progressive,* http://www.maineprogressive.org, accessed 2006, no longer available.

46.   Litwack, *North of Slavery,* 31.

47.   Leon F. Litwack, "The Federal Government and the Free Negro, 1790-1860," *The Journal of Negro History* 43, no. 4 (October 1958): 274.

48.   Ibid., 271.

49.   Ibid., 272.

50.   Litwack, *North of Slavery,* 47.

51.   Joseph G. Rayback, "The American Workingman and the Antislavery Crusade," *The Journal of Economic History* 3, no. 2 (November 1943): 155.

52. Ibid., 156.

53. Ibid., 157.

54. Litwack, *North of Slavery*, 171, 224.

55. *Congressional Globe*, 36th Cong., 1st sess., 29 December 1859, 285.

56. Leslie H. Fishel, Jr., "Northern Prejudice and Negro Suffrage 1865-1870," *The Journal of Negro History* 39, no. 1 (January 1954): 18-19.

57. Voegeli, 246-47.

58. Ibid.

59. *Congressional Globe*, 37th Cong., 2nd sess., 9 January 1862, 243.

60. Voegeli, 250.

61. Harper.

62. *Congressional Globe*, 36th Cong., 1st sess., 12 April 1860, 1679-80.

63. Litwack, *North of Slavery*, 117, 129.

63A. Farrow, 158.

64. Ibid., 47-48.

65. *Congressional Globe*, 33rd Cong., 2nd sess., 11 January 1855, 236.

66. Litwack, *North of Slavery*, 67.

67. Ibid., 85-86.

68. Ibid., 93.

69. Ibid., 86-87.

70. Iowa Legislature, General Assembly and Secretary of State, *Iowa Official Register, 1999-2000*, http://www.sos.state.ia.us/publications/redbook/toc.html.

71. West Virginia Statehood, West Virginia Division of Culture and History, 2004, http://wvculture.org/history/statehoo.html.

72. Stephen B. Weeks, "The History of Negro Suffrage in the South," *Political Science Quarterly* 9, no. 4 (December 1894): 676.

73. Roger Walace Shugg, "Negro Voting in the Ante-Bellum South," *The Journal of Negro History* 21, no. 4 (October 1936): 357-59.

74. Samll Goldsmyth et al., "Colored Freemen as Slave Owners in Virginia," *The Journal of Negro History* 1, no. 3 (June 1916): 238.

75. C. W. Birnie, "Education of the Negro in Charleston, South Carolina, Prior to the Civil War," *The Journal of Negro History* 12, no. 1 (January 1927): 17-18.

76. Shugg, 363.

77. William Lloyd Imes, "The Legal Status of Free Negroes and Slaves in Tennessee," *The Journal of Negro History* 4, no. 3 (July 1919): 270.

78. Illinois Historical Preservation Agency, http://www.state.il.us/HPA/lovejoy/illinois.htm.

79. Ibid.

80. William Furry, "Historic Hullabaloo," *Illinois Times*, 8-14 May 1997, http://www.illinoishistory.com/itosh.html.

81. Harper.

82. Edgar J., McMannus, *Black Bondage in the North* (Syracuse, NY: Syracuse University Press, 1973), 178, 181.

83. *Congressional Globe*, 36th Cong., 1st sess., 12 December 1859, 101.

84. Ibid., 102.

85.　Litwack, *North of Slavery,* 279.

86.　*Utah History Encyclopedia* (University of Utah), http://www.media.utah. edu/UHE/UHEindex.html.

87.　Michael Fellman, *Citizen Sherman* (Lawrence: University Press of Kansas, 1995), 260-61.

CHAPTER THREE

1.　Brian Holden Reid, "On the Road to Total War: The American Civil War and the German Wars of Unification, 1861-1871," *The Journal of Military History* 62, no. 3 (July 1998): 631.

2.　Fogel and Engerman, 33-34. Slavery was not abolished on the Arabian Peninsula until 1962.

3.　Heinrich H. Maurer, "The Earlier German Nationalism in America," *The American Journal of Sociology* 22, no. 4 (January 1917): 534.

4.　Theodore S. Hamerow, "History and the German Revolution of 1848," *The American Historical Review* 60, no. 1 (October 1954): 29.

5.　Carl Wittke, "The German Forty-Eighters in America: A Centennial Appraisal," *The American Historical Review* 53, no. 4 (July 1948): 714-15.

6.　Maurer, 528, 534-35.

7.　Wittke, 716-17.

8.　Victor S., Yarros, "The German and the Anglo-American View of the State," *International Journal of Ethics* 28, no. 1 (October 1917): 43-45.

9.　The reader will recall from the previous chapter that there was no actual emancipation of slaves at any time in any Northern state. Manumission laws that ended slavery in the North freed no slaves at the time the manumission law was passed. It freed only the children of slaves born after a certain date at a predetermined age, usually around twenty-five. Slaves in the North when manumission laws went into effect remained legally enslaved for the rest of their lives.

10.　Maurer, 529.

11.　Charles M. Wiltse, "A Critical Southerner: John C. Calhoun on the Revolutions of 1848," *The Journal of Southern History* 15, no. 3 (August 1949): 304.

12.　Edwin E. Scharf, "'Freethinkers' of the Early Texas Hill Country," *Freethought Today,* http://www.ffrf.org/fttoday/1998/april98/scharf.html.

13.　Ibid.

14.　It presently takes five years to become a naturalized U.S. citizen after permanent residence status is obtained. The U.S. Citizenship and Immigration Services advises that it takes at least six months to process applications for permanent residence.

15.　Wittke, 723.

16.　German-American History & Heritage, Web site, http://www. germanheritage.com.

17.　Mark Mayo Boatner, III, *The Civil War Dictionary* (New York: David McKay Co., Inc., 1959), 727.

18.　German-American History & Heritage.

19.　Ibid.

20.　Wittke, 715, 718, 723.

21. Boatner, 69.

22. W. T. Block, "Some Notes on Our Texas Germanic Heritage," http://www.wtblock.com/wtblockjr/texas.htm.

23. German-American History & Heritage.

24. Ibid.

25. Boatner, 588.

26. Ibid., 761, 934.

27. Ibid., 718-19.

28. International Institute of Social History, http://www.iish.nl.

29. German-American History & Heritage.

30. Ibid.

31. Ibid.

32. Boatner, 929-30.

33. German-American History & Heritage.

34. Boatner, 898-99.

35. Ibid., 725-26.

36. Ibid., 726.

37. Texas State Historical Association, *Handbook of Texas Online*, http://www.tshaonline.org.

38. "Julius Froebel," Virtual American Biographies, http://www.famousamericans.net/juliusfroebel/.

39. *Handbook of Texas Online*.

40. Boatner, 613.

41. Andreas Dorpalen, "The German Element and the Issues of the Civil War," *The Mississippi Valley Historical Review* 29, no. 1 (June 1942): 72.

42. Donnal V. Smith, "The Influence of the Foreign-Born of the Northwest in the Election of 1860," *The Mississippi Valley Historical Review* 19, no. 2 (September 1932): 204.

43. William E. Dodd, "The Fight for the Northwest, 1860," *The American Historical Review* 16, no. 4 (July 1911): 788.

44. Ibid., 786-87.

45. Thomas J. DiLorenzo, *The Real Lincoln*, (Roseville, CA: Prima Publishing, 2002), 15.

46. Dodd, 787.

47. Smith, 193.

48. Wittke, 723, 732.

49. German-American History & Heritage.

50. Smith, 198.

51. Dorpalen, 75.

52. Smith, 198-199; Wittke, 723.

53. Smith, 204.

54. James, G. Randall and David Donald, *The Civil War and Reconstruction* (Lexington, Mass.: D.C. Heath, 1969), 707-47.

55. Dodd, 788.

56. Mauer, 534.

**CHAPTER FOUR**

1. Joanna D. Cowden, *Heaven Will Frown on Such a Cause as This* (Lanham, MD: University Press of America, 2001), 5.

2. "Some Papers of Franklin Pierce, 1852-1862," *The American Historical Review* 10, no. 2 (January 1905): 365-66.

3. Christopher Phillips, *Missouri's Confederate: Claiborne Fox Jackson and the Creation of Southern Identity in the Border West* (Columbia: University of Missouri Press, 2000), 251.

4. Randall and Donald, 233.

5. Daniel W. Crofts, *Reluctant Confederates* (Chapel Hill: University of North Carolina Press, 1989), 254.

6. Ibid., 19, 21.

7. Ibid., 149.

8. Robert H. White, *Messages of the Governors of Tennessee 1857-1869,* vol. 5 (Nashville: Tennessee Historical Commission, 1959), 274.

9. Boatner, 299-300.

10. Richard M. Ketchum, ed., *The Civil War* (New York: American Heritage Publishing Co., 1960), 60.

11. Randolph was a pro-secessionist delegate to the Virginia Secession Convention. Subsequently he was commissioned a major in the Confederate army, organized the legendary "Richmond Howitzers," and was later promoted to brigadier general and appointed Confederate secretary of war by President Davis.

12. Randall and Donald, 181-82.

13. Gray Wood, *The Hidden Civil War* (New York: Viking Press, 1942), 57.

14. Randall and Donald, 144-45.

15. Jean Baker, *James Buchanan* (New York: Henry Holt and Company, 2004), 125.

16. *Proceedings of the Governor,* ed. William Sumner Jenkins, Maryland State Archives, Early State Records Microfilm Index # M3162, 1861, 1196.

17. Randall and Donald, 233.

18. Crofts, 333.

19. U.S. War Department, *The War of the Rebellion: A Compilation of the Official Records of the Union and Confederate Armies,* ser. 3, vol. 1 (Washington, D.C.: Government Printing Office, 1880-1901): 76. Hereafter cited in all chapter notes as *Official Records.*

20. Randall, 180-82.

21. Crofts, 149, 152.

22. Boatner, 684.

23. *Official Records,* ser. 1, vol. 1, 687.

24. Randall and Donald, 184.

25. *Official Records,* ser. 3, vol. 1, 81.

26. Randall and Donald, 185.

27. White, 277.

28. Ibid., 305-6.

29. Randall and Donald, 187.

30. Ibid., 197.

31. Jack T. Hutchison, "Bluegrass and Mountain Laurel: The Story of Kentucky in the Civil War," Cincinnati Civil War Round Table, http://www.users.aol.com/CintiCWRT/bluegrass.html, 6.
32. Ibid., 6.
33. Ibid., 7.
34. Phillips, 245.
35. Ibid., 252.
36. *Proceedings of the Governor,* 1190.
37. *Proceedings of the Governor,* 1196.
38. Randall and Donald, 233.
39. *Proceedings of the Governor,* 1194.
40. Gray, 57-58.
41. Ibid., 58.
42. Ibid., 59.
43. Randall and Donald, 293.
44. Baker, 126.
45. Clement Eaton, *A History of the Old South,* 2nd ed. (New York: Macmillan Co., 1966), 505.
46. DiLorenzo, 142.
47. Boatner, 894-95.
48. *Congressional Globe,* 37th Cong., 1st sess., 4 July 1861, 1.
49. DiLorenzo, 15.


**CHAPTER FIVE**
1. Randall and Donald, 646.
2. *Texas* v. *White,* 74 U.S. 700, 725, 743 (1869).
3. John Niven, *Salmon P. Chase* (New York: Oxford University Press, 1995), 382, 390, 411.
4. Ibid., 384-96.
5. Ibid., 407.
6. Ibid., 437.
7. *Texas* v. *White,* 738-39.
8. Ibid., 725.
9. Ibid., 726.
10. Ibid., 706.
11. *Lane County* v. *Oregon,* 74 U.S. 7 Wall., 76 (1868).
12. *Hickman* v. *Jones,* 76 U.S. 9 Wall. 197, 200 (1869).
13. *White* v. *Hart,* 80 U.S. 13 Wall. 646, 20 L.Ed 685, 648 (1871).
14. Ibid., 650.
15. *Daniels* v. *Tearney,* 102 U.S. 415, 418 (1880).
16. Boatner, 412.
17. *Ex Parte Milligan,* 71 U.S. 4 Wall. 2, 122 (1866).
18. Ibid., 127.
19. Ibid.

20.	*Fletcher* v. *Peck,* 10 U.S. 87 (1810).

21.	*Merrion* v. *Jicarilla Apache Tribe,* 455 U.S. 130 (1982).

22.	*United States* v. *Winstar Corp.,* 518 U.S. 839, 872, 860 (1996)

23.	*Jefferson Branch Bank* v. *Skelly,* 66 U.S. 1 Black 436, 446 (1861).

24.	*Home Tel. & Tel. Co.* v. *Los Angeles,* 211 U.S. 265 (1908).

25.	*Bowen* v. *Agencies Opposed to Social Security Entrapment,* 477 U.S. 41 (1986).

26.	*United States* v. *Cherokee Nation of Oklahoma,* 480 U.S. 700 (1987).

27.	*Hughes Communications Galaxy, Inc.* v. *U.S.,* 271 F.3d 1060 (Fed. Cir. 2001).

28.	*Martin* v. *Hunter's Lessee,* 14 U.S. 304, 326 (1816).

28A. John Remington Graham, *A Constitutional History of Secession* (Gretna, LA: Pelican Publishing Company, 2002), 286-87

29.	Catherine Fisk and Erwin Chemerinsky, "The Filibuster," *Stanford Law Review* 49 (January 1997): 247.

30.	Sir William Blackstone, *Commentaries on the Laws of England,* vol. 1 (1765): 90-91.

31.	Michael B. Rappaport and John McGinnis, "Systematic Entrenchment: A Constitutional and Normative Theory," *Public Law and Legal Theory Papers* no. 3 (Northwestern University School of Law, 2003), 5.

32.	*Fletcher* v. *Peck,* 135.

33.	*Ohio Life Insurance & Trust Company* v. *Debolt,* 57 U.S. 16 How. 416, 431 (1853).

34.	*Newton* v. *Mahoning County Commissioners,* 100 U.S. 548, 559 (1879).

35.	Eric A. Posner and Adrian Vermeule, "Legislative Entrenchment: A Reappraisal," *Yale Law Journal* 111, no. 7 (2002): 1665.

36.	Ibid., 1688.

37.	Ibid., 1694-1701.

38.	Fisk, 250.

39.	Rappaport, 6, 11.

40.	Fisk, 250.

41.	Rappaport, 10.

42.	Ibid., 9.

43.	H. Newcomb Morse, "The Foundations and Meaning of Secession," *Stetson Law Review* 15 (1986): 426.

44.	Rappaport, 9.

45.	Kenneth M. Stampp, "The Concept of a Perpetual Union," *The Journal of American History* 65, no. 1 (June 1978): 14.

46.	Ibid., 14.

47.	Ibid., 17.

48.	Ibid., 18.

49.	Fisk, 248.

50.	*Fletcher* v. *Peck,* 135.

51.	*Ohio Life Insurance & Trust Company* v. *Debolt,* 431.

52.	*Connecticut Mutual Life Insurance Co.* v. *Spratley,* 172 U.S. 602, 621 (1899).

53.	*Reichelderfer* v. *Quinn,* 287 U.S. 315, 318 (1932).

54.	Fisk, 248-49.

55.	*United States* v. *Ballin,* 144 U.S. 1, 5 (1892).

56. *Coyle* v. *Smith*, 221 U.S. 559, 566-67, 574 (1911).

57. *Pollard* v. *Hagan*, 44 U.S. 3 How) 212, 221, 223-24 (1845).

58. *Permoli* v. *First Municipality*, 44 U.S. (3 How.) 589, 606, 609 (1845).

59. *Escanaba Co.* v. *Chicago*, 107 U.S. 678, 688-89 (1883).

60. *United States* v. *Texas*, 143 U.S. 621, 634 (1892).

61. *Coyle* v. *Smith*, 567.

62. Ibid.

63. James M., McPherson, *Battle Cry of Freedom* (New York: Oxford University Press, 1988), 240.

64. *New York Times Book Review* and *The Washington Post Book World*, review of *Battle Cry of Freedom*, by James M. McPherson, http://search.barnesandnoble.com/ Battle-Cry-of-Freedom/James-M-McPherson/e/9780195168952/?itm=1.

65. Adolf Hitler, *Mien Kampf*, trans. Ralph Manheim (New York: Houghton Mifflin Company, 1999), 566.

66. Jean Baker, *James Buchanan* (New York: Henry Holt and Company, 2004), 12.

67. Ibid., 126.

68. *Chisholm* v. *Georgia*, 2 U.S. 419 Dall., 454-55 (1793).

69. Ibid., 457.

70. *Stone* v. *State of Mississippi*, 101 U.S. 814, 819 (1879).

71. New Jersey Archives Online, http://www.njarchives.org/links/treasures/ usconstitution/14thamend.html.

72. *New York* v. *Miln*, 36 U.S. 11 Pet. 102-3 (1837).

73. Stampp, 27-28.

74. *Thurlow* v. *Comm. of Massachusetts*, 46 U.S. 504, 528-29 (1847).

75. Ibid, 529.

76. *United States* v. *Darby*, 312 U.S. 100 (1941).

77. *Senate Journal*, 36th Cong., 2nd sess., 4 December 1860, 15-16.

**CHAPTER SIX**

1. Claude H. Van Tyne, "Sovereignty in the American Revolution: An Historical Study," *The American Historical Review* 12, no. 3 (April 1907): 537.

2. Ibid., 537-38.

3. Ibid., 539-40.

4. *Congressional Globe*, 36th Cong., 2nd sess., 17 December 1860, 107.

5. Ibid., 598.

6. Ibid., 854.

7. Ibid., 1370.

8. Morse, 426.

9. Ibid., 428.

10. Ibid., 429.

11. James Ronald Kennedy and Walter Donald Kennedy, *The South Was Right!* (Gretna, LA: Pelican Publishing Company, 1994), 209.

12. Stampp, 10.

13. Ibid.

14.  Ibid., 12-13.

15.  Ibid., 6, 33.

16.  H. Arthur Scott Trask, "A Northern Man of Southern Principles: President Franklin Pierce of New Hampshire on Politics and the Sectional Conflict," *League of the South Papers* no. 10 (2000), League of the South Institute, http://www.lsinstitute.org/Pierce.htm.

17.  Ibid.

18.  Joseph G. Rayback, "Martin Van Buren's Desire for Revenge in the Campaign of 1848," *The Mississippi Valley Review* 40, no. 4 (March 1954): 707.

19.  Jeffrey Rogers Hummel, "Martin Van Buren, the Greatest American President," *The Independent Review* 4, no. 2 (fall 1999): 275.

20.  U.S., The Whitehouse, "About the White House Presidents," http://www.whitehouse.gov/about/presidents/MillardFillmore/.

21.  "Some Papers of Franklin Pierce, 1852-1862," *The American Historical Review* 10, no. 2 (January 1905): 366-67.

22.  Trask, 2000.

23.  "Papers of Franklin Pierce," 368.

24.  Baker, 142.

25.  Frank Wysor Klingberg, "James Buchanan and the Crisis of the Union," *The Journal of Southern History* 9, no. 4 (November 1943): 455, 458.

26.  Jonas Viles, "Sections and Sectionalism in a Border State," *The Mississippi Valley Historical Review* 21, no. 1 (June 1934): 21-22.

27.  Klingberg, 459, 461.

28.  Ibid., 463.

29.  Baker, 121.

30.  Ibid., 137-38.

31.  John Seigenthaler, *James K. Polk* (New York: Henry Holt and Company, 2004), 109.

32.  Ibid., 110.

33.  Ibid., 111.

34.  Klingberg, 474.

35.  Morse, 431, 433.

36.  Ibid., 432.

37.  Ibid., 431-33.

38.  Ibid., 433.

CHAPTER SEVEN

1.  Lance Janda, "Shutting the Gates of Mercy: The American Origins of Total War, 1860-1880," *The Journal of Military History* 59, no. 1 (January 1995): 7.

2.  Ibid., 7-8.

3.  Ibid., 8, 11-12.

4.  Ibid., 10.

5.  Daniel E. Sutherland, "Abraham Lincoln, John Pope, and the Origins of Total War," *The Journal of Military History* 56, no. 4 (October 1992): 573.

6.    Janda, 12.
7.    Burrus M. Carnahan, "Lincoln, Lieber and the Laws of War: The Origins and Limits of the Principle of Military Necessity," *The American Journal of International Law* 92, no. 2 (April 1998): 215.
8.    Janda, 12.
9.    Ibid., 13.
10.   Sutherland, 581.
11.   Ibid., 582.
12.   Ibid.
13.   Ibid., 583-84.
14.   Francis Lieber was a German immigrant and legal scholar. He was born in Berlin in 1800 and joined the Prussian Army at the age of fifteen. He fought at the battle of Waterloo and later immigrated to the United States in 1829. His code, "Instructions for the Government of Armies of the United States in the Field," was approved by Lincoln in 1863 and was adopted by the Prussians in 1870.
15.   Carnahan, 219.
16.   Ibid.
17.   Janda, 13-14.
18.   Ibid., 15.
19.   Carnahan, 226.
20.   John F. Marszalek, *Sherman's Other War* (Kent, OH: Kent State University Press, 1999), 43.
21.   Stanley P. Hirshson, *The White Tecumseh: A Biography of General William T. Sherman* (New York: John Wiley & Sons, Inc., 1997), preface.
22.   Stephen E. Bower, "The Theology of the Battlefield: William Tecumseh Sherman and the U.S. Civil War," *The Journal of Military History* 64, no. 4 (October 2000).
23.   John F. Marszalek, *Sherman: A Soldier's Passion for Order* (Carbondale: Southern Illinois University Press, 2007), 350.
24.   Michael Fellman, *Citizen Sherman* (Lawrence: University Press of Kansas, 1995), 5, 8, 11.
25.   Marszalek, *A Soldier's Passion,* 351.
26.   Marszalek, *Sherman's Other War,* 65.
27.   Fellman, 98-99.
28.   Ibid., 107-8.
29.   Bower, 1009.
30.   Fellman, 237.
31.   Marszalek, *Sherman's Other War,* 76, 78.
32.   Hirshson, preface.
33.   Fellman, 8-11.
34.   Ibid., 12, 21.
35.   Ibid., 89-90.
36.   Ibid., 236-37.
37.   Ibid., 107.
38.   Marzalek, *Sherman's Other War,* 44.

39. Fellman, 40-41.

40. Ibid., 45.

41. Louisiana State University, Web site, http://www.lsu.edu/visitors/history.shtml.

42. Hirshson, 235.

43. Ibid.

44. Fellman, 260-61.

45. Marszalek, *A Soldier's Passion,* 379

46. Ibid., 381

47. Fellman, 271.

48. Marszalek, *A Soldier's Passion,* 379, 382.

49. Fellman, 261.

50. Hirshson, 336.

51. John Embry Parkerson, Jr., "United States Compliance with Humanitarian Law Respecting Civilians During Operation Just Cause," *Military Law Review* 133 (summer 1991): 36, 39.

52. Ibid., 36.

53. George B., McCellan, *McCellan's Own Story: The War for the Union* (New York: Charles L. Webster, 1887), 326.

54. Ibid., 326-27.

55. U.S. Army, *Enemy Prisoners of War, Retained Personnel, Civilian Internees and Other Detainees,* Army Regulation 190-98, (Washington, D.C.: Government Printing Office, 1997), see 4-5a "Unauthorized work," 16.

56. *Official Records,* ser. 1, vol. 17, 122.

57. Marszalek, *A Soldier's Passion,* 190, 192.

58. Ibid., 192-93.

59. *Official Records,* ser. 1, vol. 17, 240.

60. John Bennett Walters, "General William T. Sherman and Total War," *The Journal of Southern History* 14, no. 4 (November 1948): 462-63.

61. Edward F. Williams III, "Early Memphis and its River Rivals," reprinted from *The West Tennessee Historical Society Papers* no. 22 (1968): 15-16.

62. *Official Records,* ser. 1, vol. 17, 235-36.

63. Boatner, 883.

64. Walters, 464.

65. Williams, 17.

66. Walters, 464.

67. Michael W. Rich, "Henry Mack: An Important Figure in Nineteenth-Century American Jewish History," *American Jewish Archives* (fall-winter 1995): 268. (Special thanks to Jacob Rader Marcus Center of the American Jewish Archives, Cincinnati Campus Hebrew Union College).

68. Bertram Wallace Korn, *American Jewry and the Civil War* (Philadelphia: The Jewish Publican Society of America, 1951), 272.

69. Selma S. Lewis, *A Biblical People in the Bible Belt: The Jewish Community of Memphis, Tennessee, 1840s-1960s* (Macon, GA: Mercer University Press, 1998), 39.

70. Korn, 279-80.

71. Stephen V. Ash, "Civil War Exodus: The Jews and Grant's General Orders No. 11," *The Historian* 49 (August 1982): 510.

72. Isaac Markens, "Lincoln and the Jews," *American Jewish Historical Society* no. 17 (1909): 122.

73. Korn, 122-23.

74. Ibid., 143.

75. Jewish-American History Documentation Foundation, Inc., "Resignation of Captain Philip Trounstine, 5th Ohio Cavalry, in Protest against 'General Orders #11,'" http://www.jewish-history.com/civilwar/trnstine.htm.

76. Korn, 123.

77. John E. L. Robertson, *Paducah: Frontier to the Atomic Age,* (Charleston, SC: Arcadia Publishing, 2002), 44.

78. Korn, 124.

79. Ibid., 123-24.

80. Ash, 513.

81. Boatner, 817.

82. James A. Wax, "The Jews of Memphis: 1860-1865," *The West Tennessee Historical Society Papers* no. 3 (1949): 74.

83. Korn, 125.

84. *Congressional Globe,* 37th Cong., 3rd sess., 9 January 1863, 245-46.

85. Korn, 168.

86. Ibid., 283, note 93.

87. Isaac Wolfe Bernheim, *History of the Settlement of Jews in Paducah and the Lower Ohio Valley* (Paducah, KY: Temple Israel, 1912), 24-25.

88. Walters, 467.

89. Ibid., 467-68.

90. Boatner, 951.

91. Ibid., 877.

92. Randall, 411.

93. Walters, 468.

94. Michael R. Bradley, *With Blood and Fire: Life behind Union Lines in Middle Tennessee, 1863-65* (Shippensburg, PA: Burd Street Press, 2003), 58-59.

95. Ibid., 60-61.

96. Ibid., 61.

97. Ibid.

98. Wax, 75.

99. Ibid.

100. Korn, 154.

101. *Official Records,* ser. 1, vol. 17, 141.

102. *Official Records,* ser. 3, vol. 2, 724.

103. Lewis, 39.

104. Korn, 154.

105. Boatner, 420.

106. Walters, 470.

107. Ibid., 471.

108. Boatner, 543-44.

109. Walters, 471.

110. Ibid., 472.

111. Ibid., 473.

112. *Official Records,* ser. 1, vol. 32, 117-19.

113. Ibid.

114. Ibid.

115. Ibid.

116. Phillip H. Sheridan, *Personal Memoirs of P.H. Sheridan* (New York: Charles L. Webster & Co., 1888), 380.

117. Army Regulation 190-8, 4-5a "Unauthorized work," 16.

118. Bradley, 76-79.

119. Ibid., 80.

120. Boatner, 616.

121. *Official Records,* ser. 1, vol. 38, 68.

122. *Official Records,* ser. 1, vol. 38, 76-77.

123. Walters, 474.

124. *Official Records,* ser. 1, vol. 39, 494.

125. Boatner, 325, 895.

126. *Official Records,* ser. 2,vol. 7, 567.

127. Army Regulation 190-8, 4-5a "Unauthorized work," 16.

128. Thomas G. Robisch, "General William T. Sherman: Would the Georgia Campaigns of the First Commander of the Modern Era Comply With Current Law of War Standards?" *Emory International Law Review* 9, no. 459 (1995): 461.

129. Department of State Publication, "Laws of War: Laws and Customs of War on Land, Annex to the Convention," 18 October 1907, see articles 23, 42, 46, and 53 (Hague Resolutions); "Geneva Convention Relative to the Protection of Civilian Persons in Time of War," 1949, in Robisch, 1995, 475-76.

130. *Official Records,* ser. 1, vol. 39, 358.

131. Robisch, 483-84. See Department of the Army, FM 27-10 Change 1, *The Law of Land Warfare, Change 1* (1956).

132. Hirschson, 255.

133. James C. Bonner, "Sherman at Milledgeville," *Journal of Southern History* 22, no. 3 (August 1956): 289.

134. *Official Records,* ser.1, vol. 44, 799.

135. Robisch, 480-81.

136. Robisch, 500.

137. Ibid., 501-2.

138. *Official Records,* ser.1, vol. 38, 579.

139. Robisch, 503.

140. 18 USC 2331, sec. 2331 (January 2004).

141. *Official Records,* ser.1, vol. 32, 278-81.

142. Fellman, 180-81.

143. Randall, 431.

144. Harold M. Hyman, *The Reconstruction Justice of Salmon P. Chase* (Lawrence, KS: The University of Kansas Press, 1997), 74.


CHAPTER EIGHT

1. Alexander H. Stephens, *A Constitutional View of the Late War Between the States,* vol. 2 (Philadelphia: National Publishing Co., 1868-70), 669.

2. I prefer the terminology "Second War of Secession" to the term "Civil War," as explained in the introductory chapter of this book, but I use the latter term for the sake of clarity.

3. Likewise, I prefer the term "First War of Secession" to describe the war in which the original thirteen states seceded and won their independence from England.

4. See David Fischer's *Historians' Fallacies* (London: Routledge and Kegan Paul, 1970).

5. Edward L. Ayers, *What Caused the Civil War?* (New York: W.W. Norton & Co., 2005), 114.

6. *Congressional Globe,* 39th Cong., 1st sess., 27 February 1866, 1056-57.

7. Burrus M. Carnahan, "Lincoln, Lieber and the Laws of War: The Origins and Limits of the Principle of Military Necessity," *The American Journal of International Law* 92, no. 2 (April 1998): 221.

8. James M. McPherson, *Battle Cry of Freedom* (New York: Oxford University Press, 1988), 331-33.

9. *Connecticut Mutual Life Insurance Co.* v. *Spratley,* 172 U.S. 602 (1899).

10. *Permoli* v. *First Municipality,* 44 U.S. (3 How.) 589, 609 (1845).


CHAPTER NINE

1. Federal Bureau of Investigation, official Web site, http://www.fbi.gov/hq/cid/pubcorrupt/pubcorrupt.htm.

2. Georgia, *The Official Code of Georgia Annotated.*

3. Paul Craig Roberts, "Going to Jail for Being a Democrat: How Alabama Gov. Don Siegelman Got Roved," *Counter Punch,* 3 March 2008, http://www.alternet.org/rights/78407.

4. David E. Kaplan, "Spies Among Us," *U.S. News & World Report,* 8 May 2006.

5. Siobhan Gorman, "Satellite-Surveillance Plan Aims to Mollify Critics," *The Wall Street Journal,* 20 December 2007, sec. A4.

6. Chalmers Johnson, *The Sorrows of Empire* (New York: Henry Holt and Company, 2004), 165.

7. Eric Lichtblau, "Error Gave F.B.I. Unauthorized Access to E-Mail," *New York Times,* 17 February 2008.

8. Ibid.

9. Reporters Committee for Freedom of the Press, http://rcfp.org.

10. Ibid.

11.   Radley Balko, *Overkill: The Rise of Paramilitary Police Raids in America* (Washington, D.C.: Cato Institute, 2006), 7-8.

12.   Ibid., 8.

13.   Ibid., 9.

14.   The Pew Center on the States, "One in 100: Behind Bars in America 2008," Pew Public Safety Performance Project, *Report,* 2008, 3, 5.

15.   Ibid., 7.

16.   U.S. Northern Command (USNORTHCOM), Web site, http://www.northcom.mil.

17.   U.S. Congressional Research Service Report for Congress, "National Emergency Powers," Congressional Research Service, *Report,* Order Code 98-505 GOV, August 30, 2007, 1.

18.   National Security and Homeland Security Presidential Directive, U.S. National Security Presidential Directive 51 (NSPD-51)/Homeland Security Presidential Directive 20 (HSPD-20), http://www.fas.org/irp/offdocs/nspd/nspd-51.htm; Federal Continuity Directive 1 (FCD 1), "Federal Executive Branch National Continuity Program and Requirements," http://www.fema.gov/pdf/about/offices/fcd1.pdf.

# Index

Alabama, 151, 173
Alaska, 279
Arizona Territory, 116
Arkansas, 103-6, 184-85, 196, 222
Aurora Colony, 26

Badeau, Adam, 203
Bell, John, 101-2
Benjamin, Judah P., 227
Blackstone, William, 140
Blagojevich, Rod, 279
Blair, Frank P., 228-29
Blenker, Louis, 81, 84
Breckenridge, John C., 89, 99
Brown family, 33
Brownlow, William G., 227
Buchanan, James, 105, 124, 138-39, 154, 168, 185, 191-92
Burned-over District, 25
Bush, George W., 287, 295, 298, 300
Butler, Benjamin, 233

California, 54, 57, 66, 99, 173, 227
Cameron, Simon, 109
Campbell, John, 50
Cass, Lewis, 48
Chase, Salmon P., 38, 52, 68, 120, 122-28, 262-63, 273
Cherokee Nation, 116
Chivington, John Milton, 66
Clayton, John M., 48
Colfax, Schuyler, 50
Connecticut, 56, 61, 68, 173
*Connecticut Mutual Life Insurance Co.* v. *Spratley,* 148

continuity of government, 297
Council on Foreign Relations, 294
Cox, Samuel S., 51
Crenshaw, John, 63
Crittenden, John J.,193
Cuomo, Mario, 11, 14

Degener, Edward, 87
de Tocqueville, Alexis, 39
Doolittle, James R., 174
Douai, Karl Adolph, 81

E-Cycle Management, 280
Early, Jubal, 106
Ellis, John W., 109
emancipation, 11, 19, 30, 38, 51, 54, 63, 68
English, W. H., 50
equal footing, 16, 126, 150-52, 271
equality of the states, 16, 153
Ewing, Thomas, 208
*Ex Parte Milligan,* 133, 260
Experian, 290

Fayetteville, Tennessee, 239
Federal Bureau of Investigation, 12, 279
Ferry, Orris S., 174
Fillmore, Millard, 185, 189, 193, 195
final solution, 21, 67, 270
Florence, Thomas B., 174
Florida, 115, 196
Ford, John N., 285
Forrest, Nathan Bedford, 236-38
Forsyth, John, 48
Forty-Eighters, 23, 72-75, 78, 80, 84, 87, 90-97

Foster, John G., 242
Fourteenth Amendment, 158
Froebel, Julius, 87

Garfield, James A., 26
Georgia, 16, 130, 132, 146, 153, 156-57, 171, 210, 237, 240-41, 244-47, 260, 280, 286
Germany, 72-73, 78, 81-82, 84, 87, 89, 91, 96-97
Grant, Ulysses S., 22-23, 67, 100, 199, 202-4, 206, 216, 218, 220, 224-27, 229, 231-32, 235-36, 244, 260
Grier, Robert Cooper, 124, 132

Harlan, James, 52
Harmony Society, 25
Harris, Isham G., 108-9, 238
Hecker, Frederich Karl Franz, 80, 84, 90-91
*Hickman* v. *Jones,* 129
Hicks, Thomas Holliday, 105, 112-13
Hitler, Adolf, 23, 67, 154, 198, 257, 270, 296
Holly Springs, Mississippi, 224
Hovey, Alvin P., 133
Huntington, Ellsworth, 194
Hurlbut, Stephen, 224, 233, 235, 244
Hurst, Fielding, 238

Illinois, 20, 36, 38, 41, 62, 67, 79-80, 89-90, 92-93, 113, 152, 173
Illinois Central Railroad, 91, 117
Illinois Constitution, 56
*Illinois Staatsanzeiger,* 92
Indiana, 20, 38, 41, 50-54, 57-58, 62, 67, 79, 89-92, 133-34
Iowa, 20, 38, 41, 51, 54, 58, 68, 90, 92, 173

Jackson, Claiborne Fox, 111
Jefferson, Thomas, 144, 169-70, 256-66
Jews, 21-22, 100, 222, 224-28, 232-33, 235
Johnson, Andrew, 64-65

Kapp, Frederich, 80-81, 90, 92
Kaskel, Cesar, 225-26, 228
Kennesaw, Georgia, 247
Kentucky, 16, 19, 68, 99, 101, 103, 109, 111, 113, 116, 150, 184, 193
King, Horatio, 193
Kudlich, Hans, 86

LaGrange, Tennessee, 224
*Lane County* v. *Oregon,* 123, 128, 130
*lebensraum,* 23, 269-70
legislative entrenchment, 15, 139-41, 143-44, 146, 157, 159, 271-73
Letcher, John, 106
Lieber Code, 22, 202, 205-6, 212, 213-16, 218-19, 229, 231-32, 235-41, 244, 268
Lincoln, Abraham, 11-12, 14, 19, 21-23, 27-28, 38, 41-42, 49, 60, 63-73, 79, 81, 89-93, 96-97, 99-106, 109, 111-18, 120, 124, 132-33, 135, 137-39, 149, 153-55, 161-62, 164-65, 167-69, 180-85, 187-93, 195, 197-99, 202-7, 213-16, 222, 225-26, 242, 250, 252, 255, 257-59, 261, 263-65, 267-69, 271, 279, 289, 297, 300
Little Egypt, 113
Livingston, Donald W., 24
Louisiana, 151, 159

Madison, James, 143-44, 146, 149
Magoffin, Beriah, 109, 111
Maine, 42, 67
manumission, 29-30, 36, 54, 56, 63
Marcy, William L., 48
Marx, Karl, 23, 81, 84, 95, 183
Maryland, 113
Mason, George, 144
Massachusetts, 279
Massachusetts Constitution of 1780, 172
mass execution, 22
McClellan, George B., 204-5, 207, 217, 239, 244, 247
*McCullough* v. *Maryland,* 158
McDowell, Irwin, 205

McMinnville, Tennessee, 232
Memphis, Tennessee, 217-20, 222, 224, 226-28, 232-33, 235, 237
Mencken, H. L., 18
Meridian, Mississippi, 235
Michigan, 38, 41, 56, 89-92, 173
military necessity, 204-7, 213, 219, 231, 236, 252-53
Milledgeville, Georgia, 245
Minnesota, 22, 38, 41, 58-59, 66, 68, 90-92, 173
Mississippi, 196, 224, 229, 235-36
Missouri, 19, 68, 99-100, 103, 111, 113, 116, 184-85, 193, 227
Mormon Church, 25

National Security Presidential Directive, 51, 297
Negro exclusion, 20-21, 41, 51, 67
New Jersey, 20, 29, 36, 38, 61-63, 67, 99, 158, 171
New Orleans, Louisiana, 151
New York, 25-26, 29-30, 34-35, 39, 49, 61, 67-68, 78-81, 86, 90-91, 104, 171-73, 175, 178, 187, 189, 279
*New York* v. *Miln,* 161
Niceley, Frank S., 285, 287
North Carolina, 16, 61, 103, 106, 109, 146, 153, 159, 171, 178-79, 196
Noyes, John Humphrey, 26

Obama, Barack, 295, 297, 299-300
Ohio, 20, 38, 41, 50-52, 54, 57-58, 61, 67-68, 79, 87, 90-92, 158, 173, 209
Oregon, 21, 26, 59, 99, 152, 159, 279
Osterhaus, Peter, 89
Owen, Robert Dale, 53

Paducah, Kentucky, 222-25, 228
Paine, Eleazer A., 239-40
Paul, Ron, 295
Pennsylvania, 146, 171
Pettit, John, 53
Pierce, Franklin, 18, 99-100, 115, 180, 185, 187, 189-91, 193, 195

Polk, James K., 194
Powell, Lazarus, 227
Prang, Louis, 84
Pretorius, Emil, 84

Randolph, George W., 103, 220
Rector, Henry M., 106
Reed, W. M., 237
Rhode Island, 146, 178-79, 279
right of revolution, 16
Roswell, Georgia, 240

Salomon, Charles E., 82, 84
Salomon, Edward S., 82
Salomon, Frederick S., 82, 84
Schimmelfennig, Alexander, 86
Schoepf, Albin Francisco, 86
Schurz, Carl, 78, 80-81, 84, 90-93
secession, 11, 14-19, 23-24, 27-28, 60, 99-101, 105-6, 108-9, 111, 114-16, 118-20, 123, 126, 129-30, 132, 134-35, 137-39, 144, 146, 153-55, 159, 162, 168, 173-75, 178, 181, 183-85, 188, 190-93, 197-98, 215, 227, 262, 271-72, 274-75, 278
secret docket, 291
Seigenthaler, John, 194
Semple, Ellen Churchill, 194
Seymour, Horatio, 115
Sheridan, Philip, 206, 211, 239, 244, 247
Sherman, William T., 21-23, 66-67, 199, 204, 206-12, 216, 218-20, 222, 228-29, 231, 233, 235-38, 240-41, 244-48, 250, 252, 259, 268, 270
Sickles, Daniel E., 173
Siegelman, Don, 287
Siemering, August, 87
Sigel, Franz, 82, 84
slavery, 11, 19, 29-38, 42, 49, 53-57, 60, 62-63, 67-68, 70-72, 75, 80, 86, 94, 187, 189, 213, 218, 257-59
Souter, David, 140
South Carolina, 16, 146, 149, 153, 159, 168, 171, 177, 196

sovereignty, 106, 108
Sullivan, Jeremiah C., 226
Swayne, Noah Haynes, 130, 132

Tennessee, 16, 19, 61-62, 64, 68, 101,
    103, 106, 108-9, 150, 183-84, 193,
    205, 220, 224, 226-27, 232, 237-40,
    261, 279-80, 285-86
Tenth Amendment, 16, 156-58, 262,
    275
Texas, 175-76, 271
*Texas* v. *White,* 119-20, 122, 124, 127-28,
    130, 257, 262-63, 275
total war, 200-201, 204-6, 212, 216, 237,
    252-53
Treaty of Paris, 170
Treaty of Tellico, 183
Trounstine, Phillip, 225
Trumbull, Lyman, 64
Tyler, John, 185, 188-89

unmistakability, 15, 135-36, 138-40,
    271-72
USNORTHCOM, 296

Van Buren, Martin, 185, 187, 195
Vermont, 16, 19, 54-56, 150, 172, 175-
    76, 271
Vicksburg, Mississippi, 206, 229, 235-36

Virginia, 16, 41, 61, 99, 101, 103, 106,
    132-35, 144, 146, 149, 153, 171-72,
    178, 184-85, 196, 204-5, 217, 260, 271
Virginia sovereignty convention, 103,
    106

Waco Protocol, 295
Waite, Morrison R., 157
Walcutt, Charles C., 220, 222
Warren, Earl, 299
Washington, 169
Watie, Stand, 116
Watkins, Louis, 241
Webber, Max von, 86
West Virginia, 19, 42, 60, 69, 271
Weydemeyer, Joseph, 84
*White* v. *Hart,* 130, 260
Williamsburg, Virginia, 217
Willich, August, 84, 86
Wilmot, David, 49
Wilson, Henry, 227
Wilson, Woodrow, 193, 300
Wirt, William, 48
Wisconsin, 21, 38, 41, 51, 68, 79-80, 82,
    89-92
Wise, Henry A., 82

Yellow Tavern, 239